Python®
Automation

by Alan Simpson

A Wiley Brand

Python® Automation For Dummies®

Published by: **John Wiley & Sons, Inc.**, 111 River Street, Hoboken, NJ 07030-5774, www.wiley.com

For general information on our other products and services, please contact our Customer Care Department within the U.S. at 877-762-2974, outside the U.S. at 317-572-3993, or fax 317-572-4002. For technical support, please visit https://hub.wiley.com/community/support/dummies.

Wiley publishes in a variety of print and electronic formats and by print-on-demand. Some material included with standard print versions of this book may not be included in e-books or in print-on-demand. If this book refers to media that is not included in the version you purchased, you may download this material at http://booksupport.wiley.com. For more information about Wiley products, visit www.wiley.com.

Library of Congress Control Number is available from the publisher.

ISBN 978-1-394-37142-6 (pbk); ISBN 978-1-394-37144-0 (ebk); ISBN 978-1-394-37143-3 (ebk)

Printed and bound by CPI Group (UK) Ltd, Croydon, CR0 4YY

C9781394371426__301025

Table of Contents

Introduction

Welcome to *Python Automation For Dummies,* the book designed to help you find out all about Python and the many things you can do with Python to automate tedious, mundane, and time-consuming computer tasks.

About This Book

You don't need to read this book cover-to-cover to benefit. Instead, you can treat it more like a reference for building Python automation scripts and apps as needed, just by flipping to any example in the book and using the code provided in that section. Of course, I always explain the code so you understand what's going on. That knowledge, in turn, will grow and help you come up with your own creative solutions to automation tasks and other apps.

This is not a textbook on the Python language. I don't attempt to teach you every nook and cranny of the Python language. There are plenty of books available for that, including *Python All-in-One for Dummies* and *Python Essentials For Dummies* (published by Wiley), both of which I wrote with John Shovic.

For convenience, the kinds of tasks and code you'll use often are summed up in Part 1 of this book. When you need a quick reminder on a fundamental task, such as starting a new app from scratch, you'll find all the steps there. Common error messages and such are covered in Chapter 17, so you can get clarification and advice in a jiffy.

When something in Python leaves you stumped, use this book as a reference, paging through the table of contents or index to the spot that deals with that bit of information.

Within this book, you may note that some web addresses break across two lines of text. If you're reading this book in print and want to visit one of these web pages, simply key in the web address exactly as it's noted in the text, pretending as though the line break doesn't exist. If you're reading this as an e-book, you've got it easy — just click the web address to be taken directly to the web page.

Foolish Assumptions

This book doesn't assume you're already an accomplished software engineer with years of experience writing Python code. I do assume that you're tech savvy enough to understand common tech jargon like *files, folders, icons, copy, paste, gigabytes,* and so forth.

If I assume too much, there are plenty of resources available to you to fill in the blanks. Artificial intelligence (AI) is usually your best bet for getting quick definitions and answers to tech questions. Any free AI will do. In Windows, you can use Copilot. On a Mac, you can use Apple Intelligence. Or you can use any AI that includes a free tier such as ChatGPT at `https://chatgpt.com`.

Icons Used in This Book

Throughout this book, I use icons in the margin to point out content that's perhaps a little offbeat relative to the main flow of the text. Here's the kind of content each icon represents:

TIP

The Tip icon alerts you to juicy information that makes computing easier — a time-saver or shortcut that's worth keeping in mind, for example.

REMEMBER

Don't forget to remember these important points because you're likely to need the information often. These are usually items that are easy to forget but well worth remembering.

WARNING

When an operation could have unpleasant consequences that aren't easily undone, the Warning icon alerts you to the dangers and tells you how to avoid that danger. Always pay attention to this icon.

TECHNICAL STUFF

I use the Technical Stuff icon when I get into the weeds on a particular subject. You can ignore anything marked with this icon without missing the main point.

Beyond the Book

In addition to the material in the print or e-book you're reading right now, this product also comes with a free access-anywhere Cheat Sheet that covers Python data types and keywords, arithmetic and string operators, assignment operators, and more. To get this Cheat Sheet, simply go to www.dummies.com and enter **Python Automation For Dummies Cheat Sheet** in the Search box.

In addition, I provide all the source code for this book at www.dummies.com/go/pythonautomationfd. Finally, at that same URL you'll find a bonus chapter called "Managing and Speeding Up the Big Jobs."

Where to Go from Here

Where you go from here is up to you! If you need a specific automation script, go to the section that describes the script you need to see *all* of the code for that script — not a lengthy tutorial on how to write the script. If you're new to Python and you don't have a lot of experience writing Python code, Chapter 1 is a great place to start.

1

Getting Started with Python Automation

Chapter **1**

Automating with Python

Welcome to Python automation! In this chapter, you explore why Python is the ideal language for automating mundane, time-consuming computer tasks. If you've ever found yourself stuck doing the same boring computer chores over and over — like renaming a bazillion files, sorting through spreadsheets, or downloading stuff from the web — Python may just become your new best friend. It's a programming language that's easy to pick up, even if you're not a tech wizard, and it's perfect for automating those mind-numbing tasks that eat up your time. Think of Python as a trusty robot assistant: You tell it what to do in plain, simple words (well, code), and it does your work in no time at all.

What makes Python so great for automation is the fact that it has a little something for everyone. Python has built-in tools to handle all sorts of everyday tasks — like managing files, crunching data, bossing around your computer — and a huge pile of free add-ons (called *libraries*) can do even fancier things, like scraping websites or sending emails. You don't need to be a coding genius to get started — just a few lines of Python can save you hours of clicking and typing. So, whether you're organizing your music collection or taming a messy inbox, Python's got your back, making life a whole lot easier with a few friendly commands.

Choosing a Programming Language

There are many programming languages in the world. They have names like C#, Go, Java, JavaScript, Python, and TypeScript, to name a few. The TIOBE Index (`www.tiobe.com/tiobe-index`) consistently ranks Python as the most popular language of our time.

JavaScript is great for creating web apps, but it's rarely used for anything else. Python excels at AI and automation. In fact, Python has so many ready-to-use modules designed for automation that it would probably be crazy to use any language *other* than Python for the kinds of automation scripts you'll see throughout this book.

There's a lot to like about Python — and many reasons to learn Python beyond automation. For one, many people regard Python as the easiest language for many beginners to learn. Python's syntax is clean and simple — it reads almost like English.

TIP

You're never stuck without information with Python. There are endless tutorials, forums, and free *libraries* (premade code you can borrow) to help you out. Virtually every modern AI chatbot is perfectly capable of writing Python code for you and answering any questions about Python that pop into your head.

Python lets you write short, powerful code. What may take 20 lines in another language often takes just a few lines in Python. That means less typing and fewer mistakes to try to ferret out. Plus, modern AI can debug your existing code as easily as it can write code for you.

Let's zoom in on automation — the topic of this book. When it comes to automation, Python is a superstar. Whether you're on Linux, macOS, or Windows, Python works like a charm. Write your automation script once, and it'll run anywhere. No need to reinvent the wheel for different systems.

With Python, you can write a quick script to handle many tasks in minutes. Although the following code below may not mean much to you right now, it illustrates how you can take a daunting task, like renaming hundreds of files in a folder, with just a few lines of code:

```
import os
for filename in os.listdir("."):
    os.rename(filename, filename.replace("old", "new"))
```

Tiny bits of code like that can handle big automation tasks.

Beyond file tasks, Python plays nice with application programming interface (APIs; define here), databases, Microsoft Excel files, and AI. If you're automating something like "Check my email, grab attachments, and update a spreadsheet," Python can tie it all together smoothly.

TECHNICAL
STUFF

APIs allow Python to interact with AI and other powerful online capabilities, without your having to reinvent the wheel or host huge files on your own computer. APIs are a hallmark of modern computing, and you definitely want to use a programming language that makes API access easy.

REMEMBER

Learning Python is like giving yourself a superpower. Python is easy to start, endlessly useful, and when it comes to automation, unbeatable. You'll save time, impress your friends (or boss), and maybe even have some fun along the way. Perhaps best of all, Python is completely free.

Have I convinced you to choose Python yet?

Understanding Python Syntax

Every language has certain rules of *syntax* that outline how you must arrange words in order for them to make sense. Like, "Teddy, jump three times!" If you say it all jumbled up, or leave out words, like "Jump Teddy three," Teddy may get confused and not know what to do. In programming, syntax is the same thing — you need to order the words so the computer understands what you want. Syntax is just the rules for putting words and symbols in the right order.

Some programming languages require lots of punctuation, in addition to words, as part of their syntax. That gets tiresome and makes learning more difficult. I'll give you a simple example — a piece of code that checks whether a number is even or odd and prints a message — in both JavaScript and Python.

JavaScript seems very "busy" with parentheses, curly brackets, and semicolons:

```javascript
function checkEvenOrOdd(number) {
    if (number % 2 === 0) {
        console.log("The number " + number + " is even!");
    } else {
        console.log("The number " + number + " is odd!");
    }
}

checkEvenOrOdd(7);
```

That code looks like something written by aliens. But that's what a JavaScript requires. You've got:

>> Curly brackets {} to wrap the function and the if...else blocks.

>> Parentheses () for the function definition and the if condition.

>> A semicolon (;) at the end of each line (JavaScript loves semicolons).

Now here's the same thing in Python:

```python
def check_even_or_odd(number):
    if number % 2 == 0:
        print(f"The number {number} is even!")
    else:
        print(f"The number {number} is odd!")

check_even_or_odd(7)
```

Granted, it's still not plain English. But it's much, much cleaner and simpler. Here's what's special about Python:

>> No curly brackets! Python uses *indentation* (those spaces at the start of lines) to know what's inside the function or if...else. It's like the code is breathing — it looks airy and neat.

>> Fewer parentheses — only needed for the function definition, not the if condition.

>> No semicolons — Python doesn't need them, so the code is less cluttered.

TIP

As an experienced instructor who has taught thousands of software developers, I can assure that all the curly brackets and semicolons are the toughest things for beginners to get used to — they're among the main things that drive people away from learning to code. Learning Python first lets you dodge that bullet.

Getting Python

Python is super lightweight and doesn't demand much from your hardware, which is one reason it's so popular. Think of this as the "minimum stuff" your computer needs to run Python and get started with coding or automation.

Identifying the hardware requirements

You can run Python on almost any modern computer. That doesn't include mobile devices like phones and tablets, but it does include most desktops and laptops. Here's what you'll need at the bare minimum:

>> Python works on Linux, macOS, Windows (7, 8, 10, or 11), and even some mobile systems. Basically, if it's a computer from the last 10 to 15 years, you're good!

- **»** Any modern processor, including Apple M series, or even just a basic processor like an Intel or AMD processor works fine. Even a 1 gigahertz (GHz) single-core central processing unit (CPU) can handle it, but it may feel slow for big projects.

- **»** In terms of random access memory (RAM), 512 megabytes (MB) is enough to run Python itself, but 2GB or more is better if you're doing anything practical (like automation or running other programs at the same time). Most modern computers have 8GB of RAM or more, so you're probably covered.

- **»** Python's installer is tiny — about 30MB to 50MB to download and install. You'll want at least 100MB to 200MB of free space for Python, its libraries, and your own code files. If you're adding big libraries (like for data science), a few gigabytes of free space is smart.

- **»** No special graphics card or graphics processing unit (GPU) is needed. Python runs in a text window, so any basic screen works.

TECHNICAL STUFF

To get your system specs in Windows, press Windows+I to open Settings and choose System⇨ About. On a Mac, click the Apple menu in the upper-left corner of your screen, and choose About This Mac.

If you're automating something heavy — like controlling a web browser with selenium or processing tons of files — you'll want more RAM (maybe 8GB) and a faster CPU. But for most people learning Python, and for everyday automation (like renaming files or sending emails), even a cheap laptop is probably sufficient, as long it's not a Chromebook or a similar device with a mobile operating system.

Installing Python

To use Python, you may first have to install it on your computer. Some Mac computers come with Python version 2 preinstalled. But these days, you really need to use Python 3, so plan on installing Python yourself. It's free, it's easy, and I can give you the steps. However, I *can't* tell you exactly what you'll see when you browse to the Python website, because websites change often. If you're using a Mac or Windows PC, follow these steps (if you're using Linux, see the nearby sidebar):

1. **Go to** www.python.org.

2. **Click Downloads and click either Mac or Windows.**

   You don't technically need to click Mac or Windows — the website will detect which operating system you're using and when you hover your mouse over Downloads (as I did in Figure 1-1), you'll see the option to download the correct version. As you can see in the figure, I was using Windows, so the website offered that automatically.

3. **Click the button that shows the current version number.**

   In Figure 1-1, the version is 3.13.2, but the number you see may be different.

4. **Open the folder to which you downloaded Python.**

   This is usually your Downloads folder.

5. **Double-click the icon of the downloaded file.**

6. **Follow the onscreen instructions to Install (or Upgrade Now if you're given that option).**

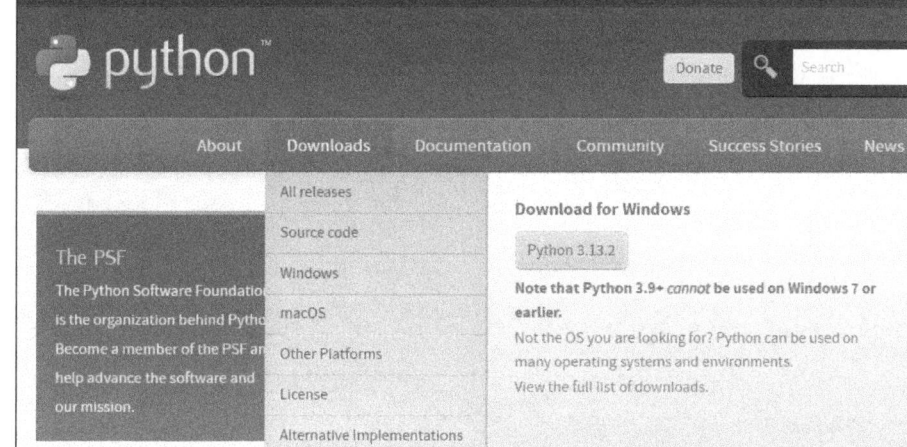

FIGURE 1-1:
Download options from the Python website.

INSTALLING PYTHON ON LINUX

Most Linux distributions come with Python preinstalled (usually Python 3). There are many different Linux distributions (or distros), including Arch, Debian, Fedora, and Ubuntu. I can't give step-by-step instructions for each. But a good starting point may be to determine whether you already have Linux installed and, if so, which version. You should be able to do so following these steps:

1. **Press Ctrl+Alt+T to open the Terminal.**

2. **Type the following and press Enter:**

   ```
   python3 --version
   ```

(continued)

(continued)

If the command returns something like Python 3.12.2, Python is installed. If you get an error, try the following command:

```
python --version
```

If you get an error message on both tries, or you want a newer version of Python, you can still install Python from the Python website. Download and install the Gzipped source tarball or XZ compressed source tarball file. Or check the documentation for your specific Linux distribution for recommendations. Optionally, you can also ask any AI for recommendations related to your specific Linux distro.

Chapter **2**

Choosing a Code Editor

To write Python code, you need a code editor. If you've been coding with Python for a while and you already have a preferred editor, you're welcome to stick with that. If you're just starting out with Python, I recommend Visual Studio Code (VS Code for short), which is the editor I use in this book. VS Code is the most widely used code editor in the world, and it's very well suited to Python coding.

TECHNICAL STUFF

On a personal front, I also use VS Code to write code in Cascading Style Sheets (CSS), Hypertext Markup Language (HTML), and JavaScript, the main languages for creating websites and web apps. If you're thinking about learning that kind of coding, VS Code will serve you well there, too.

The hardware requirements for VS Code are minimal. Here's a quick rundown:

» **Operating system:** Linux 64-bit distro (for example, Ubuntu 16.04+, Debian 9+, Fedora 24+, and so on); macOS 10.15 (Catalina) or later; or Windows 7, 8.1, 10, or 11 (32-bit or 64-bit).

» **Processor:** 1.6 GHz or faster (for example, Intel Core 2 Duo, AMD Athlon 64 X2, Apple M1, or better).

» **Random access memory (RAM):** 1GB (Linux or Windows) or 512MB (macOS). But 4GB or more is better.

>> **Storage:** About 200MB to 300MB for the basic installation.

>> **Display:** At least 1,024 x 768 resolution.

Most modern computers exceed those requirements considerably.

Installing VS Code

To use VS Code as your code editor, the first step is to download and install it. This is basically a matter of browsing to `https://code.visualstudio.com` and following the onscreen instructions. Here are step-by-step instructions — but remember, websites can change at any time, so if something is different for you, just follow any onscreen instructions you see:

1. **Browse to** `https://code.visualstudio.com.`

2. **Click Download for Windows, Download for macOS, or Download for Linux depending on which operating system you're using.**

3. **Open the folder to which you downloaded the file (usually your** `Downloads` **folder).**

4. **Double-click the icon for the downloaded file (the filename usually starts with** VSCode**).**

   If you're using Windows, follow the onscreen instructions. When you get to the page about additional tasks, feel free to check or uncheck any boxes based on your preferences. I typically set up mine as shown in Figure 2-1.

   If you're using macOS, drag the `Visual Studio Code.app` file that was extracted from the downloaded Zip file to your `Applications` folder.

VS Code should be installed at this point. In Windows, you should be able to Start it from your Start menu (you may have to search for it on the menu if it's not readily apparent). If you opted for a Desktop icon, double-click that icon to open VS Code. When VS Code is running, you can right-click its icon in the taskbar and choose Pin to Taskbar so you can easily start it right from the taskbar in the future.

On a Mac, you should be able to start VS Code from its icon in Launchpad or from the `Applications` folder. If you see a warning about VS Code being downloaded from the internet, go ahead and open it anyway. When VS Code is running, you can right-click its icon in the Dock and choose Options ⇨ Keep in Dock for easy access in the future.

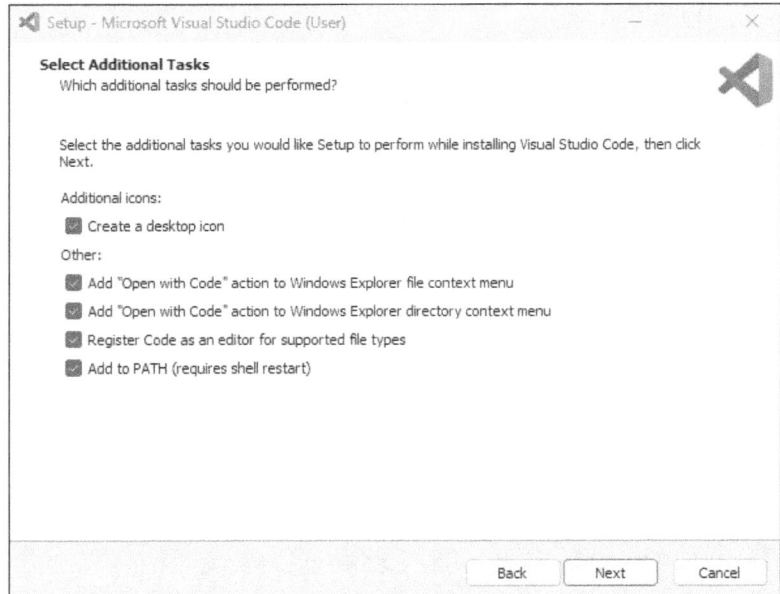

FIGURE 2-1:
Additional
options
for Windows.

TECHNICAL
STUFF

VS Code offers free artificial intelligence (AI) in the form of Copilot. The first time you start VS Code, you may see the option to set up Copilot for free. It's a great tool to help with learning to code. You'll need a GitHub account to enable it. If you have a GitHub account, you can set up Copilot now; otherwise, you can skip that option for the time being and come back to it later.

VS Code will likely default to a dark theme, which you're welcome to use if you prefer. However, throughout this book, I use a light theme, because the images just look better on paper that way. To choose your own theme, click Settings in VS Code (the gear icon in the lower-left corner) and choose Themes ⇨ Color Theme. I use the Light Modern theme throughout this book.

The bar of icons at the left side of VS Code (see Figure 2-2) is called the Activity Bar. It contains icons you'll use often. To see the name of any icon, just hover the mouse pointer over the icon. In the next section, you'll use the Extensions icon to add Python extensions to VS Code.

Activity Bar

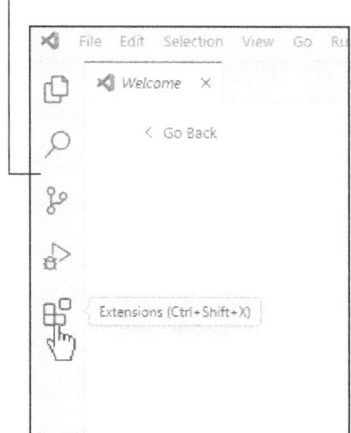

FIGURE 2-2:
The Activity Bar in
VS Code. Hover
the mouse
pointer over any
icon to
see its name.

Installing Python Extensions

To write Python code in VS Code, you'll need to install the VS Code Python extensions. Follow these steps:

1. **Click Extensions in the VS Code Activity Bar (shown near the mouse pointer in Figure 2-2).**

2. **In the Search box near the top of the left pane, type** Python.

3. **Find Python by Microsoft (it has more than 100 million downloads) and click its Install button (see Figure 2-3).**

   Don't worry about other Python extensions.

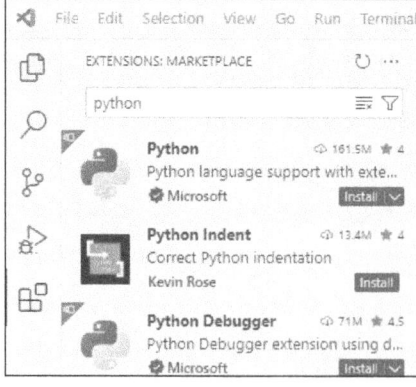

FIGURE 2-3:
Install the Python
extension from
Microsoft.

It should take only a few seconds to install the extension. When it's done, remove the search term *Python* from the Search box to see all your installed extensions. That list should now include Pylance, Python, and Python Debugger, as shown in Figure 2-4 (all three are included in the download).

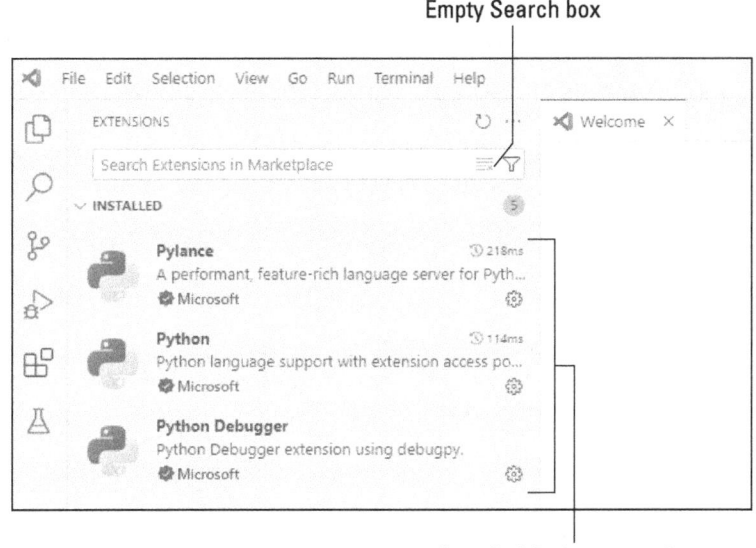

Empty Search box

Installed Python extensions

FIGURE 2-4:
Installed Python
extensions.

REMEMBER

If you hit a snag in VS Code, or you're just wondering how to do something, feel free to ask AI for help. Virtually all modern AI chatbots can tell you anything you want to know about VS Code.

Creating a Folder for a New Project

Whether you're writing a small automation script or a large app, you'll be working on a project. In Python, it's always a good idea to put each project in its own folder. That folder is referred to as the *workspace folder* in VS Code. Before we go any further, let's create a new empty folder so that you can see all the steps involved:

1. **Close VS Code if it's still open.**

    In Windows or Linux, choose File ➪ Exit from the VS Code menu bar. In macOS, choose Code ➪ Quit Visual Studio Code from the VS Code menu bar.

2. **Navigate to wherever you'd like to put your folder.**

   It can be a cloud drive, if you like. Or you can just put it on the Desktop for now and move it to another location later as convenient.

3. **Create the folder.**

   You should be able to just right-click an empty spot on the Desktop (or in the current folder) and choose New ⇨ Folder in Windows or New Folder in macOS.

4. **Name the folder** First Python **(unless you prefer a different name).**

If you don't get the folder name right on the first try, right-click the folder's icon, choose Rename, type the correct name, and press Enter.

Now that you have a new, empty folder to work with, the next step is to open that folder in VS Code.

Opening a project's folder in VS Code

Whether you're starting a new project, or returning to an existing project you've already started, the first step will be to open the project folder in VS Code.

If you're using Windows, you may be able to right-click the folder's icon and choose Open With ⇨ VS Code or Show More Options ⇨ Open with Code to open VS Code and the folder simultaneously.

Regardless of what operating system you're using, you can follow these steps to open your project folder in VS Code:

1. **Open VS Code.**

2. **Near the top of the Activity Bar at the left, click Explorer.**

3. **Click Open Folder.**

4. **Navigate to the folder's parent directory, click the folder's icon, and click Open.**

5. **If you see a message about trusting the folder, choose Yes, I Trust the Authors (because you are the author!).**

The Explorer pane remains open. The name of the folder you opened appears near the top of that pane (see Figure 2-5). That folder is the project's *root folder*, also known as the *workspace folder* in VS Code. All the subfolders and files that make up your project will be contained within that workspace folder.

Open folder

FIGURE 2-5:
A project folder
open in the
Explorer pane.

Explorer pane

TIP

Clicking the root folder name in VS Code expands and collapses it to show or hide files in that folder. Usually, you want it expanded to see subfolders and files contained within your project.

Selecting your Python version

TIP

Before you start doing any actual work with Python, it's a good idea to know what version of Python (if any) is currently active. So, the first thing you may want to do after opening a folder in VS Code is follow these steps:

1. **From the VS Code menu bar, choose View ⇨ Command Palette.**

   If you prefer, press Ctrl+Shift+P in Windows or ⌘+Shift+P in macOS. Pressing F1 may also work.

2. **Type sel and click Python: Select Python Interpreter from the drop-down menu, as shown in Figure 2-6.**

3. **Click the Recommended Python interpreter, as shown in Figure 2-7, if you have multiple versions from which to choose.**

You won't see anything on the screen indicating which Python interpreter you've chosen, but don't worry: I show you how to determine that, using the Terminal, in the next section.

FIGURE 2-6:
Selecting a
Python
interpreter.

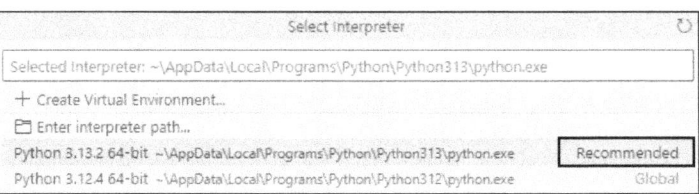

FIGURE 2-7:
Choose the
Recommended
Python
interpreter.

**TECHNICAL
STUFF**

In this chapter, I had you select the Recommended interpreter in case you're just getting started with Python and just want to use the latest Python version. In practice, some projects require specific Python versions, so VS Code lets you pick one each time you start it. You won't need this for this book, but I'm mentioning it because choosing a specific version helps advanced developers.

Opening the Terminal in VS Code

Much of the time when working with Python, you'll use the Terminal pane. The Terminal provides a *command line interface* (CLI) for entering commands from the keyboard. You can open the Terminal from the menu, or shortcut keys, as follows:

>> Choose View ⇨ Terminal from the menu bar.

>> Press F1, or press Ctrl+` in Windows or Command+` in macOS. ` is the backtick character, usually to the left of the number 1 on the keyboard.

The Terminal opens near the bottom of the VS Code window, looking something like Figure 2-8 (in Windows). The PS and path you see are the *command prompt*, where you type your commands.

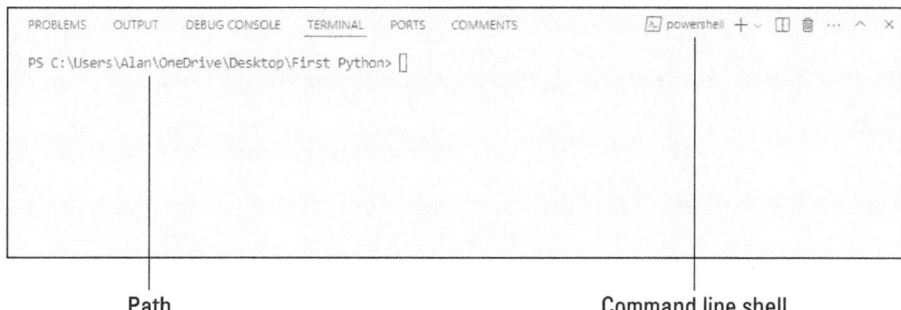

PROBLEMS   OUTPUT   DEBUG CONSOLE   TERMINAL   PORTS   COMMENTS   powershell + ∨ ☐ 🗑 ... ∧ ✕

PS C:\Users\Alan\OneDrive\Desktop\First Python> []

FIGURE 2-8:
The Terminal
in VS Code.   Path   Command line shell

**TECHNICAL
STUFF**

In Linux and macOS, the command prompt will be different, but don't worry about that right now. I explain more after we activate a virtual environment a little later in this chapter. However, it's worth noting that you're not stuck with whatever happens to be showing as your default command line shell. You can use the drop-down arrow next to the current shell name to choose a different command line shell if you like.

You always want to know what Python version you're using in VS Code, and the Terminal lets you find out, as I explain in the next section.

Checking your Python version

To see what Python version you're currently using, you can enter either the command python –version or python –V (the case matters here). But until you've set up a virtual environment (see the next section), that command may give you an error message. The trick to get around that may seem strange, but here it is:

>> In Windows, use py rather than python at the command.

>> In Linux or macOS, use python3 rather than python as the command.

The reason for this weirdness has to do with the operating system PATH that determines how system commands (which are run from the operating system) have been treated in the past, and the fact that different projects may require different Python versions. Both py and python3 are *aliases* for the python command and will use whatever python version is currently available. In VS Code, that's the Python version you chose when choosing Python: Select Python Interpreter from the command palette (see "Selecting your Python version," earlier in this chapter).

WARNING

Python code is case-sensitive, meaning you can't use uppercase and lowercase letters interchangeably. You must use the same uppercase and lowercase letters shown in this book for things to work as described in this book.

When VS Code tells you it doesn't recognize `python` as a command, you can still determine your Python version using the following:

» In Windows, enter the command `py –version` or `py –V` to determine your Python version.

» In Linux or macOS, enter the command `python3 –version` or `python3 –V` to determine your Python version.

After you type the appropriate command and press Enter, the current Python version will show just under the command you typed, as shown in Figure 2-9.

PROBLEMS   OUTPUT   DEBUG CONSOLE   TERMINAL   PORTS   COMMENTS

```
PS C:\Users\Alan\OneDrive\Desktop\First Python> python --version
Python was not found; run without arguments to install from the Microsoft Store
PS C:\Users\Alan\OneDrive\Desktop\First Python> py --version
Python 3.13.2
PS C:\Users\Alan\OneDrive\Desktop\First Python> []
```

Python version

FIGURE 2-9:
Using Python version 3.13.2 in this example.

After you've set up and activated a virtual environment, the `python` command will work as expected. Let's get started on the whole business of virtual environments now.

Using Virtual Environments

Every Python script or app should live in its own folder (its *workspace folder*) for organization and portability. Each one also needs its own virtual environment, specifying the Python version and module dependencies, to run correctly. This setup lets you execute the script on any computer — Linux, macOS, Windows — regardless of the system's Python version or installed modules.

At first, the process of creating a virtual environment may seem like a bit of a pain. But you get used to it, and the advantages are well worth the tiny effort it takes to create and activate a virtual environment.

Creating a virtual environment

The command to create a virtual environment is, technically, `python -m venv` followed by a name for the virtual environment. But, of course, that `python` command may fail, so you'll have to use the `py` alias in Windows or the `python3` alias in Linux or macOS to get it to work.

The `-m` is a *flag* the tells Python to run a module named `venv` as a script, rather than as a module (which is something we normally add to existing scripts rather than run directly). That name, venv is short for *virtual environment.*

You also need to give the virtual environment a name. The virtual environment is stored in a subfolder under the workspace folder name. You can name your virtual environment anything you like, but `.venv` is a common name. That `.venv` name offers several advantages over some name you choose at random:

>> The dot in `.venv` signals to other developers that the folder contains configuration or utility information and is not part of the actual Python code.

>> Many modern editors like VS Code and PyCharm recognize `.venv` as a virtual environment and auto-detect it for Python interpreter selection, reducing setup steps.

>> On Unix-like systems (Linux, macOS), files and folders starting with a dot are hidden unless the user specifically knows how to look for them. That prevents less experienced users from messing about in the `.venv` folder without knowing what they're doing.

In short, you can think of using `.venv` as the virtual environment folder name a "best practice," and the consistency will make it easier to recognize its purpose at a glance.

To create a virtual environment named `.venv`, open the VS Code Terminal and enter the appropriate command:

>> **Windows:** `py -m venv .venv`

>> **Linux or macOS:** `python3 -m venv .venv`

You won't get any feedback in the Terminal after you press Enter. But if you look at the Explorer pane, you'll probably see the `.venv` folder icon under the root of your workspace folder, `First Python` in our working example. You may also see the message shown in Figure 2-10 pop up in the lower-right corner of VS Code.

FIGURE 2-10:
A VS Code
message about a
newly created
virtual
environment.

> ⓘ We noticed a new environment has been created. Do you ⚙ ✕
> want to select it for the workspace folder?
>
> Source: Python
> [Yes] [No] [Don't show again]

The message is asking if you want to associate the virtual environment with the workspace folder, which is just another name for the *root folder*, or the folder that contains the entire project (including the virtual environment). Go ahead and click Yes. But if you don't get that opportunity, don't worry about it. Activating the virtual environment each time you open the project's folder will ensure that VS Code "knows" to use the Python version and add-ins from the virtual environment every time you open that folder to run or work on your script.

Activating a virtual environment

Creating a virtual environment doesn't activate the virtual environment. You always want to make sure your virtual environment is activated before you start working on your script or run a script. That you'll do in the Terminal window of VS Code. The command prompt in the Terminal should still show the path of the workspace root folder. Enter one of the commands to run the activate script within that folder, depending on your operating system:

>> **Windows:** `.venv\Scripts\activate`

>> **Linux or macOS:** `.venv/bin/activate`

WARNING

Notice that Windows uses backslashes (\), while Linux and macOS use forward slashes (/). Remember to use the same uppercase/lowercase letters shown here.

If you see a warning about the script coming from an "unknown publisher," type **A** and press Enter to always run. The publisher in this instance is the Python Software Foundation, which created the venv module, and you can certainly trust them.

When a virtual environment is active, the name of that virtual environment shows in the command prompt, so you know the virtual environment. Figure 2-11 shows how the command prompt may look in Windows, where the name `.venv` is enclosed in parentheses at the start of the command prompt.

In a Linux or macOS environment, the command prompt path won't look the same as shown in Figure 2-11. If you're using the zsh command line shell, then it will look more like this:

```
.venvalan@MacBookAir First Python %
```

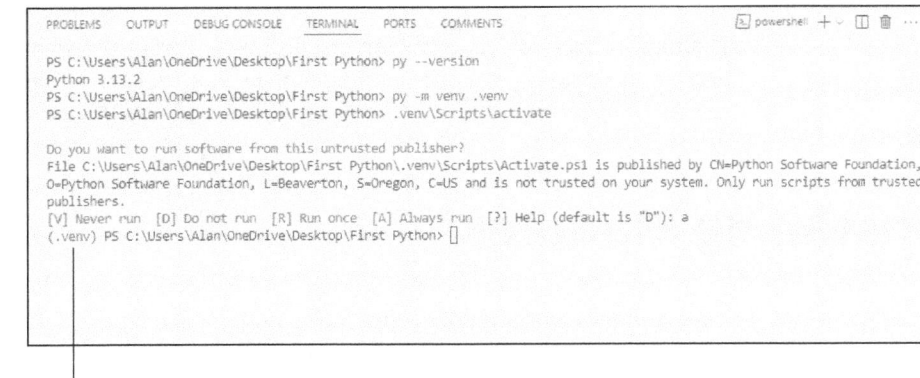

```
PROBLEMS   OUTPUT   DEBUG CONSOLE   TERMINAL   PORTS   COMMENTS                    powershell  +  ⌄  ⬚  🗑  ⋯

PS C:\Users\Alan\OneDrive\Desktop\First Python> py --version
Python 3.13.2
PS C:\Users\Alan\OneDrive\Desktop\First Python> py -m venv .venv
PS C:\Users\Alan\OneDrive\Desktop\First Python> .venv\Scripts\activate

Do you want to run software from this untrusted publisher?
File C:\Users\Alan\OneDrive\Desktop\First Python\.venv\Scripts\Activate.ps1 is published by CN=Python Software Foundation,
O=Python Software Foundation, L=Beaverton, S=Oregon, C=US and is not trusted on your system. Only run scripts from trusted
publishers.
[V] Never run  [D] Do not run  [R] Run once  [A] Always run  [?] Help (default is "D"): a
(.venv) PS C:\Users\Alan\OneDrive\Desktop\First Python> []
```

FIGURE 2-11:
The .venv
virtual
environment
is active.

Active virtual environment

If you're using the bash shell, it will look more like this:

```
.venvMacBookAir:First Python alan$
```

On your own computer, *MacBookAir* will be the name of the computer you're using, and *alan* will be your own username.

TECHNICAL STUFF

Z shell (or zsh) is a command-line interpreter shell, similar to Bash (short for Bourne Again Shell), but with more capabilities. Until macOS Catalina 10.15, released in 2019, macOS used Bash as the default shell; since then, zsh has been the default shell for macOS.

You can choose which command line shell you want to use by clicking the dropdown arrow next to the current shell name near the upper-right corner of the Terminal (refer to Figure 2-8). But Python commands should work the same way with either shell.

After you've activated a virtual environment, you no longer need to use an alias like py or python3 instead of python in a command. The python command works without the alias. So, now you can use python --version or python -V to see the version number of Python you're using for the current project.

When your workspace folder is open and your virtual environment is active, you're ready to get to work on creating or modifying your script or running a script if you've already created one. It's extremely unlikely you'll need to deactivate the virtual environment while you're in the workspace. But in the interest of completeness, I should tell you that it's easy to do. Regardless of what operating system you're using, you can just type the following command at the command prompt and press Enter:

```
deactivate
```

The name of the virtual environment disappears from the start of the command prompt in the Terminal. The command `python` goes back to being unrecognized, so you'd have to use the `py` or `python3` alias to run any Python commands.

Installing Modules

After you've created and opened your project workspace folder, selected your Python version (interpreter), and created and activated your virtual environment, you can install any modules your project might use. So, what are modules and why would you use them?

A Python *module* is Python code already written by someone else to perform certain tasks. Most modules have been around for years, have been refined and improved over the years, and are ideal for performing whatever they're designed to do. Modules help you avoid reinventing the wheel, by giving you trustworthy code to perform some common tasks.

Some modules are part of the Python standard library and installed automatically when you first install Python. You can use them any time in your code just by including an `import` statement at the top of your code. The most common and widely recognized modules include the following:

>> **math:** Mathematical functions

>> **os:** Operating system interfaces

>> **sys:** System-specific parameters and functions

>> **datetime:** Date and time handling

>> **random:** Random number generation

To keep the base Python installation lean, many larger more specialized modules are not included. But you can add them to your virtual environment using a `pip install` command at the command prompt when you're sure that virtual environment is active. The name *pip* is short for Pip Installed Packages, and that's exactly what it does. You just enter a command like this:

```
pip install modulename
```

Replace *modulename* with the name of the module you want to import. Optionally, you can install multiple modules just by separating their names with a space, like this:

```
pip install modulename1 modulename2 modulename3 modulename4
```

So, how do you know what modules to import for a script? When you're a beginner creating your own scripts, you don't. But when you're running an existing script, like those presented in this book, the import statements at the top of the code tell you exactly which modules you'll need.

```
import requests
import tkinter as tk  # For GUI
from bs4 import BeautifulSoup  # For web scraping
import pandas as pd  # For data handling
import matplotlib.pyplot as plt  # For plotting

class WeatherDashboard:
    def __init__(self, root):
        self.root = root
        self.root.title("Weather Dashboard")
        self.root.geometry("400x500")
```

The name of the module to install is always right after the word import. Don't worry about from or as names in the preceding sample code (import tkinter as tk or from bs4 import BeautifulSoup). Just use the name after import in your install command. For example, to install packages to run that script, you could enter these pip install commands:

```
pip install requests
pip install beautifulsoup4
pip install pandas
pip install matplotlib
```

Optionally, you could import them all with the following single command:

```
pip install requests beautifulsoup4 pandas matplotlib
```

Don't worry about memorizing all of that right now. I'll be sure to explain requirements with each automation script presented in this book. For now, it's sufficient to make the connection between the import statements at the top of a script, and the pip install commands for adding those to the script's virtual environment.

Writing and Running Python Scripts

The goal of everything we've done so far is to set things up to create a Python app or script. The word *app* is short for *application,* and it typically refers to larger commercial apps requiring dozens of files of code. In Python, it's common to refer to single-file apps as *scripts.* Most automation projects in this book only require one file of code, so I use the word *script* more than *app.* But regardless of whether you call it a script or an app, each one requires its own workspace folder and virtual environment.

In this section, I show you how to write and run a Python script.

Writing a Python script

Now it's time to write your first Python script. If you've been following along, you have the `First Python` workspace folder open in VS Code, and your `.venv` virtual environment is activated. You're ready to create your first script. Each script is just a file within the workspace root folder. That file must have a `.py` extension. The filename itself should follow the same rules as Python variable names. In short:

>> Use all lowercase letters.

>> Use a lowercase letter (not a number or underscore) for the first character.

>> Use an underscore (_) instead of a space.

>> Don't use any special characters (for example, !, @, #, -, and so on).

>> Don't use names of built-in modules (for example, sys, os, math, random, datetime, io, and so on).

>> Make the name as descriptive as possible and always use the `.py` extension.

Table 2-1 shows examples of good and bad filenames, where the third column indicates what's wrong in the bad example.

TABLE 2-1 **Good and Bad Python Filenames**

Good Filename	Bad Filename	Why It's Bad
`main.py`	`Main.py`	It has an uppercase letter.
`calculate_stats.py`	`math.py`	It has the same name as a built-in module.
`file_reader.py`	`File Reader.py`	It has uppercase letters and a space.
`process_images.py`	`9images.py`	It starts with a number.

REMEMBER

You can ask any AI, "What are names of Python built-in modules?" if you're not sure about a filename.

With all the rules and guidelines out of the way, the actual process to create the file is quite simple in VS Code. Make sure the root folder is selected in the Explorer pane. From there, follow these steps:

1. **Click the root folder name** (First Python **in our working example) to select it.**

   If the folder collapses, you can click again to expand the folder and keep it selected.

2. **Click the New File icon just to the right of the root folder name.**

   It looks like a document with a plus sign (+).

3. **Type a filename with a** .py **extension.**

   For this example, use hello.py.

4. **Press Enter.**

The filename should be visible under the root folder name, at the same level of indentation as the .venv folder. The file opens in the editor to the right. If you've enabled AI, you'll see a prompt at the top of the new file inviting you to tell AI what code you want to write, as shown in Figure 2-12.

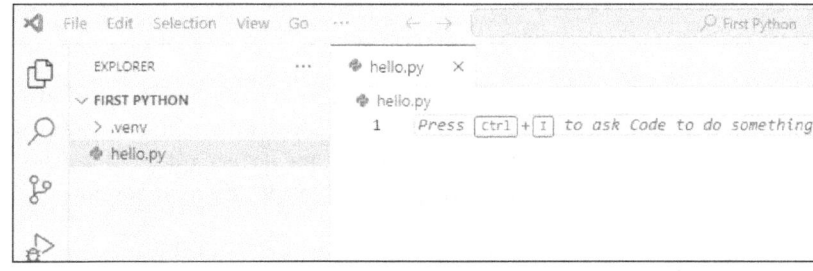

FIGURE 2-12:
A file named
hello.py
added to
the project.

TIP

If you ever need to rename or delete a file in the Explorer pane, just right-click the filename for a shortcut menu of options. If you accidentally put a file in the .venv folder rather than the root folder, you can simply drag the file to the root folder name and drop it there.

If you don't want to use AI to write your code, just start typing your code. For the first example, you'll create a Hello World script that includes a Python comment. Follow these steps:

1. **Click inside the editor to the right of the Explorer pane and type** # My first Hello World script.

2. **Press Enter and type the following Python code:**

```
print("Hello, World!")
```

Note that this is code so you must type it exactly as shown or it won't work.

3. **Press Enter.**

Figure 2-13 shows how things should look now. The name of script appears in a tab at the top of the Editor pane. The code you typed into the script appears below that.

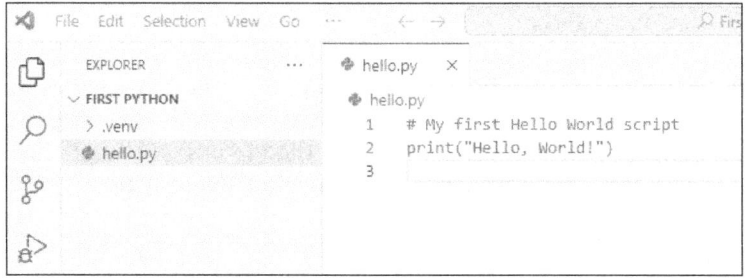

FIGURE 2-13:
A Python comment and some code typed into hello.py.

The print() command in Python tells Python to output something to the Terminal when you *execute* (run) the script. In the example print("Hello, World!"), we expect that line to show Hello, World! as the output. To test it, you need to run the script, as I explain in the next section.

Running a Python script

Running a Python script is simple, and you have a couple of choices. In this section, I describe the most common.

If you haven't already done so, click the script filename (hello.py in the example) to see its code in the editor. Then click Run Python File (see Figure 2-14) near the upper-right corner of the VS Code window.

The script runs, and any output from a print() command appears in the Terminal, such as where you see Hello, World! in Figure 2-15.

FIGURE 2-14:
The Run Python
File button near
the upper-right
corner of
VS Code.

FIGURE 2-15:
Result of
running hello.py.

```
PROBLEMS   OUTPUT   DEBUG CONSOLE   TERMINAL   PORTS   COMMENTS

(.venv) PS C:\Users\Alan\OneDrive\Desktop\First Python> & C:/Users/Alan/AppDat
/python.exe "c:/Users/Alan/OneDrive/Desktop/First Python/hello.py"
Hello, World!
(.venv) PS C:\Users\Alan\OneDrive\Desktop\First Python> []
```

As an alternative to using the Run Python File button, you can type **python** *scriptname* at the command prompt in the Terminal. For example, to run `hello.py`, you'd type the following in the Terminal and press Enter:

```
python hello.py
```

The script runs and displays any `print()` output in the usual manner.

OPENING AN EXISTING PROJECT

After you've created a script, you don't need to go through all these steps every time you want to run or work with the script. In fact, all you really need to do is open the workspace folder and activate its virtual environment. The steps are simple:

1. **Open the script's workspace folder in VS Code.**

2. **Choose View ⇨ Terminal from VS Code's menu bar to open the Terminal.**

3. **Activate your virtual environment: In Windows, enter** .venv\Scripts\activate. **In Linux or macOS, enter** .venv/bin/activate.

   Make sure not to enter the period at the end.

4. **To edit a script, click its name.**

5. **To run a script, click its name and click the Run Python File, or use the syntax** `python filename.py` **to run the script from the command prompt in the Terminal.**

That should do the trick for any existing project.

Chapter **3**

Python Basics for Automation

n this chapter, you discover the concepts, commands, and structures for writing Python code. If you're an experienced Python developer, most of this won't be news to you. If you're experienced with other programming languages, the terms and concepts will be familiar — you'll just be learning the Python way of doing things. And if you're new to writing code, *all* of this will be new.

REMEMBER

This one chapter isn't a replacement for an entire book on Python. (If that's what you need, check out *Python All-in-One For Dummies* by John C. Shovic and Alan Simpson [published by Wiley]) The goal of this chapter is to give you a quick overview of Python and a quick reference to code you'll see in this book's automation scripts.

Understanding Python Comments

Python comments aren't really Python code. Instead, they're plain-English notes embedded in code. Comments have no effect on how the code runs or is executed. When writing your own code, you can include comments as notes to yourself, for reminders about what the code is doing. Throughout this book, I use comments to describe what's going on and help you learn.

To type a single-line comment, start by typing **#**. All text to the right of the # on the same line (only) is a comment. For example, looking at the following line, the x=10 part is actual Python code, and the text to the right of the # is a plain-English comment.

```
x=10 # Store the number 10 in the variable named x.
```

TECHNICAL STUFF

You can also add longer multiline comments to your code by placing the comment text between two sets of triple quotation marks (" " ") or triple apostrophes (' ' '). For example, all the text between the two sets of triple quotation marks is comment text, not code:

```
"""
In Python, any text between triple quotation marks or triple apostrophes is
    a comment.
"""
```

Mastering Variables and Data Types

Virtually all Python scripts (and code in other languages) use *variables* to store data (information). Think of a variable as a cubbyhole in which you can store things. Every variable in a script must have a unique name. You can make up your own variable names, as long as you play by the following rules:

>> A variable name must start with a letter (a–z or A–Z).

>> After the first letter, a variable name can contain any letter (a–z or A–Z), any digit (0–9), or one or more underscores (_).

>> A variable name can't contain spaces or special characters like !, @, #, $, -, and so on.

>> Python variable names are case-sensitive, which means myVar, MyVar, and myvar are treated as different variables.

>> Variable names can't match any of Python's commands or keywords, such as if, for, while, class, def, True, False, and so on.

Beyond the hard-and-fast rules, there are some best-practice style guidelines, defined in PEP 8 (https://peps.python.org/pep-0008). That guide is a set of recommendations for writing clean, readable, and consistent code. It was authored by Guido van Rossum (Python's creator) and others. PEP stands for Python Enhancement Proposal, and most Python developers follow it. PEP 8 recommends the following for variable names:

>> Use lowercase with underscores for variable names (for example, my_variable).

>> For *constants,* variables whose values never change, use all uppercase (for example, TAX_RATE).

>> Avoid starting with an underscore unless it's for a special case (for example, private variables in classes).

>> Use descriptive names that indicate the variable's purpose (for example, user_age instead of x).

TIP

There's no strict limit on the length of a variable name, but it's best to keep them concise and meaningful for readability.

Each variable contains some *value.* Here's an example where the variable user_name contains the value alan:

```
user_name = "alan"
```

The value you store in a variable has a *data type*. Computers store different kinds of information differently for efficiency and speed. The next sections describe each data type and present examples of their use.

Working with numbers

Computers, as you probably know, are great for working with numbers. In Python, there are two data types for numbers:

>> **Integer (**int**):** Whole numbers with no decimal point, such as 2, 11, 1,345, or –11

>> **Floating point (**float**):** Numbers that contain a decimal point, such as 3.12, 99.98, or –1.075. The range of values goes from 2.35×10^{-308} to 1.797×10^{308}.

TIP

When typing numbers, never include a dollar sign or comma, even if the number represents a dollar amount. For example, you must type the dollar amount $1,234.57 as 1234.57. Your script can *show* the number with a dollar sign and comma in its output. But you need to leave those out when assigning the number value to a variable.

Here are some examples of variables being assigned number values, with explanatory comments:

```
quantity = 10      # integer
unit_price = 1.98       # floating-point number
sales_tax_rate = 0.065       # floating-point number
temperature = 98.6       # floating-point number
offset = -10       # integer
```

A number always represents some quantity and you can do math with them, such as add, subtract, multiply, or divide.

Working with text (strings)

To store text in a variable, use the string (str) data type. The term *string* refers to a string of characters; it doesn't represent some number you would use for doing math. You must enclose the string in single quotation marks (' ') or double quotation marks (""), so Python recognizes it as a string.

TIP

Strings are typically things like names, email addresses, product names, even whole sentences. Here are some Python variables being assigned string values:

```
name = "Alice"  # string
greeting = 'Hello, world!'  # string
email_address = "someone@somewhere.com"  # string
message = 'Please insert a USB drive to continue.'  # string
```

TIP

When typing your own code, it doesn't matter if you enclose a string in single or double quotation marks. Python will treat it as a string either way. However, the PEP 8 guidelines recommend you use one or the other consistently throughout any given script for consistency and readability.

If the string itself contains a single or double quotation mark, like the word *don't* (the apostrophe is the same as a single quotation mark), that could cause an error because it looks like the string ends at the apostrophe:

```
warning = 'Don't do that!'  # Three single quotation marks confuses Python.
```

There are two ways around this problem. If you enclose the string in double quotation marks, there's no conflict because Python "knows" the string ends at the last double quotation mark:

```
warning = "Don't do that!"
```

Another way around the problem is to precede the embedded quotation marks with a backslash. In that case, you could enclose the entire string in single quotation marks because the backslash tells Python that the apostrophe is part of the string and not the end of the string:

```
warning = 'Don\'t do that!'  # The \' represents an embedded apostrophe.
```

Deciding true or false with Booleans

The Boolean (bool) data type is a value that can be True or False, and no other value. Booleans are often used in decisions. You must type **True** or **False** with an initial capital letter for Python to recognize it as a Boolean data type.

TECHNICAL STUFF

Though not required, it's common to start the name of any variable that stores a Boolean value with is_ as in these examples:

```
is_member = False  # Boolean
is_active = True  # Boolean
```

The is_ in front of the name signals that the variable represents a Boolean value, which helps make your code more readable.

Using lists

A variable doesn't always have to contain just one value. A variable can also contain a list of values. The rules for defining a list are pretty straightforward:

>> The list must be enclosed in square brackets: [ ].

>> Each value in the list must be separated by a comma (,).

>> Values in the list can be any data type, and they don't all have to be the same data type.

TECHNICAL STUFF

Some programming languages use the term *array* to describe a list. But an array is the same thing — a numbered list of values.

Here are examples of Python variables being assigned lists of values:

```
fruits = ["apple", "banana", "orange"]  # list of strings
player_numbers = [11, 26, 28, 41]  # list of integers
data_type_examples = [1, 3.14, "string here", False]  # list of values
```

Each item in a list has an index number or subscript, indicating its position in the list. However, unlike normal counting, where you always start with 1, Python starts at 0. So, in the first example, fruits[0] is "apple". In the second example, player_numbers[1] is 26 (even though it may seem like it should be 11).

Making immutable lists with tuples

The data types I explain in the previous sections cover just about anything you'll ever need to do in Python or any other programming language for that matter. But Python does have some more advanced data types, which are sometimes used in more advanced apps.

TECHNICAL STUFF

A *tuple* (tuple) is a data type that's like a list, but with one big difference: Tuples are *immutable,* meaning that after you define a tuple in your code, other code in the script can't change any values or rearrange values. To indicate that a list of values is a tuple rather than a list, enclose the values in parentheses rather than square brackets.

The main reason tuples exist is because the computer can work with them faster than it can work with lists because no considerations for possible changes need to be made. Also, tuples are secure in the sense that, after the list is defined, nothing in the code can change the list. Here is an example of a tuple:

```
ny_coordinates = (40.7128, -74.0060)  # map coordinates for New York
```

As with lists, the values in a tuple are numbered starting at 0. Even though you use parentheses, rather than square brackets, you still use square brackets to access items in the list. In the following code, a variable named latitude receives the value 40.7128 and a variable named longitude receives the value -74.0060:

```
latitude = ny_coordinates[0]   # first value in tuple 40.7128
longitude = ny_coordinates[1]  # second value in tuple -74.0060
```

Defining key–value pairs in dictionaries

A Python dictionary (dict) is another list-like structure, but instead of individual values, a dictionary contains a list of key–value pairs. Unlike lists, which are enclosed in square brackets, and tuples, which are enclosed in parentheses, a dictionary is always enclosed in curly braces ({}).

Typically, the key in each pair is the name of what the value represents; the value is a number or string assigned to that name. Use a colon (:) to separate the key from the value. As with other list types, use a comma to separate each key–value pair. Here's an example where a variable named person contains a dictionary with key–value pairs about a person:

```
person = {"name": "Angela", "age": 47, "country": "USA"}
```

The nice thing about a dictionary is that you can tell what's going on just by looking at the code: In this case, the person is named Angela, she's 47 years old, and she lives in the United States.

To access values in a dictionary, you don't have to deal with zero-based index numbers. Use the key name, in square brackets, to indicate which item you want. For example, the code stores information about a person in three separate variables.

```
user_name = person["name"]   # Angela
user_age = person["age"]   # 47
user_locale = person["country"]   # USA
```

Data dictionaries are often used to store data extracted from a database. The key names in the data dictionary represent field names from a row within the database.

Leaving things hanging with None

None is a special data type that indicates "nothing," not even data type. It's sometimes used to create a placeholder variable whose actual value and data type may be determined later in code. In your code, you can use None in decision-making (described a little later in this chapter) to determine whether a variable has been assigned a value yet.

Let's say you've built a web app that always starts with a user who isn't logged in yet. In your code, you could set the username variable to None, to make it clear that no user is logged in yet:

```
# Variable user_name no data type or value
user_name = None
```

Subsequent code that shows a page header can show a message to sign in if the user hasn't logged in yet. Otherwise, it can show Hello followed by the user's name, as follows:

```
# If no logged in user, set prompt to sign in.
if user_name is None:
    prompt = ("Sign In")
```

```
# Otherwise, set prompt to Hello and the user's name.
else:
    prompt = ("Hello " + user_name)
```

I know we haven't discussed if...else yet, so this example may be a little advanced if you're new to Python. But don't worry — I explain all about if...else in the "Making Decisions" section, later in this chapter.

REMEMBER

Artificial intelligence (AI) knows all about Python and data types. Any time you have a question about that, consider asking any free AI for clarification first. You'll get an answer immediately.

Formatting Output

When writing scripts, Python developers often use print() to output data to the Terminal to check on things, such as the value of some data or condition. The print statement uses the simple syntax:

```
print(value)
```

where the *value* is a literal string or number or a variable name. If the value is literal text, it must be enclosed in single or double quotation marks:

```
print('Hello world!')
```

That line of code "prints" Hello World! on the screen. In the following example, a variable named user_name is set to Wanda. The print() statement displays Wanda onscreen because the variable named user_name is not in quotation marks, so Python treats it as a variable name rather than literal text:

```
# Put Wanda in a variable named user_name.
user_name = "Wanda"
# Display the contents of the user_name variable.
print(user_name)
```

When you want to display both literal text and variable data in output, you can use a formatted string literal, or f-string. To use such a string, put a lowercase letter f right after the opening parenthesis after print. Inside the quotation marks, put the literal text you want to show, with variable names enclosed in quotation marks. For example, the following code is similar to the preceding code, but it displays the literal text Hello there along with the user_name variable's value using an f-string:

```
# Put Wanda in a variable named user_name.
user_name = "Wanda"
# Display the contents of the user_name variable.
print(f"Hello there, {user_name}!")
The output from the above code is Hello there, Wanda!
```

Your f-string can contain any number of variables. The following example includes two variables, a string and a number. The f-string prints them both:

```
# Two variables, one a string the other a number
user_name = "Wanda"
age = 25
# Display the contents of the user_name variable.
print(f"Hi, {user_name}! I see you are {age} years old.")
```

The output from the above code is:

```
Hi, Wanda! I see you are 25 years old.
```

When displaying numbers, the output you get may not be exactly what you want. For example the following code prints the value of pi (from Python's built-in math module) and a floating-point number named unit_price:

```
# Import the built-in math module.
import math
# Show the value of pi in an f-string.
print(f"Pi is equal to {math.pi}")
# Now do a dollar amount.
unit_price = 12345.67
print(f"The unit price is {unit_price}")
```

The output from that code is the following two lines:

```
Pi is equal to 3.141592653589793
The unit price is 12345.67
```

To gain some control over the numbers (as well as strings), you can use format directives, shown in Table 3-1, to specify exactly how you want the number to look. In the f-string example, x represents a variable that contains the value shown in the Example Input column. Underscores in the Output column will display as blank spaces in the output. The table also includes directives for aligning strings with spaces and for truncating strings to a maximum length.

TABLE 3-1   **Formatting Directives Used with Python f-strings**

Directive	Description	Example Input	f-String Example	Output
d	Integer (decimal)	42	f"{x:d}"	42
5d	Integer, width 5	42	f"{x:5d}"	___42
<5d	Integer, width 5 (left-aligned)	42	f"{x:<5d}"	42___
>5d	Integer, width 5 (right-aligned)	42	f"{x:>5d}"	___42
^5d	Integer, width 5 (centered)	42	f"{x:^5d}"	_42__
03d	Integer, three digits, zero-padded	7	f"{x:03d}"	007
f	Float (default six decimals)	3.14159	f"{x:f}"	3.141593
.2f	Float, two decimals	3.14159	f"{x:.2f}"	3.14
8.2f	Float, width 8, two decimals	3.14159	f"{x:8.2f}"	3.14
<8.2f	Float, width 8, two decimals, left	3.14159	f"{x:<8.2f}"	____3.14
x	Integer as hexadecimal (lower)	255	f"{x:x}"	ff
X	Integer as hexadecimal (upper)	255	f"{x:X}"	FF
o	Integer as octal	8	f"{x:o}"	10
b	Integer as binary	5	f"{x:b}"	101
s	String (default)	Python	f"{x:s}"	Python
10s	String, width 10 (left-aligned)	Python	f"{x:10s}"	Python____
>10s	String, width 10 (right-aligned)	Python	f"{x:>10s}"	____Python
.3s	String, truncated to three chars	Python	f"{x:.3s}"	Pyt
%	Percentage (multiply by 100)	0.75	f"{x:%}"	75.000000%
0.10%	Percentage, one decimal	0.75	f"{x:.1%}"	75.00%
,	Thousands separator (integers)	1234567	f"{x:,d}"	1,234,567
,.2f	Thousands separator (floats)	12345.6789	f"{x:,.2f}"	12,345.68

Dealing with Dates and Times

Python doesn't have a data type for working with dates and times, but it does have powerful built-in modules to help with them. The main built-in module is named `datetime`. To use it, include the following statement at the top of your script:

```
from datetime import datetime
```

TECHNICAL STUFF

Notice that the preceding code is `from datetime import datetime`, rather than just `import datetime`. That allows you to define a date without repeating `.datetime` in the variable assignment. Had I used `import datetime` as the first line of code, the second line would have needed to be `dt = datetime.datetime(2026, 11, 28, 15, 30, 0)` in order to work. Not a big deal. But it's a common syntax, so I used it here as an example.

To get values from `datetime`, you typically follow *variablename* = with `datetime.`, followed by code specifying exactly what you want. For example, take a look at the following:

```
from datetime import datetime
current_time = datetime.now()
print(current_time)
```

Running that code produces output that looks something like this, but with the current date and time according to your computer's internal clock:

```
2025-04-12 10:10:51.644321
```

To create your own dates and times, use the syntax `datetime.date(year, month, day)`. For example, this line stores 12/25/2026 in a variable named `my_date`:

```
my_date = datetime.date(2026, 12, 25)   # Year, Month, Day
```

To specify both a date and a time use the syntax `datetime.datetime(year, month, day, hour, minute)`. Use the 24-hour clock for the hour (for example, 15 for 3:00 p.m.). Here's an example where we're setting a variable named deadline to November 30, 2026, at 3:30 p.m.:

```
deadline = datetime.datetime(2026, 11, 30, 15, 30)
```

To make dates and times easier for people to read, you can use `strftime()` with the directives shown in Table 3-2. They work similarly to the f-string directives shown in Table 3-1, but you have to put the directive inside the parentheses of `.strftime()` inside the f-string. In the Code Example column, `dt` represents any datetime value.

TABLE 3-2 **The Directives for .strftime() Formatting with datetime Values**

Directive	Description	Code Example	Output Example
%Y	Year with century (four digits)	`f"{dt.strftime('%Y')}"`	2025
%y	Year without century (two digits, 00–99)	`f"{dt.strftime('%y')}"`	25
%m	Month as zero-padded number (01–12)	`f"{dt.strftime('%m')}"`	03
%B	Full month name	`f"{dt.strftime('%B')}"`	March
%b	Abbreviated month name	`f"{dt.strftime('%b')}"`	Mar
%d	Day of month (01–31)	`f"{dt.strftime('%d')}"`	27
%A	Full weekday name	`f"{dt.strftime('%A')}"`	Thursday
%a	Abbreviated weekday name	`f"{dt.strftime('%a')}"`	Thu
%H	Hour (00–23, 24-hour clock)	`f"{dt.strftime('%H')}"`	14
%I	Hour (01–12, 12-hour clock)	`f"{dt.strftime('%I')}"`	02
%M	Minute (00–59)	`f"{dt.strftime('%M')}"`	35
%S	Second (00–59)	`f"{dt.strftime('%S')}"`	22
%p	AM/PM indicator	`f"{dt.strftime('%p')}"`	PM
%j	Day of year (001–366)	`f"{dt.strftime('%j')}"`	086
%w	Weekday as number (0–6, where 0 is Sunday)	`f"{dt.strftime('%w')}"`	4
%U	Week number of year (00–53, Sunday start)	`f"{dt.strftime('%U')}"`	12
%W	Week number of year (00–53, Monday start)	`f"{dt.strftime('%W')}"`	13

Directive	Description	Code Example	Output Example
%c	Locale's date and time representation	`f"{dt.strftime('%c')}"`	Thu Mar 27 14:35:22 2025
%x	Locale's date representation	`f"{dt.strftime('%x')}"`	3/27/2025
%X	Locale's time representation	`f"{dt.strftime('%X')}"`	14:35:22
%%	Literal % character	`f"{dt.strftime('%%Y')}"`	%Y

As an example, the following code sets a datetime to November 15, 2026, at 3:30 p.m.:

```python
from datetime import datetime  # Import the datetime class
dt = datetime(2026, 11, 28, 15, 30, 0)  # No need for datetime.datetime
print(dt)
print(dt.strftime('%B %d, %Y %I:%M%p'))
```

The output is as follows:

```
2026-11-28 15:30:00
November 28, 2026 03:30PM
```

The first line shows how the datetime looks if you don't use any formatting. The second line shows the output with the `strftime()` formatting.

Manipulating Data with Operators

Python contains all the operators you'd expect to find in any programming language. If you need more information for any operator in this section, you can ask AI or refer to the official Python documentation at the www.python.org.

Using arithmetic and string operators

By far, the most-used operators are the arithmetic and string operators, shown in Table 3-3. These operators are used for addition, subtraction, multiplication, division, exponentiation, and string concatenation. The order shown in the table is also the order of operations, as defined in standard math. You may have learned it as PEMDAS (Parentheses, Exponents, Multiplication, Division, Addition, Subtraction) in school.

TABLE 3-3 **Arithmetic and String Concatenation Operators**

Precedence	Operator	Description	Example	Result
1	( )	Parentheses (grouping)	(2+3)*4	20
2	**	Exponentiation	2**3	8
3	*	Multiplication	2*3	6
3	/	Division	6/2	3
3	//	Floor division	7//2	3
3	%	Modulus (remainder)	7%2	1
4	+	Addition	2+3	5
4	+	String concatenation	'a'+'b'	'ab'
4	–	Subtraction	5–2	3

Operators that have the same order of operations are executed left to right in an expression. The + operator, when used with strings, simply joins the strings into one string. For example, in the following example, the user_name variable contains Sarah. That's then joined to the string "Hello, " (which includes a space at the end), to form a new string named Greeting that contains Hello, Sarah.

```
# Combining strings with the + operator
user_name = "Sarah"
greeting = "Hello, " + user_name
print(greeting)
```

TIP

People sometimes use Please Excuse My Dear Aunt Sally (PEMDAS) as a mnemonic for memorizing order of operations. PEMDAS stands for parentheses, exponents, multiplication, division, addition, subtraction, which is the order in which operations should be performed.

Using assignment operators

Use Python assignment operators to assign values to variables. Earlier, I provide examples of using the = operator to assign a value to a variable. For example, user_name = "Sarah" assigns the string value Sarah to a variable named user_name. Table 3-4 shows the assignment operators. In the Example column, the semicolon separates two separate lines of code. The Result column shows the result of executing both lines of code.

TABLE 3-4   **Python Assignment Operators**

Operator	Description	Example	Result
=	Assigns a value to a variable	x = 5	x is 5
+=	Adds and assigns	x = 5; x += 3	x is 8
-=	Subtracts and assigns	x = 5; x -= 2	x is 3
*=	Multiplies and assigns	x = 5; x *= 2	x is 10
/=	Divides and assigns	x = 6; x /= 2	x is 3.0
//=	Floor divides and assigns	x = 7; x //= 2	x is 3
%=	Modulus and assigns	x = 7; x %= 2	x is 1
**=	Exponentiates and assigns	x = 2; x **= 3	x is 8
&=	Bitwise AND and assigns	x = 5; x &= 3	x is 1
|=	Bitwise OR and assigns	x = 5; x |= 2	x is 7
^=	Bitwise XOR and assigns	x = 5; x ^= 3	x is 6
>>=	Right shifts and assigns	x = 8; x >>= 2	x is 2
<<=	Left shifts and assigns	x = 2; x <<= 2	x is 8

TECHNICAL STUFF

Don't worry about understanding all the assignment operators in Table 3-4. Many are very advanced and specialized and not used in Python automation. I'm showing them here in the interest of being thorough. As always, AI or any reference book can fill you in on the details of any operator.

Recognizing other operators

In addition to all those assignment operators, Python offers operators for comparison, like == for "is equal to," and logical operators like "and" for `country == "USA" and birth_year < 2000`. Those operators are summarized in Table 3-5. I know it's a lot to take in when you're first learning this stuff. But you don't need to memorize them — just refer back to this chapter if you encounter one in an automation script presented in this book.

TIP

If you need more information on any operator, you can also ask any AI or refer to the Python documentation at `www.python.org`.

TABLE 3-5 Python Unary, Comparison, and other Operators

Category	Operator	Description	Example	Result
Unary arithmetic	"+x"	Unary plus (identity)	"+5"	"5"
Unary arithmetic	"-x"	Unary minus (negation)	"-5"	"-5"
Comparison	"=="	Equal to	"3 == 3"	"True"
Comparison	"!="	Not equal to	"3 != 4"	"True"
Comparison	">"	Greater than	"5 > 3"	"True"
Comparison	"<"	Less than	"2 < 4"	"True"
Comparison	">="	Greater than or equal to	"5 >= 5"	"True"
Comparison	"<="	Less than or equal to	"3 <= 4"	"True"
Logical	"and"	Logical AND	"True and False"	"False"
Logical	"or"	Logical OR	"True or False"	"True"
Logical	"not"	Logical NOT	"not True"	"False"
Bitwise	"&"	Bitwise AND	"5 & 3" (0101 & 0011)	"1" (0001)
Bitwise	"|"	Bitwise OR	"5 | 2" (0101 | 0010)	"7" (0111)
Bitwise	"^"	Bitwise XOR	"5 ^ 3" (0101 ^ 0011)	"6" (0110)
Bitwise	"~"	Bitwise NOT (complement)	"~5" (~0101)	"-6"
Bitwise	"<<"	Left shift	"2 << 1" (0010 << 1)	"4" (0100)
Bitwise	">>"	Right shift	"4 >> 1" (0100 >> 1)	"2" (0010)
Identity	"is"	Object identity (same object)	"a = [1]; b = a; a is b"	"True"
Identity	"is not"	Object nonidentity	"a = [1]; b = [1]; a is not b"	"True"
Membership	"in"	Membership (contained in)	"'a' in 'abc'"	"True"
Membership	"not in"	Nonmembership	"'x' not in 'abc'"	"True"

Getting Loopy with Loops

Loops are common in all programming languages. They're used to repeat one or more lines of code multiple times. You can use them to access items in a list one at a time, folders on a drive, or files in a folder. Python provides two main types of loops: `for` loops and `while` loops.

Looping with for

The `for` loop is useful when counting or when there is a known number of items to iterate over. The loop executes a block of code for each item in the sequence. The syntax is as follows:

```
for variable in sequence:
    # Code to repeat
```

Replace *variable* with a variable name of your choosing. This value keeps count with each iteration of the loop. Replace *sequence* with the name of the list or collection of items to loop through. The colon (:) marks the start of the loop block, and indentation defines what code belongs inside the loop. Indentation is critical, because only the code that's indented under the `for` statement is repeated for each loop iteration. The first un-indented line under `for` isn't executed until the looping is completed.

Here's an example where I define a list of three values and then use a `for` loop to go through the list and print each item on a separate line:

```
# Define a list and loop through the list.
fruits = ["apple", "banana", "cherry"]
for fruit in fruits:
    print(fruit)
```

TIP

With Python automation, you're more likely to loop through all files in a folder, or something similar. Here's an example where the `folder_path` variable indicates the location and name of a hypothetical folder. Then the `for` loop iterates through each file in the folder and displays its name. The script imports the built-in `pathlib` module, which contains the code to allow such looping to work.

```
from pathlib import Path
# Specify the directory path (you can change this to your desired directory).
directory = Path(r"C:\Users\Alan\Documents\Practice") # Windows example
#directory = Path("/Users/Alan/Practice") # Mac example
```

```
# Loop through all files in the directory.
for file_path in directory.iterdir():
    if file_path.is_file():  # Check if it's a file (not a directory).
        print(f"Found file: {file_path.name}")
```

Looping for a while

The while loop repeats a block of code as long as a condition is true. It's like saying, "Keep doing this until something changes." There is no variable keeping track of how many times you've gone through the loop, so you don't want to use this loop where counting is required. The syntax of the while loop is:

```
while condition:
    # Code to repeat
```

The condition statement can be anything that evaluates to either True or False. The loop runs for as long as the condition remains True. All code that's indented below the while line is executed with each pass through the loop. When the condition evaluates to False, the loop stops and code execution resumes at the first non-indented line of code below the loop.

WARNING

If the condition never evaluates to False, the script will get stuck in an infinite loop. If you find yourself in that predicament, press Ctrl+C to cancel the loop. You may have to press Ctrl+C a few times.

A while loop can be used to repeatedly ask a user for input until some condition is met. In the following example, a prompt asks the user to enter a number between 1 and 10. If the user ignores the prompt and enters something else, the loop keeps asking until the user complies with the requests (or presses Ctrl+C to bail out of the loop):

```
# Start with user_input at some number that's not between 1 and 10.
user_input = 0
# Loop until the input is a number between 1 and 10.
while user_input < 1 or user_input > 10:
    try:
        # Get input from the user and convert it to an integer.
        user_input = int(input("Enter a number between 1 and 10: "))
    except ValueError:
        # Handle non-numeric input (for example, letters or symbols).
        print("Invalid input! Please enter a valid number.")

# After the loop ends, confirm the valid input.
print(f"You entered a valid number: {number}")
```

The try: and except: statements in the sample code are covered in the "Handling Exceptions" section, later in this chapter.

Bailing out of loops

Though rarely needed, Python offers three special keywords for bailing out of loops before the loop ends naturally or for detecting whether a loop completed naturally:

» break: Exits the loop immediately.

» continue: Skips the rest of the current iteration and moves to the next one.

» else: Runs a block of code when the loop finishes normally (not when break is used).

Use the break statement with an if condition to break out of a loop if some condition is met. In the following example, the fruits variable contains some fruit names, one of which is an empty string (""). The sample code breaks out of the loop when it encounters such a string.

```
# A list of fruit names
fruits = ["Apple", "Banana", "", "Grape"]
# Print the list of fruits.
for fruit in fruits:
    if fruit=="":
        break
    print(fruit)
print("All Done")
```

The output from that code is:

```
Apple
Banana
All Done
```

The continue statement also works with an if condition. However, instead of stopping the loop, it simply avoids executing the code at that pass through the loop. For example, the following code is identical to the preceding code, but it uses continue in place of break:

```
# A list of fruit names
fruits = ["Apple", "Banana", "", "Grape"]
# Print the list of fruits.
```

```
for fruit in fruits:
    if fruit=="":
        continue
    print(fruit)
print("All Done")
```

Unlike with break, this code skips over printing the null string, but continues on with the rest of the items in the list before exiting. So, the output is as follows:

```
Apple
Banana
Grape
All Done
```

The else keyword doesn't stop a loop from executing. Instead, if the for loop iterates through all its items and doesn't encounter a break, the code in the else block runs. If the loop is exited prematurely with a break, the else block is skipped. This can be useful for scenarios where you want to confirm that a loop completed fully or to handle a "not found" case after searching through a sequence.

```
numbers = [1, 2, 3, 4, 5]
target = 6
for num in numbers:
    if num == target:
        print(f"Found {target}!")
        break
else:
    print(f"{target} not found in the list.")
```

When executed, the preceding code displays 6 not found in the list because the break condition never happened, because the number 6 is not in the list.

Here's the same code where the condition is met because the number 3 is in the list.

```
numbers = [1, 2, 3, 4, 5]
target = 3
for num in numbers:
    if num == target:
        print(f"Found {target}!")
        break
else:
    print(f"{target} not found in the list.")
```

When executed, this code shows Found 3! because the number 3 is in the list. The loop also stops searching right after it finds 3. It's an efficient way to search a list, because the loop doesn't need to analyze every item in the list before determining whether the 3 is found.

REMEMBER

Indentation is critical in Python, and none of the loops above will work unless the code is properly indented. Code that executes inside a loop must be indented under the for statement, and code that executes when the if condition proves true must be indented under the if statement.

Making Decisions

Virtually all Python scripts involve decision-making (also called *branching*) so code only executes under certain conditions. Python offers three main tools for decision-making: if...else, ternary operator, and a match (as of version 3.10 of Python). You'll mostly use comparison and logical operators (refer to Table 3-5) to define a condition that evaluates to either True or False.

Deciding with if...else

The most common way to make decisions in Python is the if...else block of code. Indentation is critical in these blocks. Code that's indented under an if statement executes only when the if condition proves true. Code indented under an else statement executes only when the if condition proves false.

Let's start with a simple example where a variable named age receives some numeric value. In the code below, the if statement prints one thing if age is greater than or equal to (>=) 18. Otherwise, it prints a different message.

```
# Define a variable and assign a number.
age = 18
# Make a decision based on the value in the age variable.
if age >= 18:
    print("You can vote!")
else:
    print("You're too young to vote.")
```

That code illustrates the importance of indentations in Python. The text "You can vote!" displays only if the age variable contains a number that's greater than or equal to 18. If the age value is less than 18, then the else condition is true and the text "You're too young to vote." shows.

Sometimes if...else may not be enough, because there are more than two possible outcomes. That's where the elif statement comes into play. As you may have guessed, elif is short for else if. Each elif statement can have its own condition that proves either True or False. The final else statement only executes if none of the elif conditions proves True.

Once again, indentations are critical for the code to work properly. As soon as one if or elif statement proves True, no other conditions are considered. Code execution resumes at the next un-indented line under the if...elif...else block. Here's an example:

```python
# Define a variable named score and give it a numeric value between 0 and 100.
score = 92
# Assign a letter grade to the score based on the following rules:
if score >= 90:
    print("Grade: A")
elif score >= 80:
    print("Grade: B")
elif score >= 70:
    print("Grade: C")
elif score >= 60:
    print("Grade: D")
else:
    print("You have failed the exam.")

# The following code is outside the if...elif...else block.
print("Thanks for playing!")
```

When executed, only the if or one elif or the else statement will execute. The last line of code isn't indented under else so that line executes no matter what.

Compacting decisions with a ternary operator

The Python ternary operator is a compact way to write simple if...else statements in one line. You cannot use elif conditions. But it's great for assigning values based on a condition. The basic syntax is:

```python
variable = value_if_true if condition else value_if_false
```

The following code assigns values to two variables — one named age and the other named status. The status variable gets its value from a ternary operator that assigns a value of "adult" if the age is greater than or equal to 18. Otherwise, status gets a value of `"minor"`. So, it works the same way as `if...else`, but it's very compact and it executes in a single line of code. There's no need for indentations because it's just one line of code.

```
# The age variable gets a numeric value.
age = 20

# The status variable gets a string value dependent on the age variable's value.
status = "adult" if age >= 18 else "minor"
print(status)
```

Deciding with match

Python version 3.10 added the `match` statement as another way to handle decision-making when there are multiple possibilities. The `match` statement is a block of code that starts with `match` followed by a variable name. Below that are generally two or more indented `case` statements followed by values and a colon. Indented below each `case` statement is one or more lines of code that execute only if the value in the `case` statement matches the value of the variable.

At the bottom of the `match` block you can use `case _:` — the underscore represents a *wildcard* that matches anything that wasn't already covered in a previous case. It's like an `else` that executes only if none of the previous case statements proved true.

The following code shows a relatively simple example in which the `day` variable contains a number between zero and six:

```
# Define a variable named day and assign it number 0-6.
day = 6

match day:
    case 1:
        print("Monday")
    case 2:
        print("Tuesday")
    case 3:
        print("Wednesday")
    case 4:
        print("Thursday")
    case 5:
        print("Friday")
```

```
# The following case executes only if no previous case proved true.
case _:
    print("Weekend")
```

TIP

You can use comparison and logical operators from Table 3-5 to set up more complex conditions. For more compact code, use the Bitwise ampersand (&) for and and the Bitwise pipe (|) for or.

The following code shows an example where the first case statement proves True if the day variable contains a weekday (Monday, Tuesday, Wednesday, Thursday, or Friday). The second case statement proves True if the day variable contains Saturday or Sunday. The wildcard case statement with the underscore (_) proves True if no previous case statement proved True. The day. lower() expression makes the day name all lowercase to match the letters in the case statements.

```
# Assign a day name (string) to the day variable.
day = "Tuesday"
# Make a decision based on the day value converted to lowercase.
match day.lower():
    # The pipe operator (|) represents "or."
    case "monday" | "tuesday" | "wednesday" | "thursday" | "friday":
        print("Weekday")
    case "saturday" | "sunday":
        print("Weekend")
    case _:
        print("I don't recognize that day")
# Any code from this point on is outside the match block.
```

Defining Python Functions

Much of the Python code you encounter will be organized into Python functions. Functions are a fundamental tool in programming, allowing you to write reusable, organized, and efficient code. A *function* is a block of code that performs a specific task and can be reused whenever needed. Think of it like a recipe: You define the steps once, and then you can use it anytime without rewriting everything.

In Python, functions are defined using the def keyword. Here's the basic structure:

```
def function_name(parameters):
    # Code block (what the function does)
    return result  # Optional: Returns a value
```

The word def is short for *define,* and it tells Python to treat the following code as a function. The code isn't executed immediately. Instead, other code in the script can call the function at any time to execute its code.

The *function_name* part is a name you make up. Use lowercase letters and under-scores instead of spaces. The name should describe what the function does, such as calculate_area or authenticate_user.

The *parameters* are optional and are names of variables that can receive data when the function is called.

The return statement marks the end of the function. The *result* is optional; it's the name of a variable that contains any data sent back to the code that called the function. If you omit *result*, the function returns None).

As with other blocks of code, indentations are critical. All code that's part of the function, including the return statement, must be indented below the initial definition def statement.

Subsequent code in your script can *call* the function by name followed by parentheses.

Most functions accept one or more parameters as input. Code within the function then performs some operation on that input and returns a single value as the result. Here's an example where a function named calculate_area accepts two values: width and height (presumably of a rectangle). Code inside the function then multiplies width and height to calculate the area of the rectangle and stores it in a variable named area. The value of area is then returned to the calling code in the last line, return area.

```
# A function to calculate and return the area of a rectangle
def calculate_area(width, height):
    area = width * height
    return area
```

After it's defined, subsequent code can call the function, pass values into its parameters, and store the result in a variable. The following code calls the calculate_area function, passing in the values 5 and 10, and then storing the result in a variable named rectangle_area.

```
# Calling the calculate area function.
side_a = 5
side b = 10
rectangle_area = calculate_area(side_a, side_b)
```

REMEMBER

Functions are used heavily in most Python code, because they allow a large script to be broken down into smaller, more manageable chunks.

Defining default values for parameters

You can define default values for parameters. The default is used if you call the function without providing a value for a parameter. Here's an example where the default value for a variable is set to the string `"friend"`:

```
def greet(name="friend"):
        greeting = "Hi, " + name
        return greeting
```

Here's an example of calling the function, and providing the value `"John"` for the parameter:

```
print(greet("John"))
```

The result of executing that code is:

```
Hi, John.
```

Here's an example where I don't pass in anything for the parameter. Note that you still have to include the parentheses as in `greet()`. You just don't put anything inside the parentheses:

```
print(greet())
```

That code displays:

```
Hi, friend
```

The default value is used in place of the missing parameter value.

Using type hints in Python functions

Python also allows you to use *type hints* in function definitions. These are mainly informative to people reading the code to understand what to pass into the function or what the function returns. Use a colon followed by a type name inside the parameter list to indicate a data type for parameters. Use an arrow (formed by typing a hyphen and a tight angle bracket) to indicate the data type of what the function returns.

For example, in the following function, `quantity` is expected to be an integer, and `unit_price` is a floating-point number. The function returns a floating-point number:

```
def calculate_total(quantity: int, unit_price: float) -> float:
    return quantity * unit_price
```

TIP

To keep large apps organized and easy to understand, it's best for each function to perform a single task and return only one value or no value at all. You'll see many examples throughout this book. The main point being: Keep functions simple to make even the largest apps into collections of relatively simple chunks of code.

Creating Classes and Objects

Functions are one way to organize code. Classes are another. In coding we use classes to manage objects. An *object* is a unit of information about one item. For example, an object representing a user of an app may include data about that user's username (`user_name`), email address (`email_address`), enrollment date (`date_enrolled`), login status (`is_logged_in`), and other information. Keeping all that information associated with the user as a single object makes it easier to keep track of and manage the user data.

A *class* is a chunk of code that allows you to create objects. For example, to have user objects in your app, you'd define a `User` class that defines exactly what data is associated with each user. The class also allows you to create user objects. The class can also contain methods, which are like functions, but designed specifically for use with user objects.

TECHNICAL STUFF

Organizing code into classes is sometimes called object-oriented programming (OOP). You may have already heard that term in relation to other programming languages such as Java.

Classes in Python are defined using the `class` keyword. Unlike variables, the name of a class usually starts with an uppercase letter. A class is like a factory used to create objects. Within a class, you define a *constructor*, which lets you define which variables, called *instance variables* (or *properties*), to associate with each object. You can define functions inside a class. However, these functions are accessible only to objects that you create using the class; they're called *methods* to distinguish them from regular functions.

Here's a sample class named `User` that says each user will have a `user_name`, `email_address`, and `date_joined`. The class contains one method, which, when called, returns a string showing the instance variables (properties) for one user. Note that all the code contained within the class, including the method definition, must be indented within the class.

```
class User:
    # Constructor method (initializer)
    def __init__(self, user_name, email_address, date_joined):
        self.user_name = user_name   # Instance variable
        self.email_address = email_address
        self.date_joined = date_joined


    # Method
    def info(self):
        return f"{self.user_name}, {self.email_address} joined {self.
    date_joined}"
```

TIP

A User class could contain a lot more information about each user, including address, phone number, and other information. I'm keeping the example simple here to show you how to code a class and to help you recognize classes in other people's code.

For the sake of example, let's suppose that User class is stored in a file named user.py. You want to be able to create user objects from another file, which I'll call main.py for this example. The following code shows how you could create a user object from main.py. First, import the User class from user.py (the .py is assumed after from user in the code). Then use the correct syntax to create a new user named new_user. To test the code, the script then called the .info() method of the class to print information about the new user.

```
# Import the User class from user.py
from user import User
from datetime import date


# Create a new user named Mary with an email and today's date
new_user = User("Mary","someone@somewhere.com",date.today())


# Print the new user's information
print(new_user.info())
```

Handling Exceptions

No matter how good your code is, people using your code can make errors that could potentially crash your script. For example, perhaps your code asks the user for a number. But the user inputs a string instead. Such a simple error could stop your script in its tracks and display some arcane technical error message to your user.

Handling errors that could cause your script to crash is called *exception handling*. The technique allows your script to keep running smoothly and hide any technical error messages from your user.

Use `try`, `except`, `else`, and `finally` keywords to handle exceptions in your code. Here's the basic structure:

>> `try`: The block of code you want to monitor for exceptions

>> `except`: The block that runs if a specific exception occurs, specifying how to handle it

>> `else` (optional): Runs if no exception occurs in the `try` block

>> `finally` (optional): Runs no matter what, whether an exception occurred or not (useful for cleanup tasks)

Also related to exception handling, but not limited to being inside a `try` block is the `raise` keyword, which explicitly *raises* (triggers) an exception in your code. It allows you to signal that an error or exception condition has occurred. You can raise built-in exceptions or custom exceptions defined in your own code. Python has about 30 built-in exceptions, including the following:

>> `TypeError`: Raised when an operation or function is applied to an object of inappropriate type (for example, adding a string and an integer).

>> `ImportError`: Raised when an `import` statement fails to find or load a module.

>> `ModuleNotFoundError`: Raised when a module cannot be found (for example, `import nonexistent_module`).

>> `FileNotFoundError`: Raised when a file or directory is requested but doesn't exist (for example, `open("missing.txt")`).

>> `PermissionError`: Raised when an operation lacks sufficient permissions (for example, trying to write to a read-only file).

>> `EOFError`: Raised when trying to read beyond the end of a file or input stream.

>> ValueError: Raised when a function gets an argument of the right type but an inappropriate value (for example, int("abc")).

>> Exception as e: Catches any exception and stores the exception object in a variable named e. Use print(f"An error occurred: {e}") to display the error object text.

Custom exceptions are classes you create yourself using the class keyword and (Exception). The syntax for defining such a class is:

```
class Exceptioname(Exception):
```

Replace *Exceptioname* with a name of your own choosing (as long as it doesn't match any of the existing built-in exception names). As with regular classes, Python suggests using an initial uppercase letter in the class name to identify the code as a class. The word Exception in parentheses means your class will inherit the capabilities of all exceptions from the Exception class that's built into the Python language.

REMEMBER

Using exception handling in scripts is a best practice for writing Python scripts. You'll see many examples throughout the automation scripts in this book.

The following script asks the user to enter two numbers. The try block checks for various errors and displays appropriate error messages so that the script can keep running without crashing, regardless of what the user enters.

```
# Function to ask for two numbers, handle exceptions, and divide.
def divide_numbers():
    try:

        # Get input from user
        num1 = input("Enter the first number: ")
        num2 = input("Enter the second number: ")

        # Convert user entries to floats
        number1 = float(num1)
        number2 = float(num2)

        # Perform division
        result = number1 / number2

    # Handle exception if user inputs non-numeric values.
    except ValueError:
        print("Error: Please enter valid numbers")
        return None
```

```python
    # Handle exception if second number is zero.
    except ZeroDivisionError:
        print("Error: Cannot divide by zero")
        return None

    # Handle any other exceptions that may occur.
    except Exception as e:
        print(f"Unexpected error occurred: {str(e)}")
        return None

    # This block executes only if no exceptions occur.
    else:
        print(f"The division was successful!")
        return result

    # This block always executes, regardless of exceptions.
    finally:
        print("Calculation attempt completed")

# Main function to run the division calculator function.
def main():
    print("Welcome to the Division Calculator!")
    result = divide_numbers()

    if result is not None:
        print(f"Result: {result}")
    print("Thank you for using the calculator!")

# Call the main function to start the program.
if __name__ == "__main__":
    main()
```

Here's how the script works:

>> try: Contains the code that may raise exceptions. In this example, the try block asks the user to enter two numbers. Then the code attempts to convert whatever the user entered into two floating-point numbers and perform division on them.

>> except: Handles specific exceptions that may occur:

- ValueError: Raised if the user enters a value that can't be converted to a float (such as a string).

- ZeroDivisionError: Raised if the second number is zero.

- Exception: Raised for any other unexpected error.

» else: Executes only if no exceptions occur. Prints a success message and returns a result.

» finally: Executes no matter what. Prints a completion message.

The script contains a second function named main() that displays a welcome message and then calls the divide_numbers() function. Whatever that function returns is stored in a variable named result. If result is anything other than None, that result is displayed. Then, no matter what, the script shows the text "Thank you for using the calculator!"

The very last block calls the main() function, which, in turn, runs the entire script.

Throughout Python, you'll see variable names and values that start and end with double underscores like __init__ and __name__ and __main__. These are sometimes called *dunder names* (*dunder* being short for *double underline*). They're built-in variable names that have special meaning in Python. The common use of them is this statement, shown near the end of the previous sample code:

```
if __name__ == "__main__":
```

__name__ is a special, built-in variable that automatically gets its value when you run Python code. In a script that you run directly (for example, using the Run Python File icon in VS Code or a python command followed by the script's filename), the __name__ variable gets the value __main__.

In code that's imported into a script with an import statement, the __name__ variable gets the value of the imported module's name, never __main__. Using if __name__ == "__main__": ensures that any code indented below the if statement is executed only when that script is executed directly, not when it's imported into another script that was run directly.

TIP

The last code example in this chapter is typical in that it allows you to organize code into functions, each of which performs a specific task and returns a value. Then it calls functions, as needed at the end, but only if the current script was run directly and not imported as a module via import statements.

2

Automating Common Computer Tasks

IN THIS PART . . .

Automate and organize files and folders.

Back up files, find duplicates, and delete old files.

Manage files for images and videos.

Automate the mouse, the keyboard, and typing text.

Automate the office and office apps.

IN THIS CHAPTER

» **Talking the talk**

» **Playing it safe with automation scripts**

» **Walking through directory trees**

» **Grouping files according to file type**

» **Batch file naming**

Chapter **4**

Automating Files and Folders

M any automation scripts save you time and effort by navigating through folders and files to make changes to files. Python offers many tools and techniques for working with *directories* (folders) and files. Three modules are key:

» os: Provides ways to interact with the operating system (Linux, macOS, Windows) including navigating folders and files, and working with paths and environment variables

» shutil: Utilities for copying, moving, renaming, and deleting folders and files

» pathlib: Provides a newer, object-oriented way to work with folders and files, making it easier to create scripts that work on any operating system

These modules are part of the standard library, which means they're built in. When you want to use any of these modules, you don't need to pip install them. Instead, just put your import statement(s) right at the top of your code.

Note: Like the rest of the world, I use the terms *directory* and *folder* interchangeably, because they mean the same thing: a container for storing files.

Demystifying the Buzzwords

Most people probably use File Explorer in Windows or Finder on macOS to work with files and folders.

In Windows, File Explorer directories are indicated by manila file folder icons (hence, the name *folder*). In the File Explorer navigation pane, built-in folders like Desktop, Downloads, Documents, Pictures, and Videos may not look like folder icons, but those are all folders.

Files are indicated by document icons, or by a thumbnail image if the file is an image or video. The path to the current folder is shown in the Address Bar at the top of the window in a friendly format, such as *Alan Simpson > Documents > Practice* (see Figure 4-1).

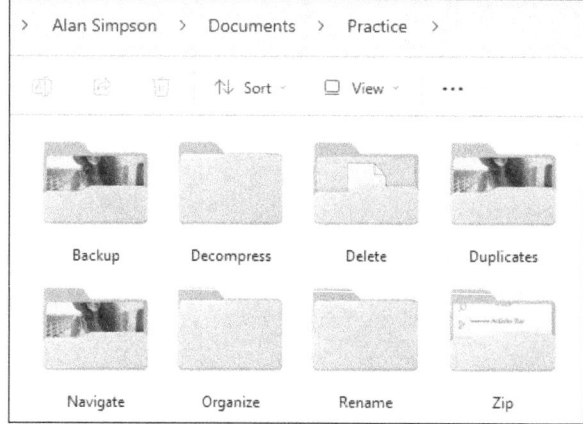

FIGURE 4-1:
Windows
File Explorer.

TIP

If you click after the last named folder in the Windows Address Bar's friendly path, you'll see the path converted to a format more suitable for writing code. So, typically, you can just copy and paste that path into your code — though, in Python, you'll have to change it a little, as I explain in the "Drives, directories, folders, and files" section, later in this chapter.

On macOS, you use Finder to navigate folders and files. Directories are indicated by folder icons. Files are indicated by document icons or a thumbnail image for images and videos. The path to the current folder is displayed near the bottom of the Finder window, such as *Macintosh HD > Users > alan > Practice* (see Figure 4-2). That path is a little misleading because, from Python's perspective, the *actual* path is Users/*username*/Practice.

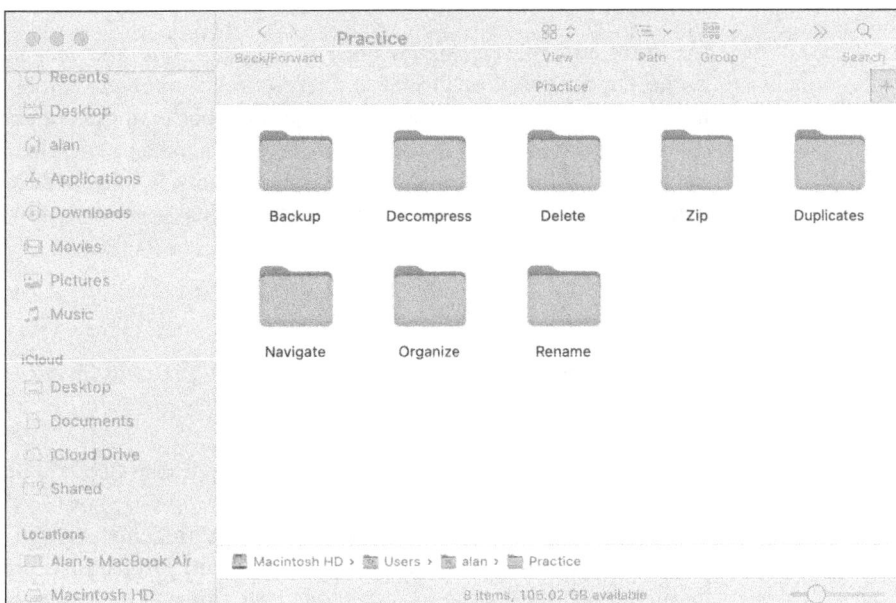

FIGURE 4-2:
macOS Finder.

WARNING

Folders under iCloud in Finder's navigation pane are read-only in relation to Python code. So, if you're on a Mac, you're better off creating your Practice folder under your username under Macintosh HD. Copy the files you intend to modify to that Practice folder first, for safety. The path to a folder named Practice under your username will look like /Users/Alan/Practice without Documents as part of the name.

Drives, directories, folders, and files

Working with files and folders in code requires working with paths. A *path* is the path required to get to a certain file or folder. For example, in Windows, a path may look something like this:

```
C:\Users\Alan\Documents\Practice\photo.jpg
```

The path above refers to a file named photo.jpg. To get to that file you need to navigate to the C: drive, and then down through the folders named Users, Alan, Documents, and Practice.

In a Windows path, the C: is the disk *drive* (the actual storage device). The names that follow, separated by backslashes (\), are folder and subfolder names. If the path leads to a specific file in the last folder, the filename is at the end of the path. The filename always ends with an extension, like .jpg, to indicate the file type and to differentiate it from a folder name.

In Linux and macOS, paths omit the drive name and just start with a folder name. On macOS, I recommend putting your `Practice` folder under your username, rather than in the `Documents` folder, because the `Documents` folder under iCloud is read-only to Python. Use forward slashes (/) rather than backslashes to separate folder names in the path. If the path is to a specific file, the filename comes last in the path, and it always has a filename extension. Here's an example of a path on macOS:

```
/Users/Alan/Practice/photo.jpg
```

You don't need a drive letter like `C:`, because the path always refers to the main startup disk (named Macintosh HD in Finder, by default).

REMEMBER

When you right-click a file in any folder and choose Get Info in Finder, you'll see a path like `Macintosh HD` > `Users` > *username* > `Practice` (it's in the General section, next to Where). Right-click that path and choose Copy As Pathname. The Clipboard will contain the proper path, so when you paste it into your code, it will be the correct pathname for your code in the format `/Users/username/Practice`.

For Linux, you usually start the path with `/home` which is the *root* (top) folder of the entire directory tree. Unlike on macOS, there's rarely a `Users` subfolder in Linux. So, the Linux path will look more like this:

```
/home/Alan/Practice/photo.jpg
```

Absolute versus relative paths

All the paths shown in the preceding section are *absolute paths,* because they all start at the top of the directory tree, indicated by / on macOS and Linux, and by `C:\` in Windows.

In Python, you can use relative paths, which are always expressed relative to the current working directory. Two symbols are used for relative paths:

» `.`: Refers to the current working directory

» `..`: Refers to the parent of the current working directory

For example, if the current working directory in Windows is `C:\Users\Alan\Documents\Practice`:

» `.` refers to `C:\Users\Alan\Documents\Practice`

» `..` refers to `C:\Users\Alan\Documents`

If the current working directory on macOS is /Users/Alan/Practice:

» . refers to /Users/Alan/Practice

» .. refers to /Users/Alan

Backslashes in Windows paths

Windows paths use single backslashes to separate folder names and filenames in paths. Python uses the backslash in strings as an escape character, giving special meaning to the character that follows the backslash. Here are some examples:

Code	Description
\n	Newline (ends the current line, or inserts a blank line when used alone)
\t	Tab (inserts a tab character)
\"	A literal quotation mark embedded in a string
\'	A literal apostrophe (single quotation mark) embedded in a string
\\	A literal backslash embedded in a string

In Python code, use \\ as a separator in a string like the following, when you're storing a variable:

```
path = "C:\\Users\\Alan\\Documents\\Practice"
```

Optionally, you can define the string as a raw string by prefixing the first quotation mark with a lowercase r like this:

```
directory = r"C:\Users\Alan\Documents\Practice"
```

If you're using pathlib, you can pass the variable directly into pathlib.Path without worrying about the backslashes. In the preceding example, the Windows path is stored in a variable named directory. If you import Path from pathlib, you can write:

```
from pathlib import Path
directory = r"C:\Users\Alan\Documents\Practice"
directory = Path(directory)
```

With `pathlib`, you can also specify Windows paths using forward slashes, like this:

```
directory = Path("C:/Users/Alan/Documents/Practice")
```

You'll see that used throughout the scripts in this chapter.

Playing It Safe

Some scripts in this chapter delete or rename files in ways that you can't easily undo. So, it's a good idea to always work with a `Practice` folder that contains copies of files. If you make a mess of things, there's no loss. All your original files and folders will still be intact in their original location.

Throughout this book, I use a folder named `Practice`. On Windows, I put it in the `Documents` folder for easy access. So, the path, in Windows is:

```
C:\Users\Alan\Documents\Practice
```

On macOS, I'm not using `Documents` because it syncs to iCloud and can't be written to from Python without changing permissions. When working with scripts that change files, you want to play it safe and minimize the impacts of any unforeseen errors. So, on a Mac, I put the `Practice` folder under my username. The path is:

```
/Users/Alan/Practice
```

Most Linux distros don't have a built-in `Documents` folder. There, I just put the `Practice` folder under my username. That path in most Linux distros would be:

```
/home/Alan/Practice
```

Navigating Folders and Files

Any operation that involves file automation is likely to involve navigating through directories and files. Python's `os` and `pathlib` modules both provide many tools for that. `pathlib` is the more modern, object-oriented tool for navigating files and folders, so I focus on that for much of the work in these scripts.

Here's an example script that lets you pass any folder path as the starting point. The script then shows the name of every folder and every file in each folder. The script also shows the name of the current operating system. Admittedly, the code doesn't automate any tasks — it just prints the names of folders and files. But you're likely to use similar code whenever you write a script that automates working with files and folders.

```python
import platform
from pathlib import Path

def walk_directory(directory_path):
    # Convert string path to Path object if necessary.
    root_dir = Path(directory_path.strip())

    # Check if the directory exists.
    if not root_dir.exists():
        print(f"Error: Directory '{directory_path}' does not exist")
        return

    # First, show the files in the root directory.
    print(f"\n{root_dir.name}:")
    for item in root_dir.iterdir():
        if item.is_file():
            print(f"    {item.name}")

    # Then walk through the subdirectories.
    for folder in root_dir.rglob("*"):
        if folder.is_dir() and folder != root_dir:    # Skip the root
directory itself.
            # Print the folder name with a colon.
            print(f"\n{folder.name}:")

            # Get all the files in the current folder.
            for file in folder.rglob("*beach*"):
                if file.is_file():
                    # Print the filename indented
                    print(f"    {file.name}")

def main():
    # Set the directory to a Windows, macOS, or Linux path.
    directory = r"C:\Users\Alan\Documents\Practice"
    # directory = "/Users/Alan/Practice"
    # directory = "/home/Alan/Practice"
```

```
        # If no input, use the current directory.
        if not directory:
            directory = "."

        # Show the operating system name.
        os_name = platform.system()
        print(f"\nOperating System: {os_name}")
        print(f"Scanning directory: {directory}")
        walk_directory(directory)

        print("Done.\n")

if __name__ == "__main__":

        # Call the main function to start the script.
        main()
```

When you run the script on Windows, the output will look something like this, but with your own folder names and filenames:

```
Operating System: Windows
Scanning directory: C:\Users\Alan\Documents\Practice

Practice:
        Photo (1).jpg
        Photo (2).jpg
        Photo (3).jpg

01 Sample Folder:
        beach (1).jpg
        beach (2).jpg
        beach (3).jpg
        beach (4).jpg

02 Sample Folder:
        biz (1).jpg
        biz (2).jpg
        biz (3).jpg
        biz (4).jpg
Done.
```

TIP

In this example, I used Windows and my own `Practice` folder. The `Practice` folder contains three image files and two subfolders: `01 Sample Folder` and `02 Sample Folder`. Each subfolder contains four image files.

Next, I'll walk you through the code, explain what it does, and show you how to adapt it to your own operating system and needs.

Near the top of the code, you see two `import` statements:

```
import platform
from pathlib import Path
```

I'm using the `platform` module just to show the operating system name in the script. I'm using the `Path` class from `pathlib` to walk the directory tree.

Next comes the `walk_directory` function, which does all the work of walking down through all the subfolders and files and printing their names. It accepts one parameter, `directory_path`, which is the path to the folder at which you want to start walking, defined later in this code.

```
def walk_directory(directory_path):
    # Convert string path to Path object.
    root_dir = Path(directory_path)

    # Check if the directory exists.
    if not root_dir.exists():
        print(f"Error: Directory '{directory_path}' does not exist")
        return

    # First, show files in the root directory.
    print(f"\n{root_dir.name}:")
    for item in root_dir.iterdir():
        if item.is_file():
            print(f"    {item.name}")

    # Then walk through the subdirectories.
    for folder in root_dir.rglob("*"):
        if folder.is_dir() and folder != root_dir:   # Skip the root
directory itself.
            # Print folder name with a colon.
            print(f"\n{folder.name}:")

            # Get all the files in the current folder.
            for file in folder.iterdir():
                if file.is_file():
                    # Print the filename indented.
                    print(f"    {file.name}")
```

REMEMBER

Any Python line that starts with a # is a comment, not actual code. The comment is just there to tell you about the code.

The first step in the function is to convert the string passed in (stored in the variable directory_path) to a Path object. The rest of this function then uses root_dir to refer to that path.

```
# Convert string path to Path object.
root_dir = Path(directory_path)
```

The next line checks to make sure the path exists. This prevents the script from crashing with a Python error message in case someone provides a bad pathname. The exception handler displays an error message and then exits the function before it attempts to walk through a nonexistent directory:

```
# Check if the directory exists.
if not root_dir.exists():
    print(f"Error: Directory '{directory_path}' does not exist")
    return
```

Assuming no error occurred, the function prints the root_dir name and then loops through each item in that folder. The line for item in root_dir. iterdir(): tells Python to start stepping through everything in that folder and assign the variable name item to whatever it finds. Then if item.is_file(): checks to see if the current item is a file; if it is a file, it uses the line print(f"   {item.name}") to print the name indented a few spaces.

```
if item.is_file():
    print(f"    {item.name}")
```

The next line tells Python to loop through all the folder names in root_dir. The .rglob("*") means "Don't filter out anything." That rglob stands for *recursive global search,* but it's really just a way of filtering for specific items. For example, .rglob(*folder*) would access only folders that have the word *folder* in their name.

Inside the loop, the next two lines print the current folder name (as long as it isn't the root_dir, which was already printed) followed by the names of the files in that folder. The if statement, if folder.is_dir() and folder != root_dir:, makes the decision and the print statement, print(f"\n{folder.name}:"), prints the folder name on a new line.

```
# Then walk through subdirectories.
for folder in root_dir.rglob("*folder*"):
```

```
if folder.is_dir() and folder != root_dir:  # Skip the root directory.
    # Print folder name with a colon.
    print(f"\n{folder.name}:")
```

Next, a new loop starts, to iterate through all the items in the subfolder. The loop for file in folder.iterdir(): says to refer to each item in encounters as *file,* and then, within that loop, the line if file.is_file(): proves True if the item is a file (and not another subfolder), which then allows the following statement to print the filename indented a few spaces.

```
print(f"    {file.name}")
```

TIP

The .iterdir() (iterate directory) method in the for loop will look at every filename, with no filtering. You can replace .iterdir() with .rglob() to filter for specific types of files, if you like. For example, for file in folder.rglob("*.png"): would only print the names of files that have a .png filename extension. Using .rglob("*beach*"): would print only files that have the word *beach* in their filename.

That's it for the walk_directory function. As mentioned, it only prints folder names and filenames. But you can change it up a bit to automate folder and files tasks. Plus, it's designed to work with any operating system, and any starting path you pass into it. The main() function shows different ways you can pass in a path:

```
def main():
    # Optionally, set directory to a Windows, macOS, or Linux path.
    directory = r"C:\Users\Alan\Documents\Practice"
    # directory = "/Users/Alan/Practice"
    # directory = "/home/Alan/Practice"
    # If no input, use current directory
    if not directory:
        directory = "."

    print(f"Scanning directory: {directory}")
    walk_directory(directory)


    print("Done.\n")
```

The main() function accepts no parameters. Instead, it just allows you to define your starting directory. In real life, it could contain two lines like:

```
directory = r"C:\Users\Alan\Documents\Practice"
walk_directory(directory)
```

The first line sets the variable directory to the name of the path you want to walk. Then it passes that path to walk_directory. But I've included a lot of commented code to show you other ways of passing in values. If you want the script to ask you for the starting directory when you run the script, uncomment the following line:

```
# directory = input("Enter the directory path to walk (press Enter for current
    directory): ").strip()
```

Make sure you comment any later lines in main() that define a path, so they don't override what you type in. In case you're wondering about the .strip() at the end of the input statement, that just strips that input of any trailing spaces you may accidentally type in, so they don't cause any errors in subsequent processing.

If you don't want to specify the path at runtime, leave that input() line commented, and define your path in one of the following lines:

```
# Optionally, set the directory to a Windows, macOS, or Linux path.
# directory = r"C:\Users\Alan\Documents\Practice"
# directory = "/Users/Alan/Practice"
# directory = "/home/Alan/Practice"
```

Uncomment only one line, depending on the operating system you're using. Then assign your path to the directory variable using proper syntax.

REMEMBER

For Windows, make sure you precede the string with r (short for *raw string*), which tells Python not to treat the backslashes as an escape character, but instead to accept the string as is. Linux and macOS use forward slashes, so you don't need to precede those strings with the r.

This next bit of code handles errors. If the directory string is empty, it sets the directory to ".". Passing ".". into walk_directory tells it to start at the current working directory (the folder where you launched the app).

```
# If no input, use current directory
if not directory:
    directory = "."
```

By now, the directory variable has a value. Before you call the main function to walk the entire tree, these lines print the name of the operating system and the path to the directory tree you'll be walking:

```
# Show the operating system name.
os_name = platform.system()
print(f"\nOperating System: {os_name}")
# Show the directory being walked.
print(f"Scanning directory: {directory}")
# Show all folders and files in the directory.
walk_directory(directory)

print("Done.\n")
```

The function displays Done. after all the folder names it printed.

The very last bit of code then gets the whole process going by calling the main()
function, but only if you're running the script yourself and not at a module you
imported into some other script:

```
if __name__ == "__main__":
    # Call the main function to start the script.
    main()
```

Organizing Files by Type

In this script, I'll make changes to one folder. There's no need to walk through
subfolders. Technically, you could write the script that way, but this script creates
a subfolder for every file type within the current folder. You probably want to work
with only one folder so as not to generate massive numbers of folders across
multiple directories as the script is running.

When you run this script, it creates a subfolder for each file type in the current
directory and moves all files of that type into the appropriate subfolder. Make sure
you test and debug with a Practice folder with copies of files you have elsewhere.
And make sure you have read/write permissions on the folder.

The folder I'll be using is named Organize, and it's inside the Practice folder.
The Organize folder contains copies of some Microsoft Excel spreadsheets,
Microsoft Word documents, videos, and images, as shown in Figure 4-3.

After running the script, the Organize folder will look like Figure 4-4 with four
subfolders: docx for Word documents, mp4 for videos, png for PNG images, and
xlsx for Excel spreadsheets. You can rename these folders to your liking
if you like.

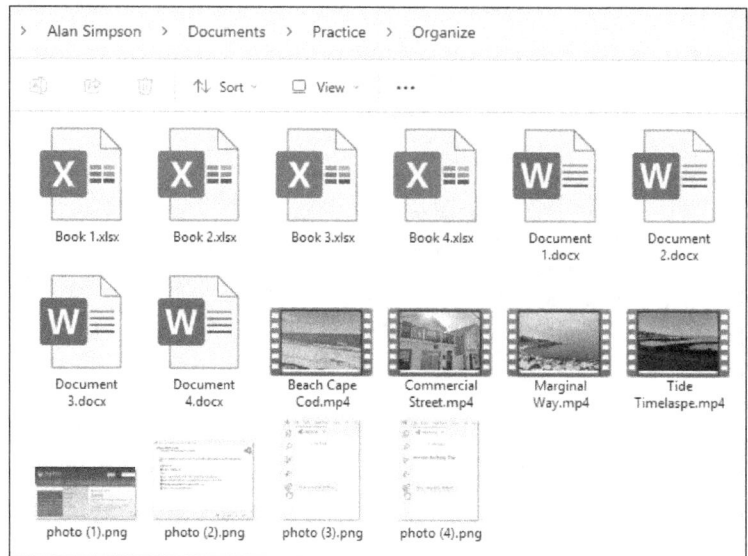

FIGURE 4-3:
The Organize
folder for this
script example.

FIGURE 4-4:
The Organize
folder after
running the
Organize script.

For this script, I'll add the shutil module. The name is short for *shell utilities,* and it has commands for creating directories, moving and copying files, and more — as long as you're working in a folder where you have write permissions.

WARNING

When moving or copying files, shutil will overwrite existing files without warning. Here, I'll only be moving files into new, empty folders, so it's not an issue. But make sure you don't overwrite anything important in your own existing folders.

First, I'll show you the entire script. Then I'll explain key parts in more detail.

```python
import shutil
from pathlib import Path

def organize_files(directory):
    # Convert directory to Path object for easier handling.
    dir_path = Path(directory)

    # Check if the directory exists.
    if not dir_path.exists():
        print(f"Error: Directory '{directory}' does not exist.")
        return

    # Get all files in the directory.
    files = [f for f in dir_path.iterdir() if f.is_file()]

    if not files:
        print("No files found in the directory.")
        return

    # Process each file.
    for file_path in files:
        # Get the file extension (converted to lowercase).
        extension = file_path.suffix.lower()

        # Skip files without an extension.
        if not extension:
            print(f"Skipping '{file_path.name}' (no extension)")
            continue

        # Remove the dot from the extension (for example, '.txt' -> 'txt').
        extension = extension[1:]

        # Create a new folder name based on the extension.
        new_folder = dir_path / extension

        # Create the folder if it doesn't exist.
        try:
            new_folder.mkdir(exist_ok=True)
        except Exception as e:
            print(f"Error creating folder '{new_folder}': {e}")
            continue
```

```
        # Define the new file path.
        new_file_path = new_folder / file_path.name

        # Move the file.
        try:
            shutil.move(str(file_path), str(new_file_path))
            print(f"Moved '{file_path.name}' to '{extension}' folder")
        except Exception as e:
            print(f"Error moving '{file_path.name}': {e}")

def main():
    # Specify your directory. I'm using a Windows path as an example.
    directory = r"C:\Users\Alan\Documents\Practice\Organize"
    # If you're using macOS, use a path like this:
    # directory = "/Users/Alan/Documents/Practice/Organize"
    # If you're using Linux, use a path like this:
    # directory = "/home/Alan/Documents/Practice/Organize"

    # Print an opening message, organize the files, and print a
    completion message.
    print(f"Organizing files in: {directory}")
    organize_files(directory)
    print("File organization complete!")

if __name__ == "__main__":
    main()
```

Like most scripts, this one starts with `import` statements for modules the script uses. Here, I use `shutil` to create directories and move files, and `Path` from `pathlib` to navigate.

The `organize_files()` function does all the work. It accepts one parameter named `directory`, which is the string specifying the path to the directory in which to work.

```
def organize_files(directory):
```

Inside the `organize_files()` function, the `directory` string is converted to a `Path` object named `dir_path`, which ensures the path is in the proper format for Python. An `if` statement then checks whether the path exists. If the path does not exist, a `print()` statement displays an error message, and a `return` statement exits the function before attempting to do any further work.

```
# Convert directory to Path object for easier handling.
dir_path = Path(directory)

# Check if the directory exists.
if not dir_path.exists():
    print(f"Error: Directory '{directory}' does not exist.")
    return
```

Assuming we haven't exited the function, the next lines create a list named `files` containing all the files in the current directory. If there are no files, then the list will be empty. The block that begins with `if not files:` will print an error message and exit the function because there are no files to work with:

```
if not files:
    print("No files found in the directory.")
    return
```

Assuming we make it through the error trapping, this next loop goes through each file in the folder. For each file, it first grabs the filename extension and stores that, in lowercase letters, to a variable named `extension`:

```
# Process each file
for file_path in files:
    # Get the filename extension (converted to lowercase).
    extension = file_path.suffix.lower()
```

Then we set up an `if` statement to ignore any filenames that don't have an extension. But if the file does have an extension, we remove the dot, so in the script the extension name is just `txt` or `png` or whatever, without the dot:

```
# Skip files without an extension.
if not extension:
    print(f"Skipping '{file_path.name}' (no extension)")
    continue

# Remove the dot from the extension (for example, '.txt' -> 'txt').
extension = extension[1:]
```

Next, we create a path to a folder that has the same name as the filename extension:

```
# Create a path to a possible new folder name based on the extension.
new_folder = dir_path / extension
```

TECHNICAL STUFF

If this line looks unusual, remember that the code is using `pathlib`. The `/` operator with a `pathlib` object intelligently joins `dir_path` and `extension` to form a valid file path.

Using mkdir for subfolders

So far, the script has done a lot of work picking apart text to come up with a folder name, such as `png` for PNG files. So, how and when does it actually create the subfolder? It does so in the next `try` block, using `.mkdir(exist=True)`.

```
# Create the folder if it doesn't exist.
try:
    new_folder.mkdir(exist_ok=True)
except Exception as e:
    print(f"Error creating folder '{new_folder}': {e}")
    continue
```

TIP

That `.mkdir()` is a method of `pathlib`, the same module we've been using to walk directory trees. The argument `exist_ok=True` tells Python that if the directory already exists, `mkdir()` should do nothing and silently continue without raising an error. Python creates the directory only if the directory doesn't already exist. The `try: except:` is just to cover any other unforeseen error, such as having insufficient permissions to create a subfolder within the current folder.

The script then creates a variable named `new_file_path`, which is the new folder name followed by `/` and the filename:

```
# Define the new file path.
new_file_path = new_folder / file_path.name
```

Moving files with shutil

At this point, a subfolder with a name that matches the current file's extension exists. So, the next step is to simply move the current file into that folder. The following code uses the `.move()` method of `shutil` for that task:

```
# Move the file.
    try:
        shutil.move(str(file_path), str(new_file_path))
        print(f"Moved '{file_path.name}' to '{extension}' folder")
    except Exception as e:
        print(f"Error moving '{file_path.name}': {e}")
```

The line that reads shutil.move(str(file_path), str(new_file_path)) moves the file. The print() statement that follows simply shows that fact onscreen, so you get some feedback as the script is running. The exception handling is there only to catch unexpected errors, which would usually involve insufficient permissions in the current folder.

TIP

Despite all the code for navigating the folder and catching exceptions, the actual folder creating and moving the file is really just two lines of code that use mkdir() from pathlib and .move() from shutil.

Making the script your own

To use the script in your own work, you can simply set parameters in the main() function. Keep in mind that I intentionally left out recursion on this script, because it has such a huge impact on the directory in which it's running. So, basically, your main option is to specify in which directory you want to organize files in one of the subsequent lines.

REMEMBER

I've shown syntax for Linux, macOS, and Windows paths in the code, and I've commented out the ones I didn't use, so you can see them as examples. You'll want to do the same, by commenting out the two paths you don't want to use, and defining your path using the proper syntax for your operating system.

```
def main():
    # Specify your directory. I'm using a Windows path as an example.
    directory = r"C:\Users\Alan\Documents\Practice\Organize"
    # If you're using macOS, use a path like this:
    # directory = "/Users/Alan/Documents/Practice/Organize"
    # If you're using Linux, use a path like this:
    # directory = "/home/Alan/Documents/Practice/Organize"
```

The rest of the code you can leave unchanged, because it just presents a little text onscreen, runs the script, shows some text onscreen, and calls the organize_files() function to do the actual work.

Renaming Files in Bulk

The next script allows you to rename files in bulk in a single directory or an entire directory tree. It's handy when you have a lot of auto-generated filenames that look like _7f729bae-9c77-4ce1-8e84-bafc8ae741cb.png or some other random name. You can rename all the files so they match the folder name. Optionally, you can provide a filename of your choosing, like Beach.png. The files will be given that name followed by a number in parentheses, such as Beach (1).png, Beach (2).png, and so forth.

WARNING

Don't attempt to change filename extensions with this script. Filename extensions indicate the file type and should never be changed arbitrarily.

As an alternative to renaming all the files in the folder, you can specify a pattern. For example, the pattern "_*" will rename only files whose first character is an underscore. The pattern "*.txt" will rename only files that have a .txt extension.

WARNING

There is no Undo for this massive renaming. So, as always, your best bet is to put a copy of all the folders and files you want to rename inside a Practice folder. That way, if you make a mistake and mess up your filenames, you still have the originals in their original location. Here's the entire script:

```python
from pathlib import Path

def rename_files(root_dir, pattern, recursive, preferred_name):
    try:
        root_path = Path(root_dir)
        # If None is provided for preferred_name, use the folder name.
        rename_to_folder = True if preferred_name is None else False

        # Check if the root directory exists.
        if not root_path.exists():
            raise FileNotFoundError(f"The specified directory '{root_dir}'
does not exist.")

        # Set iteration method based on 'recursive' flag.
        files = root_path.rglob("*") if recursive else root_path.glob("*")

        # Dictionary to track count for each folder
        folder_counts = {}

        for file_path in files:
            if file_path.is_file():
                try:
                    if not pattern or file_path.match(pattern):
                        folder = file_path.parent
                        # Update the count for the folder.
                        count = folder_counts.get(folder, 0) + 1
                        folder_counts[folder] = count
```

```
                    if rename_to_folder:
                        base_name = folder.name
                    else:
                        base_name = preferred_name

                    new_name = f"{base_name} ({count}){file_path.suffix}"
                    new_path = folder / new_name

                    file_path.rename(new_path)
                    print(f"Renamed '{file_path.name}' to '{new_
    path.name}'")

                except PermissionError:
                    print(f"Permission denied: Unable to rename '{file_path}'")

        except FileNotFoundError as fnf_error:
            print(fnf_error)
        except PermissionError as perm_error:
            print(perm_error)
        except Exception as ex:
            print(f"An unexpected error occurred: {ex}")

def main():
    # Example usage. Path to the folder where you want to rename files.
    root_dir = r"C:\Users\Alan\Documents\Practice Rename"
    # None to rename all files, or pattern in quotation marks.
    pattern = None
    # True to rename files in subfolders; otherwise, False.
    recursive = True
    # None for folder name; otherwise, name in quotation marks.
    preferred_name = None

    print(f"\nRenaming files in '{root_dir}' , recursive={recursive}")
    rename_files(root_dir, pattern, recursive, preferred_name)
    print("Renaming completed.\n")

if __name__ == "__main__":
    main()
```

To understand how the script works, take a look at Figure 4-5, which contains a bunch of subfolders.

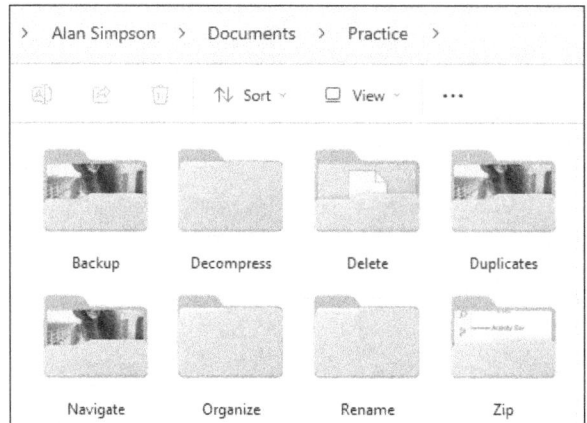

FIGURE 4-5:
The Practice folder contains subfolders of files.

Running this script against that folder would rename all the files in the Backup folder to Backup (1), Backup (2), and so forth (or some other filename you specified), with their original extensions. All the files (or at least the files you specified) would be named the same. The files in Decompress would be named Decompress (1), Decompress (2), and so forth.

TIP

In short, the effect of bulk-renaming files with this script is to give each file within a folder a similar name, instead of just some random name or whatever name you previously assigned. It's especially helpful with files that were given a random filename by some app or artificial intelligence (AI).

Renaming files with Python

Like other automation scripts in this book, this script uses pathutil to walk the directory tree. Of course, there's also a lot of exception handling to deal with permissions errors and such to keep the script from crashing without a descriptive error message. The actual renaming of each file happens with this one line of code:

```
file_path.rename(new_path)
```

The script uses the .rename() method of pathutil to do the renaming. The code that came before has already set file_path to the complete path to the file to be renamed. The new_path variable has already been given the correct name for the new file, based on user specifications defined in the main() function.

Using the bulk renaming script

To use this script, you don't need to change any code outside of the `main()` function. Instead, specify your parameters in the following lines:

```
def main():
    # Example usage. Path to the folder where you want to rename files.
    root_dir = r"C:\Users\Alan\Documents\Practice Rename"
    # None to rename all files, or pattern in quotation marks.
    pattern = None
    # True to rename files in subfolders; otherwise, False.
    recursive = True
    # None for folder name; otherwise, folder name in quotation marks.
    preferred_name = None
```

Set the `root_dir` variable to the directory that contains the files that you want to bulk rename. My example shows a Windows path. Make sure you use the proper syntax for your operating system, such as `Users/alan/Practice    Rename` for macOS.

If you want to rename all files in the directory, leave the `pattern` variable set to `None`. If you want to limit renaming, then specify a pattern of files to rename. For example, if you want to rename only files that have a `.bak` extension, assign `"*.bak"` (with the quotation marks) to that `pattern` variable. If you want to rename only files whose names start with an underscore, set the pattern to `"_*.*")`.

Use the recursion variable to control recursion. If you leave that set to `True`, the script will rename all files in that directory and all its subdirectories. If that's too extreme for you, set `recursive` to `False`. The script will ignore subdirectories and rename only files in the root directory.

Lastly, if you rename each file in a folder to have the same filename as the folder, leave the `preferred_name` variable set to `None`. Otherwise, specify a filename. Don't use a pattern, and don't try to change the filename extension. For example, if you want all the files to be named something like `Beach (1)`, `Beach (2)`, and so on (with their current extensions), then simply specify `"Beach"` as the preferred name, like this:

```
preferred_name = "Beach"
```

Chapter **5**

Automating File Management

n this chapter, you explore more techniques for navigating through directories and subdirectories to automate file management. The powerful `pathutil` and `shutil` modules make quick work of many mundane, time-consuming tasks. You discover scripts for dealing with old and temporary files, backing up files, removing duplicate files, and more.

Deleting Old and Temporary Files

This script can delete old and temporary files. In fact, it can delete files of any age, which, of course, could be dangerous. To play it safe, we won't let this script actually delete any files. Instead, we'll have it send the files to the trash — that is, to the Recycle Bin in Windows or to the Trash on Linux or macOS. That way, you can review all the files, and recover any files you want to keep before deleting them forever.

Luckily, sending to the trash is easy thanks to the `send2trash` module. This cross-platform module determines which operating system your code is running on and then sends the file to the appropriate location. You don't have to worry about any of that in your own code.

Not all Linux implementations are the same. But ~/.local/share/Trash/ is a fairly common location for files waiting to be deleted.

The send2trash module is not part of the standard library, but it is free — you just have to install it yourself. After you create a folder for this script, set up and activate your virtual environment, verify your Python version, and enter this command in the Terminal:

```
pip install send2trash
```

If you get an error message about the file not being found, try the alternative syntax:

```
python -m pip install send2trash
```

Here's the script in its entirety. Keep reading to find out how it works, and how to adapt it to your own needs.

```python
from pathlib import Path
from datetime import datetime, timedelta
# Need to pip install send2trash.
from send2trash import send2trash

def safe_delete_to_trash(root_dir, pattern, recursive, days_old):
    try:
        root_path = Path(root_dir)

        # Check if the root directory exists.
        if not root_path.exists():
            raise FileNotFoundError(f"The specified directory '{root_dir}'
does not exist.")

        # Calculate cutoff date if days_old is provided.
        cutoff_date = datetime.now() - timedelta(days=days_old) if days_old
else None

        # Set iteration method based on 'recursive' flag.
        files = root_path.rglob("*") if recursive else root_path.glob("*")

        for file_path in files:
            if file_path.is_file():  # Process only files.
                try:
                    # Check if the file matches the pattern and/or is older
than the cutoff date.
```

```python
                    matches_pattern = not pattern or file_path.match(pattern)
                    is_old = not cutoff_date or datetime.fromtimestamp
    (file_path.stat().st_mtime) < cutoff_date

                    if matches_pattern and is_old:
                        # Send file to the system Trash/Recycle Bin
                        send2trash(str(file_path))
                        print(f"Sent '{file_path}' to the trash.")

                except PermissionError:
                    print(f"Permission denied: Unable to move '{file_path}'
    to the trash.")
                except Exception as ex:
                    print(f"An error occurred while processing '{file_
    path}': {ex}")

    except FileNotFoundError as fnf_error:
        print(fnf_error)
    except PermissionError as perm_error:
        print(perm_error)
    except Exception as ex:
        print(f"An unexpected error occurred: {ex}")


# Usage example:
def main():
    # Define the parameters for the safe delete operation.
    root_dir = r"C:\Users\Alan\Documents\Practice Delete"
    pattern = "*.tmp"
    recursive = True
    days_old = 1

    global_str = "recursively" if recursive else ""
    print(f"\nDeleting {pattern} files in '{root_dir}' {global_str} older than
    {days_old} days.")
    safe_delete_to_trash(root_dir, pattern, recursive, days_old)
    print("Safe delete operation completed.\n")


if __name__ == "__main__":
    main()
```

This script uses `pathlib` to traverse folders and files. It uses `datetime` and `timedelta` to determine how old a file is. The `send2trash` module, mentioned earlier, handles all the business of sending files to the Recycle Bin or Trash first, so you can review, and possibly recover, any files you want to keep before permanently deleting them.

TIP

The function that does all the work is named `safe_delete_to_trash`, and it starts with the following line:

```
def safe_delete_to_trash(root_dir, pattern, recursive, days_old):
```

When you use the function, you pass the starting folder as `root_dir`. Optionally, you can define a pattern such as `*.tmp` to delete only temporary files (which usually have the `.tmp` extension), though you can specify any pattern you like. The `recursive` option lets you delete files from subfolders of the root directory. The `days_old` option lets you define how old a file must be before it can be deleted.

REMEMBER

Much of the code inside the function resembles the preceding code in that it walks through folders and files from the root. Exception handling is there to catch any errors, such as in improper path that doesn't lead to an actual folder.

Identifying old files

The `days_old` parameter that's passed to the `safe_delete_to_trash()` function is an integer, 365 (for one year). The `cutoff_date` variable gets a value that's 365 days prior to the current date (when the script is running). If `days_old` is set to None, then `cutoff_date` also gets a value of None.

```
# Calculate cutoff date if days_old is provided.
cutoff_date = datetime.now() - timedelta(days=days_old) if days_old else None
```

Later in the code, as a loop is looking at one file at a time, a variable named `is_old` gets a value of either True or False from this line of code:

```
is_old = not cutoff_date or datetime.fromtimestamp(file_path.stat().st_mtime) <
    cutoff_date
```

That's a lot to unpack, but basically it says that if no `cutoff_date` was specified, or if the file's date modified is less than (older than) the `cutoff_date`, then set `days_old` to True. That makes the file a candidate for deletion. But that's not the only criterion for deletion. We also look at the file pattern, as described next.

TECHNICAL
STUFF

The `.fromtimestamp()`, `.stat()`, and `.st_mtime()` methods are all from `pathutil`, the same module used to walk the directory tree.

Matching the file pattern

In addition to setting a cutoff date, the script allows the user to specify a file pattern. For example, `*.tmp` deletes only files with a `.tmp` filename extension, which is a common extension for temporary files. The variable `matches_pattern` is set to `True` if the file matches the pattern, or if the pattern passed to the function is `None`:

```
matches_pattern = not pattern or file_path.match(pattern)
```

WARNING

The user can also specify `None` for a pattern — a dangerous option, because it leaves only the age of the file to determine as a criterion for deletion. So, be careful with that.

The `file.path.match(pattern)` syntax is courtesy of `pathutil`, the module allowing you to walk directories and check the file date. If the variable `is_old` is `True` and the variable `matches_pattern` is `True`, the file is a candidate for deletion.

Sending files to the trash

The file is sent to the trash if both `matches_pattern` and `is_old` are `True`. We'll use the `send2trash` module, which is much safer than permanently deleting the file immediately, because you can open the Trash or Recycle Bin and restore any files you think you should keep before permanently deleting them.

```
if matches_pattern and is_old:
    # Send file to the system Trash/Recycle Bin.
    send2trash(str(file_path))
```

TIP

With `send2trash`, you don't need to worry about what operating system is in use or how to copy the file to the trash, because `send2trash` already has that worked out for you.

As with all scripts, we have some exception handling in there to exit the script gracefully if something unexpected comes up.

Using the deletion script safely

To use the script for deleting old and temporary files, define your parameters in the `main()` function by assigning values to the variables shown here:

```
def main():
    # Define the parameters for the safe delete operation.
    root_dir = r"C:\Users\Alan\Documents\Practice Delete"
    pattern = "*.tmp"
```

```
recursive = True
days_old = 90
```

In the working example, `root_dir` is set to a Windows path pointing to a folder named `Practice Delete` in my Documents folder. Make sure to specify a starting folder that matches your operating system (for example, `/Users/Alan/Practice Delete` on macOS).

The pattern I've used is `*.tmp` because that's a common extension for temporary files. You can use any pattern you like, but be careful — you're deleting files here. I set the `recursive` option to `True` to delete from subfolders as well. Set that option to `False` if you only want to delete from the `root_dir` directory.

I set `days_old` to 90 days for this example, but you can set yours to whatever you want.

When you run the script, this line calls the `safe_delete_to_trash()` function with the parameters defined in your variables:

```
safe_delete_to_trash(root_dir, pattern, recursive, days_old)
```

The `print()` statements above and below this line provide a little feedback on the screen.

TIP

After the script runs, remember to check your system's Trash or Recycle Bin to review all the files that were deleted. Recover any files you think you may need in the future before permanently deleting the files.

Backing Up Files

Next we'll automate backing up files. You'll probably want to back up to an external medium, like a USB drive, though you could also back up files to any cloud drive, secondary hard drive, or even a folder on your primary hard drive to move them to a backup medium later.

As with the other scripts, you'll be able to pick a starting directory and choose whether to include subfolders in the backup.

As an added twist, this script allows you to define multiple file types, such as `*.docx` (for all Microsoft Word documents), `*.xlsx` (for all Microsoft Excel files), and `*.py` (for all Python scripts). You can define whatever file types you want, and as many as you want. This script also lets you choose whether you want to overwrite existing files from previous backups.

This script uses the shutil (short for *shell utilities*) module for copying files. Much of the code may look familiar, because we'll be walking directories and catching unanticipated errors and exceptions, as with previous scripts.

Here's the entire script:

```python
from pathlib import Path
import shutil
import sys

def backup_files(root_dir, backup_dir, file_types, recursive, overwrite):
    try:
        # Ensure the root directory exists.
        if not Path(root_dir).exists():
            raise FileNotFoundError(f"Root directory '{root_dir}' does
not exist.")

        # Ensure the backup directory exists or create it.
        Path(backup_dir).mkdir(parents=True, exist_ok=True)

        # Convert file_types to a lowercase set for lookups.
        file_types = {ext.lower() for ext in file_types}

        # Determine the search method.
        search_method = Path(root_dir).rglob if recursive else
Path(root_dir).glob

        for file in search_method("*"):
            try:
                if file.is_file() and file.suffix.lower() in file_types:
                    backup_path = Path(backup_dir) / file.relative_to(root_dir)

                    # Create parent directories if they don't exist.
                    backup_path.parent.mkdir(parents=True, exist_ok=True)

                    # Check if there's enough disk space.
                    if shutil.disk_usage(backup_dir).free < file.stat().st_size:
                        raise OSError(f"Not enough space to back up
file: {file}")
```

```
                    if overwrite or not backup_path.exists():
                        shutil.copy(file, backup_path)
                        print(f"Copied: {file} -> {backup_path}")
                    else:
                        print(f"Skipped (already exists): {backup_path}")
                except PermissionError as e:
                    print(f"Permission error: {e} (File: {file})")
                except OSError as e:
                    print(f"OS error: {e} (File: {file})")
        except FileNotFoundError as e:
            print(f"Error: {e}")
        except PermissionError as e:
            print(f"Permission error: {e}")
        except Exception as e:
            print(f"An unexpected error occurred: {e}")
            sys.exit(1)  # Exit with an error code.


def main():
    # Directory from which to back up
    root_dir = r"C:\Users\Alan\Documents\Practice Backup"
    # Directory to which to back up
    backup_dir = r"D:\\"
    # Define the file extensions to back up, separated by commas.
    file_types = [".docx", ".xlsx", ".png"]
    # Set to True for recursive backup or False for non-recursive.
    recursive = True
    # Set to True to overwrite existing files or False to skip them.
    overwrite = True

    # Call the backup function with the defined parameters.
    print("\nStarting backup...")
    backup_files(root_dir, backup_dir, file_types, recursive, overwrite)
    print("Backup completed.\n")


if __name__ == "__main__":
    main()
```

The code starts by importing the modules that the script needs in order to perform the backup. The code to do the backup is in the `backup_files()` function defined in the following line:

```
def backup_files(root_dir, backup_dir, file_types, recursive, overwrite):
```

As with the other code examples, this one uses exception handling to prevent the script from crashing if some unanticipated problem occurs, like trying to access a nonexistent folder.

In the following sections, I focus on the real meat — the parts that make this script unique.

Creating folders from Python

When backing up files recursively, this script needs to create folders on the backup medium to match folders in the starting directory. After it creates such a folder, it can't attempt to create it again because doing so would generate an error message.

The trusty `pathlib` module makes this easy. Assuming that `backup_dir` contains all the path information needed to create the directory, this one line of code creates the folder (if it doesn't already exist). It even creates any parent folders that may need to be created without ever generating an error message:

```
# Ensure the backup directory exists or create it.
Path(backup_dir).mkdir(parents=True, exist_ok=True)
```

TECHNICAL STUFF

The `parents=True` part means that if the path to the directory is something like `/backups/2026/April`, then the script can create both the parent directories and the `April` directory. The `exist_ok=True` means that if the directory already exists, the script will use the existing directory without throwing an exception.

Copying files with Python

After the backup folder exists, the script can copy the next file to be backed up to that directory, assuming there's room for the file. In the script, we use this code to make sure there's enough room and, if there isn't, raise an exception to prevent the script from crashing:

```
if shutil.disk_usage(backup_dir).free < file.stat().st_size:
    raise OSError(f"Not enough space to back up file: {file}")
```

REMEMBER

The script allows the user to retain existing backup files without overwriting them with newer backups. So, before you overwrite an existing file, the script needs to check the `overwrite` variable, which is `True` to allow overwriting or `False` to prevent overwriting. This next `if` statement ensures that either overwrite is True or the file doesn't already exist on the backup medium before copying the file:

```
if overwrite or not backup_path.exists():
```

In this script, we use the .copy() method of shutil to copy the file, as shown here. The file variable contains the path of the file to be copied, and backup_path contains the complete path to the backup location and filename:

```
shutil.copy(file, backup_path)
```

Some print() statements provide feedback as the script is running. As in all our automation scripts, most of the rest of the code is just about walking the directories and catching any unforeseen exceptions.

Personalizing the backup script

To use the script to back up files, define your parameters as variable names in the main() function:

```
def main():
    # Directory from which to back up
    root_dir = r"C:\Users\Alan\Documents\Practice Backup"
    # Directory to which to back up
    backup_dir = r"D:\\"
    # Define the file extensions to back up, separated by commas.
    file_types = [".docx", ".xlsx", ".png"]
    # Set to True for recursive backup or False for non-recursive.
    recursive = True
    # Set to True to overwrite existing files or False to skip them.
    overwrite = True
```

To specify the location of files to back up, define the root_dir variable as a path. In my working example, I've used a Windows path to a folder named Practice Backup as my root directory.

REMEMBER

When defining your own root_dir, make sure your path is valid and expressed in Linux or macOS format with forward slashes if you're using one of those operating systems.

Set the backup_dir variable to the location where you want to copy files. In the example, I've set it to drive D:\ (a USB drive in my case). On Windows, the leading r and double backslashes are required in the string, even though we typically write the path as D:\.

WARNING

On a Mac or Linux, you use the volume name under /Volumes/ rather than a drive letter. The volume name is one you make up yourself when formatting the disk. That name also appears under Locations in the Finder on macOS (see Figure 5-1). So, the correct path to that would be /Volumes/Backup.

FIGURE 5-1:
A USB drive with the volume name Backup in the Finder.

To define the types of files you want to back up, set the file_types variable to a list (enclosed in square brackets) of comma-separated patterns. Enclose each pattern in quotation marks. In the example, I've specified Word documents (.docx), Excel spreadsheets (.xlsx), and Python scripts (.py). Of course, you can specify any file types you like. Feel free to list as many, or as few, as you like — there isn't an upper limit. Just make sure to get all the quotation marks and commas in the right place when writing your patterns.

If you want to include subfolders under the root directory, set recursive to True. Otherwise, to copy only files from the root directory and none of its subdirectories, set recursive to False.

Lastly, if you want to replace any previous backups on the backup drive with newer backup files, leave overwrite set to True. To retain previous backup files and not copy newer backup files, set overwrite to False.

Finding and Removing Duplicate Files

Finding duplicate files isn't always easy, because how can you be sure two files are exactly the same? The answer to that question, in the computer world, is by *hashing* the files. Hashing produces a *digest* of the file, which is a string of characters. No two files will produce the same digest, unless the files are identical.

The next script hashes files in any directory or directory tree and compares the hashes to find duplicates. When it finds a duplicate, the script sends one copy to the trash for deletion. From there, you can decide if you want to permanently delete the file or restore it and perhaps move it to a backup medium, so you still have an extra copy of the file.

TECHNICAL
STUFF

For this script, you'll be using a module called hashlib. As its name implies, hashlib is a hashing algorithm library that includes the MD5, SHA-1, SHA-224, SHA-256, SHA-384, and SHA-51 algorithms. You don't need to pip install hashlib because it's part of the Python standard library.

This script uses the pathlib library to walk the directory tree. We'll also use send2trash to send duplicate files to the trash rather than permanently delete the files, so you can inspect and possibly change your mind before deleting any files. Remember to pip install send2trash after you activate your virtual environment on this one. Here's the script in its entirety:

```python
# remove_dupilcate_files.py
# Identifies duplicate files and sends them to the trash
from pathlib import Path
import hashlib
from send2trash import send2trash


def calculate_file_hash(file_path):
    # Calculate hash for a given file.
    hasher = hashlib.md5()
    with open(file_path, "rb") as f:
        # Read the file in chunks.
        while chunk := f.read(8192):
            hasher.update(chunk)
    return hasher.hexdigest()


def find_duplicates(root_dir, recursive=True):
    # Find duplicate files based on file content.
    search_method = Path(root_dir).rglob if recursive else Path(root_dir).glob
    file_hashes = {}   # Maps hash to file paths
    duplicates = []    # List of duplicate file paths

    for file in search_method("*"):
        # Ensure it's a file.
        if file.is_file():
            file_hash = calculate_file_hash(file)
```

```
            if file_hash in file_hashes:
                duplicates.append(file)
                print(f"Duplicate found: {file} (same as
    {file_hashes[file_hash]})")
            else:
                file_hashes[file_hash] = file
    return duplicates

def trash_duplicates(duplicates):
    # Send duplicate files to the trash.
    for file in duplicates:
        try:
            # Safely send the file to the trash.
            send2trash(str(file))
            print(f"Sent to trash: {file}")
        except Exception as e:
            print(f"Failed to trash {file}: {e}")

def main():
    # Root directory to scan for duplicates
    root_dir = r"C:\Users\Alan\Documents\Practice Duplicates"
    # Set to False for non-recursive scanning.
    recursive = True

    # Find duplicates.
    print("\nScanning for duplicate files...")
    duplicates = find_duplicates(root_dir, recursive)

    if duplicates:
        print(f"\n{len(duplicates)} duplicate files found.")
        # Safely send duplicates to the trash.
        trash_duplicates(duplicates)
    else:
        print("\nNo duplicate files found.")

if __name__ == "__main__":
    main()
```

This script contains a lot of the same code as others in this book for walking directories and catching errors. In the following sections, I focus on the function for hashing files, which makes this script unique.

Calculating a file hash

To calculate a hash digest for any one file, this script uses the `calculate_file_hash()` function. The `file_path` parameter passed to the function will always be the path to the file to hash.

```
def calculate_file_hash(file_path):
    # Calculate hash for a given file.
    hasher = hashlib.md5()
    with open(file_path, "rb") as f:
        # Read the file in chunks.
        while chunk := f.read(8192):
            hasher.update(chunk)
    return hasher.hexdigest()
```

The line `hasher = hashlib.md5()` creates an object named `hasher` that will be used to calculate the hash using MD5. That MD5 hash works well for comparing files. But if you're familiar with hashing and need to use another algorithm, you can replace that line with any of the following:

>> `hasher = hashlib.sha256()`

>> `hasher = hashlib.sha512()`

>> `hasher = hashlib.sha1()`

>> `hasher = hashlib.blake2b()`

>> `hasher = hashlib.blake2s()`

TECHNICAL STUFF

Some of the other hashing algorithms are slower but more secure than MD5. However, when your goal is simply to compare files on your own system and you aren't trying to find malicious actors attempting to intentionally forge files, MD5 is generally considered sufficient.

The line that reads `with open(file_path, "rb") as f` opens the file to hash in *read binary* mode, which allows for byte-by-byte reading of the file. The line `while chunk := f.read(8192)` sets up a loop that reads 8,192 bytes (8KB) at a time from the file.

Each 8KB chunk of the file is stored in a variable named `chunk`. Then `hasher.update(chunk)` updates the overall calculation for the latest 8KB. When the loop is finished, the entire hash digest is complete, and the last line in the function, `return hasher.hexdigest()`, returns that value to the calling function.

Finding duplicate files

The find_duplicates() function does the actual searching for duplicate files. As it does, it populates a dictionary named file_hashes and a list named duplicates.

```python
def find_duplicates(root_dir, recursive=True):
    # Find duplicate files based on file content.
    search_method = Path(root_dir).rglob if recursive else Path(root_dir).glob
    file_hashes = {}  # Maps hash to file paths
    duplicates = []   # List of duplicate file paths

    for file in search_method("*"):
        # Ensure it's a file.
        if file.is_file():
            file_hash = calculate_file_hash(file)
            if file_hash in file_hashes:
                duplicates.append(file)
                print(f"Duplicate found: {file} (same as
{file_hashes[file_hash]})")
            else:
                file_hashes[file_hash] = file
    return duplicates
```

Each row in the file_hashes dictionary contains a file's hash digest, followed by a colon, and then the path to the file that produced that hash, as in the following example:

```python
{
    'abc123': Path('C:/Users/Alan/Documents/Practice Duplicates/file1.txt'),
    'def456': Path('C:/Users/Alan/Documents/Practice Duplicates/file2.txt'),
    'abc123': Path('C:/Users/Alan/Documents/Practice Duplicates/file3.txt')
}
```

In the preceding code, I use short strings like abc123 and def456 to represent the hash digest. In reality, each hash digest is 30 characters in length, not just six characters.

Each time a hash digest is completed, the following lines of code check whether the hash already exists in the dictionary. If it does, the path of the file that produced the hash digest is added to the duplicates list.

```python
if file_hash in file_hashes:
    duplicates.append(file)
```

In other words, if the file is identical to a previously hashed file (because its hash digest is the same), then the path to that duplicate file is added to the `duplicates` list. So, the `duplicates` list ends up being paths to files that are duplicates of other files. It may look something like this:

```
[
Path('C:/Users/Alan/Documents/Practice Duplicates/file3.txt')
]
```

When the `def find_duplicates()` function has finished, it returns the list of duplicate file paths to the function that called it.

Deleting duplicate files

So far, the script hasn't actually sent anything to the trash. The `duplicates` list just contains a list of paths to files that are duplicates. The `trash_duplicates()` function takes care of moving the duplicate files to the trash, using the `send2trash` module:

```
def trash_duplicates(duplicates):
    # Send duplicate files to the trash.
    for file in duplicates:
        try:
            send2trash(str(file))  # Safely send the file to the trash.
            print(f"Sent to trash: {file}")
        except Exception as e:
            print(f"Failed to trash {file}: {e}")
```

REMEMBER

Using the `send2trash` module is safer than permanently deleting the file immediately, because it gives the user a chance to review the file to be deleted.

Tweaking the find duplicates script

To use the script for deleting duplicates, define the path to your starting directory in the `main()` function by assigning a value to the `root_dir` variable.

REMEMBER

I've used a folder named `Practice Duplicates` in my Windows Documents folder. Make sure to use the correct syntax for your operating system (for example, `/users/alan/Practice Duplicates` for macOS).

```
def main():
    # Root directory to scan for duplicates
    root_dir = r"C:\Users\Alan\Documents\Practice Duplicates"
```

```
# Set to False for non-recursive scanning.
recursive = True
```

If you want to include subdirectories in your search, leave the `recursive` variable set to `True`. Otherwise, you can set the `recursive` variable to `False` to exclude subdirectories.

REMEMBER

Keep in mind that the duplicate files aren't deleted from your system. They'll be in the Trash or Recycle Bin for your review.

Compressing Files

The next automation script compresses any file types from any directory or directory tree. The original files remain intact. You can use the Zip files for sharing with others or for backups. Here's the script in its entirety:

```python
#compress_files.py
# This script compresses any file types into a Zip file.
import os
from pathlib import Path
import zipfile
from datetime import datetime

def compress_files(root_dir, output_path, file_types, recursive):
    try:
        # Create Zip file name from current datetime.
        current_time = datetime.now().strftime("%Y%m%d_%H%M%S")
        filename = f"{current_time}.zip"

        # Ensure output directory exists.
        base_path = Path(output_path)
        base_path.mkdir(parents=True, exist_ok=True)

        # Join the path with the filename.
        output_zip = base_path / filename

        # Verify root directory exists.
        if not Path(root_dir).exists():
            raise FileNotFoundError(f"Source directory '{root_dir}' does
not exist")
```

```python
        # Check if you have write permissions for output directory.
        if not base_path.is_dir() or not os.access(base_path, os.W_OK):
            raise PermissionError(f"No write permission for output directory:
    {output_path}")

        search_method = Path(root_dir).rglob if recursive else
    Path(root_dir).glob

        with zipfile.ZipFile(output_zip, 'w', compression=zipfile.ZIP_
    DEFLATED) as zipf:
            files_added = False
            for file in search_method("*"):
                if file.is_file() and file.suffix.lower() in file_types:
                    try:
                        zipf.write(file, file.relative_to(root_dir))
                        print(f"Added to archive: {file}")
                        files_added = True
                    except PermissionError:
                        print(f"Warning: No permission to access file: {file}")
                        continue
                    except OSError as e:
                        print(f"Warning: Failed to add file {file}: {str(e)}")
                        continue

            if not files_added:
                print("Warning: No files matching specified types were found")

        return output_zip

    except FileNotFoundError as e:
        print(f"Error: {str(e)}")
        return None
    except PermissionError as e:
        print(f"Error: {str(e)}")
        return None
    except zipfile.BadZipFile as e:
        print(f"Error: Failed to create Zip file: {str(e)}")
        return None
    except Exception as e:
        print(f"Unexpected error occurred: {str(e)}")
        return None

def main():
    try:
        # Directory to compress files from
```

```
    root_dir = r"C:\Users\Alan\Documents\Practice\Zip"
    # Where to save the Zip file
    output_path = r"C:\Users\Alan\Documents\Zip Files"
    # File types to compress
    file_types = [".docx", ".xlsx", ".png"]
    # Set to False for non-recursive compression
    recursive = True

    # Validate file_types parameter
    if not isinstance(file_types, list) or not all(isinstance(ft, str) for
 ft in file_types):
        raise ValueError("file_types must be a list of strings")

    # Compression
    print(f"\nCompressing files from {root_dir}")
    zip_file = compress_files(root_dir, output_path, file_types, recursive)

    if zip_file is not None:
        print(f"Files compressed successfully to {zip_file}.\n")
    else:
        print("Compression failed.\n")

except ValueError as e:
    print(f"Error: Invalid input - {str(e)}")
except Exception as e:
    print(f"Unexpected error in main: {str(e)}")

if __name__ == "__main__":
    main()
```

The script starts with some `import` statements, all of which are in the standard library. You don't need to `pip install` anything. Much of the script is for walking directory trees and catching errors, which I explain earlier, so I won't dwell on that.

This script uses the `datetime` module to define a filename for each new Zip file. You can see that code here near the top of the `compress_files()` function:

```
current_time = datetime.now().strftime("%Y%m%d_%H%M%S")
filename = f"{current_time}.zip"
```

In this script, you can specify where you want the Zip files to be stored. That path is passed into the `compress_files()` function as `output_path`. Next you can see the code that creates that directory if it doesn't already exist. Then the final line defines the complete path to the Zip file by combining that output path (defined as the `pathlib` object `base_path` here) with the filename:

```
# Ensure output directory exists.
base_path = Path(output_path)
base_path.mkdir(parents=True, exist_ok=True)

# Join the path with the filename.
output_zip = base_path / filename
```

When using this script, you can specify the types of files you want to zip as a series of file patterns (for example, `"*.docx"`, `"*.xlsx"`, or `"*.pptx"`). That list is passed into the `compress_files` function as the `file_types` parameter.

Compressing files with Python

The real meat of this script is the part where it zips the file types you specified. Inside a loop that walks the directory tree, this line opens that file in a way what allows Python to add one file at a time:

```
with zipfile.ZipFile(output_zip, "w", compression=zipfile.ZIP_DEFLATED) as zipf:
```

The `zipfile.Zipfile` uses the `Zipfile` class from the `zipfile` module to create a Zip file at the path defined by `output_zip` in write (`"w"`) mode. The `compression=zipfile.ZIP_DEFLATED` argument uses the DEFLATE algorithm, which compresses the files to reduce their size using the standard compression method for Zip files. The `as zipf` part provides a shortcut name that subsequent code can use to refer to that open Zip file.

The following `if` statement verifies that the current item in the directory is a file (not a folder) and checks to see whether that file's extension is in the `file_types` list of files to be included in the compression:

```
if file.is_file() and file.suffix.lower() in file_types:
```

If all the criteria are met for including the current file, that file is then added to the Zip file using this one line of code:

```
zipf.write(file, file.relative_to(root_dir))
```

That's really all it takes to add a file to a Zip file with Python.

As with other scripts in this chapter, there's lots of exception handling to catch and deal with any unforeseen problems, like insufficient permissions for writing to the Zip file. The script also prints some feedback on the screen to show its progress.

Setting your compression parameters

To use the compression script, set your parameters in the main() function, like this:

```
def main():
    try:
        # Directory to compress files from
        root_dir = r"C:\Users\Alan\Documents\Practice\Zip"
        # Where to save the Zip file
        output_path = r"C:\Users\Alan\Documents\Zip Files"
        # File types to compress
        file_types = [".docx", ".xlsx", ".png"]
        # Set to False for non-recursive compression
        recursive = True
```

Use the root_dir variable to define which folder contains the files you want to compress. Use the output_path variable to define the folder location (but not a filename) for the Zip file. In this example, I used Windows paths for both. Be sure to use the proper syntax for Linux or macOS if you're using one of those operating systems.

If you're using an external drive as the output, remember that on Windows you need to escape backslashes in string literals (for example, r"D:\\" for drive D:). On macOS, external drives appear under /Volumes/ followed by the volume name. For example, if the volume is named Zips under Locations in the Finder, the path would be /Volumes/Zips.

Use file_types to define which types of files you want to compress. Use square brackets ([]) to indicate a list. Enclose file patterns in quotation marks, and separate them in commas, as in my example.

To compress files in subfolders, set the recursive option to True. To zip only the files in root_dir, set recursive to False.

Decompressing Files

The next script decompresses all Zip files in a directory or recursively in a directory tree. Like the previous script, this one uses the `zipfile` module, as well as modules for walking the directory tree. Here's the script:

```python
from pathlib import Path
import zipfile

def decompress_files(directory_path, recursive):
    # Decompress Zip files in a directory.
    try:
        # Convert string path to Path object and ensure it exists.
        source_dir = Path(directory_path)
        if not source_dir.exists():
            raise FileNotFoundError(f"Directory '{directory_path}' does
not exist")
        if not source_dir.is_dir():
            raise NotADirectoryError(f"'{directory_path}' is not a directory")

        # Counter for processed archives
        archives_processed = 0

        # Walk through directory.
        pattern = "*.zip"
        for path in source_dir.rglob(pattern) if recursive else source_dir.
glob(pattern):
            if path.is_file():
                try:
                    # Create output directory based on Zip file name.
                    output_dir = path.with_suffix('')
                    output_dir.mkdir(exist_ok=True)

                    # Open and extract Zip file.
                    with zipfile.ZipFile(path, "r") as zipf:
                        # Check if Zip file is valid.
                        if zipf.testzip() is not None:
                            print(f"Warning: {path.name} appears to be
corrupted")
                            continue
```

```python
                # Extract all contents
                zipf.extractall(output_dir)
                archives_processed += 1

            print(f"Decompressed: {path.name} -> {output_dir.name}")
            print(f"Extracted to: {output_dir}")

        except zipfile.BadZipFile:
            print(f"Error: {path.name} is not a valid zip file")
        except PermissionError:
            print(f"Error: Permission denied while processing
{path.name}")
        except Exception as e:
            print(f"Error decompressing {path.name}: {str(e)}")

    if archives_processed == 0:
        print(f"No Zip files found in {'directory and subdirectories' if
recursive else 'directory'}")
    else:
        print(f"\nDecompression complete. Processed {archives_processed}
archive(s)")

except FileNotFoundError as e:
    print(f"Error: {str(e)}")
except NotADirectoryError as e:
    print(f"Error: {str(e)}")
except PermissionError:
    print("Error: Permission denied accessing directory")
except Exception as e:
    print(f"An unexpected error occurred: {str(e)}")

def main():
    # Set your directory path and recursive option here.
        directory = r"C:\Users\Alan\Documents\Practice Decompress"
        recursive = True


        # Execute decompression.
        decompress_files(directory, recursive)

if __name__ == "__main__":
    main()
```

The decompression script works like others in this chapter in terms or walking through folders and files. The main work takes place in a function named decompress_files(), which accepts two parameters: directory_path (the path to the directory that contain files to unzip), and recursive (a Boolean that should be set to True if you want to decompress files in subdirectories or False to skip subdirectories).

```
def decompress_files(directory_path, recursive):
```

As usual, there's lots of exception handling to exit the script gracefully if unexpected errors occur. In the following sections, I focus on what's unique to this script.

Unzipping files with Python

The main meat of this script is in this code:

```
# Open and extract zip file
with zipfile.ZipFile(path, "r") as zipf:
    # Check if zip file is valid
    if zipf.testzip() is not None:
        print(f"Warning: {path.name} appears to be corrupted")
        continue

    # Extract all contents
    zipf.extractall(output_dir)
```

The line that reads with zipfile.ZipFile(path, "r") as zipf opens the file at path as a Zip archive in read mode ("r"). That path file will always point to a Zip file because of the way pathutil is walking the current directory. The as zipf just provides the simple name zipf that subsequent code can use to refer to the open Zip file.

TECHNICAL STUFF

Next, the .testzip() method runs a quick check on the file to ensure it's not corrupted. That method returns None if there are no problems with the file. If .testzip() returns anything other than None, that indicates a corrupted file, and the script won't attempt to decompress the file. Instead, it prints an error message.

Assuming everything has gone well so far, the next code runs and the file is decompressed using the .extractall() method of zipfile in this one line of code:

```
zipf.extractall(output_dir)
```

That covers all the steps needed to extract all the files in the Zip file to the output_dir, which is a regular folder that has the same name as the Zip file, without the .zip extension. The remaining code is just to keep a count of things, present some feedback on the screen, and handle any exceptions.

Using the decompression script

To use the decompression script, you need to set only two parameters in the main() function:

```
def main():
    # Set your directory path and recursive option here.
        directory = r"C:\Users\Alan\Documents\Practice Decompress"
        recursive = True
```

Use the directory variable to set your starting directory, using proper syntax for Windows (as in my example) or Linux or macOS, both of which use forward slashes (for example, /Users/Alan/Practice Decompress).

Set recursive to True to decompress Zip files in all subdirectories; otherwise, set recursive to False.

Chapter **6**

Automating Image and Video Files

This chapter is all about Python automation for image and video files. I show you how to automatically resize, rotate, flip, and crop multiple images. You see how to convert image file types in bulk. Finally, I explain how to extract individual frames from a video into image files.

Two Python modules will help greatly in this chapter:

» **Pillow:** Often referred to as PIL (short for *Python Imaging Library*), this library offers tools for opening, manipulating, and saving many different image file formats including JPEG, PNG, and WebP. It provides tools for resizing and cropping, applying filters, and other common image tasks.

» **cv2:** This module offers a Python interface to OpenCV (short for *Open Source Computer Vision Library*), a powerful library designed for computer vision, image processing, and machine learning tasks.

I begin with a single script that can resize, rotate, flip, and crop any number of images in any folder.

Resizing, Rotating, Flipping, and Cropping Images

For the first script in this chapter, you'll create a Python class, so it's easy to reuse in other scripts. The class includes methods to resize, rotate, flip, and, crop images, using capabilities of the Pillow library.

WARNING

Pillow isn't part of the standard library. When you create and activate a virtual environment for this project, make sure to install it with `pip install Pillow`.

Here's the script in its entirety:

```python
# image_processor.py
# This script offers resizing, rotating, flipping, and cropping images.
# pip install Pillow for the following import.
from PIL import Image
from pathlib import Path
import os

class ImageProcessor:
    def __init__(self, input_dir, recursive, file_types):
        try:
            # Define input parameters in the main() function.
            self.input_dir = Path(input_dir)
            # Check if input directory exists.
            if not self.input_dir.exists():
                raise FileNotFoundError(f"Input directory '{input_dir}'
    does not exist")
            # Check if input directory is accessible.
            if not os.access(self.input_dir, os.R_OK):
                raise PermissionError(f"No read permission for directory
    '{input_dir}'")

            self.include_subdirs = recursive
            self.file_types = tuple(map(str.lower, file_types))
            self.output_dir = self.input_dir / "processed_images"

            # Create output directory with permission check.
            try:
                self.output_dir.mkdir(exist_ok=True)
                # Verify write permission for output directory.
```

```
            if not os.access(self.output_dir, os.W_OK):
                raise PermissionError(f"No write permission for output
directory '{self.output_dir}'")
        except PermissionError as e:
            raise PermissionError(f"Cannot create output directory: {e}")
        except OSError as e:
            raise OSError(f"Failed to create output directory: {e}")

    except (FileNotFoundError, PermissionError, OSError) as e:
        raise type(e)(f"Initialization failed: {e}")


def get_image_files(self):
    try:
        # Get list of image files based on specifications.
        image_files = []
        pattern = "**/*" if self.include_subdirs else "*"

        for file_type in self.file_types:
            image_files.extend(self.input_dir.glob(pattern + file_type))

        return [str(file) for file in image_files]  # Convert Path objects
to strings for compatibility
    except Exception as e:
        print(f"Error accessing image files: {e}")
        return []


def resize(self, width=None, height=None, output_suffix="_resized"):
    # Resize all images to specified width or height, maintaining aspect
ratio if either is None.
    if width is None and height is None:
        raise ValueError("At least one of width or height must be specified")

    for image_path in self.get_image_files():
        try:
            with Image.open(image_path) as img:
                orig_width, orig_height = img.size

                # Calculate dimensions based on input.
                if width is not None and height is not None:
                    new_width, new_height = width, height
                elif width is not None:
                    new_width = width
                    new_height = int((width / orig_width) * orig_height)
```

```python
                else:  # height is not None
                    new_height = height
                    new_width = int((height / orig_height) * orig_width)

                # Perform resize.
                resized_image = img.resize((new_width, new_height), Image.
Resampling.LANCZOS)
                output_path = self._get_output_path(image_path,
output_suffix)
                try:
                    resized_image.save(output_path)
                    print(f"Resized image saved to: {output_path} ({new_
width}x{new_height})")
                except (PermissionError, OSError) as e:
                    print(f"Error saving resized image {output_path}: {e}")
        except (FileNotFoundError, PermissionError, OSError) as e:
            print(f"Error resizing {image_path}: {e}")


def rotate(self, degrees, output_suffix="_rotated"):
    # Rotate all images by specified degrees.
    for image_path in self.get_image_files():
        try:
            with Image.open(image_path) as img:
                rotated_image = img.rotate(degrees, expand=True)
                output_path = self._get_output_path(image_path,
output_suffix)
                try:
                    rotated_image.save(output_path)
                    print(f"Rotated image saved to: {output_path}")
                except (PermissionError, OSError) as e:
                    print(f"Error saving rotated image {output_path}: {e}")
        except (FileNotFoundError, PermissionError, OSError) as e:
            print(f"Error rotating {image_path}: {e}")


def flip(self, direction="horizontal", output_suffix="_flipped"):
    # Flip all images horizontally or vertically.
    for image_path in self.get_image_files():
        try:
            with Image.open(image_path) as img:
                if direction.lower() == "horizontal":
                    flipped_image = img.transpose(Image.FLIP_LEFT_RIGHT)
                elif direction.lower() == "vertical":
                    flipped_image = img.transpose(Image.FLIP_TOP_BOTTOM)
```

```python
            else:
                raise ValueError("Direction must be 'horizontal' or
'vertical'")

            output_path = self._get_output_path(image_path,
output_suffix)
            try:
                flipped_image.save(output_path)
                print(f"Flipped image saved to: {output_path}")
            except (PermissionError, OSError) as e:
                print(f"Error saving flipped image {output_path}: {e}")
        except (FileNotFoundError, PermissionError, OSError,
ValueError) as e:
            print(f"Error flipping {image_path}: {e}")


def crop(self, left, top, right, bottom, output_suffix="_cropped"):
    # Crop all images using specified coordinates.
    for image_path in self.get_image_files():
        try:
            with Image.open(image_path) as img:
                cropped_image = img.crop((left, top, right, bottom))
                output_path = self._get_output_path(image_path,
output_suffix)
                try:
                    cropped_image.save(output_path)
                    print(f"Cropped image saved to: {output_path}")
                except (PermissionError, OSError) as e:
                    print(f"Error saving cropped image {output_path}: {e}")
        except (FileNotFoundError, PermissionError, OSError) as e:
            print(f"Error cropping {image_path}: {e}")


def _get_output_path(self, input_path, suffix):
    # Generate output file path with suffix.
    try:
        input_path = Path(input_path)
        filename = input_path.stem
        extension = input_path.suffix
        return str(self.output_dir / f"{filename}{suffix}{extension}")
    except Exception as e:
        print(f"Error generating output path for {input_path}: {e}")
        return str(self.output_dir / f"error{suffix}.jpg")  # Fallback path
```

```python
def main():
    try:
        # Replace with your directory path.
        input_directory = r"C:\Users\Alan\Documents\Practice\Img Process"
        # Mac path example
        #input_directory = "/Users/alan/Practice/Img Process"
        # True to include subdirectories
        recursive = True
        # Define as tuple inside parentheses. Must be raster image types.
        file_types=("*.jpg", "*.jpeg", "*.png", "*.webp")

        # Create processor instance with custom parameters.
        processor = ImageProcessor(input_directory, recursive, file_types)

        # Perform various operations on all matching images.
        # Comment out any operation you don't want to perform.
        # Resize to 512px width, auto height
        processor.resize(width=512, height=None)
        # Resize to 512px height, auto width.
        # processor.resize(width=None, height=512)
        # Resize to exactly 512x512.
        # processor.resize(width=512, height=512)
        # Rotate 90 degrees.
        processor.rotate(90)
        # Flip horizontally.
        processor.flip("horizontal")
        # Flip vertically.
        processor.flip("vertical")
        # Crop to 256x256 from (100,100).
        processor.crop(100, 100, 356, 356)

    except (FileNotFoundError, PermissionError, OSError) as e:
        print(f"Error in main execution: {e}")
        return

if __name__ == "__main__":
    main()
```

Obviously, that's a lot of code! However, much of it is for walking the directory tree and catching unforeseen errors. In the following sections, I focus on the code that does the actual work of modifying images.

The Pillow module works with raster images, which have extensions like `.bmp`, `.gif`, `.jpeg`, `.jpg`, `.png`, `.psd`, `.raw`, `.tif`, `.tiff`, and `.webp`. It won't work with vector images, which have extensions like `.ai`, `.cdr`, `.eps`, `.pdf`, and `.svg`.

This script provides four methods for processing any number of images:

» `crop()`: Crops image using specified coordinates

» `flip()`: Flips image horizontally or vertically

» `resize()`: Changes image dimensions

» `rotate()`: Rotates image by specified degrees

Each operation is defined in its own method. This script uses `pathlib` to walk directories that contain the files to process.

Because we've defined a class for the script, the functions defined with the `dif` keyword are treated as methods and called using the `.methodname()` syntax.

Resizing images

The resize method handles resizing of images. It accepts four parameters: `self`, `width`, `height`, and `output_suffix`. The `self` parameter is the image being resized. The `width` and `height` parameters are integers specifying the width and height to which to resize. You can set just the width or just the height, set the opposite side to `None` to resize along one dimension, and automatically calculate the opposite side's size to maintain the image aspect ratio.

The optional `output suffix` parameter adds `_resized` to the filename of the resized image, so the original file retains its original filename. If you want to use some word other than `_resized` as the addition to the name, you can pass that as a string to override the default:

```
def resize(self, width, height, output_suffix="_resized"):
```

Much of the code in the function is for calculating the image size. To retain the aspect ratio, you specify only `width` or `height`. As usual, there's also some exception handling. The actual resizing of the image and saving the resized image happens in this code:

```
# Perform resize
resized_image = img.resize((new_width, new_height), Image.Resampling.LANCZOS)
```

```
output_path = self._get_output_path(image_path, output_suffix)
try:
    resized_image.save(output_path)
```

The LANCZOS in the code is a reference to a high-quality image resampling method invented by Hungarian mathematician Cornelius Lanczos. Pillow offers other methods including BICUBIC, BILINEAR, BOX, HAMMING, and NEAREST.

Rotating images

The method to rotate an image accepts three parameters: self (a reference to the image being rotated), degrees, and an integer indicating how many degrees to rotate the image. The optional output_suffix parameter lets you specify text to add to the filename of the rotated image to differentiate the rotated image from the original image. The default is _rotated if no other value is passed:

```
def rotate(self, degrees, output_suffix="_rotated")
```

Rotating and saving the image is handled by the following line:

```
rotated_image = img.rotate(degrees, expand=True)
```

Adding expand=True ensures the image is enlarged enough, if needed, to avoid cropping. The rotated image is then stored in an object named rotated_image. The next two lines add the output suffix to the filename, and then save the rotated image object to that filename. Then some text prints to provide feedback on the screen, or an error message if any unforeseen exceptions prevent saving the file:

```
output_path = self._get_output_path(image_path, output_suffix)
try:
    rotated_image.save(output_path)
    print(f"Rotated image saved to: {output_path}")
except (PermissionError, OSError) as e:
    print(f"Error saving rotated image {output_path}: {e}")
```

That's the basic code for rotating and saving an image.

Flipping images

The method to flip an image accepts three parameters. The self parameter refers to the image being flipped. The direction parameter can be either "horizontal"

```
```

or "vertical"; it defaults to "horizontal" if nothing is passed in. The output_suffix is the text to add to the filename of the flipped image, and it defaults to _flipped if no parameter value is passed:

```
def flip(self, direction="horizontal", output_suffix="_flipped"):
```

Within the method, this code flips the image horizontally or vertically, depending on the value of the direction parameter, or generates an error if some unknown value was passed in:

```
with Image.open(image_path) as img:
    if direction.lower() == "horizontal":
        flipped_image = img.transpose(Image.FLIP_LEFT_RIGHT)
    elif direction.lower() == "vertical":
        flipped_image = img.transpose(Image.FLIP_TOP_BOTTOM)
    else:
        raise ValueError("Direction must be 'horizontal' or 'vertical'")

    output_path = self._get_output_path(image_path, output_suffix)
    try:
        flipped_image.save(output_path)
        print(f"Flipped image saved to: {output_path}")
```

TECHNICAL STUFF

In the preceding code, image.transpose() is the Pillow method that does the actual flipping. That one line of code is all it takes to flip the image, before subsequent code saves the flipped image with the output suffix added to the filename.

Cropping images

The method to crop an image accepts up to six parameters. The self parameter refers to the image being cropped. The left, top, right, and bottom parameters are integers specifying the number of pixels to trim from each side of the image. The optional output_suffix specifies the text to add to the filename of the cropped image; use _cropped if you don't pass a different value:

```
def crop(self, left, top, right, bottom, output_suffix="_cropped"):
```

The actual cropping of the image is simple in Pillow. It's performed with this one line:

```
cropped_image = img.crop((left, top, right, bottom))
```

Subsequent code saves the cropped image to the original filename with `output_suffix` added. The rest of the code is error handling and providing feedback onscreen.

TIP

Keep in mind that this script always saves modified images to a new filename. Your original images won't be lost or altered by this script.

Customizing the image processor

To adapt this script to your own needs, use the `main()` function to set your starting directory path accessing the image files you want to change in the `input_directory` variable.

If you want to process images in subfolders, set `recursion` to `True`; otherwise, set `recursion` to `False`. List file patterns enclosed in quotation marks and separated by commas inside parentheses (for a tuple) as shown here. You don't need to change the line that starts with `processor=` because that instantiates the processor object to get the process started:

```
# Replace with your directory path.
input_directory = r"C:\Users\Alan\Documents\Practice\Img Process"
# Mac path example
#input_directory = "/Users/alan/Practice/Img Process"
# True to include subdirectories
recursive = True
# Define as tuple inside parentheses. Must be raster image types.
file_types=("*.jpg", "*.jpeg", "*.png", "*.webp")

# Create processor instance with custom parameters.
processor = ImageProcessor(input_directory, recursive, file_types)
```

In the next lines, you can comment out any methods you don't want to use. For the methods you do use, set the parameters you want to pass into the methods.

```
# Perform various operations on all matching images.
# Comment out any operation you don't want to perform.
# Resize to 512px width, auto height.
processor.resize(width=512, height=None)
# Resize to 512px height, auto width.
processor.resize(width=None, height=512)
# Resize to exactly 512x512.
processor.resize(width=512, height=512)
# Rotate 90 degrees.
processor.rotate(90)
```

```
# Flip horizontally.
processor.flip("horizontal")
# Flip vertically.
processor.flip("vertical")
# Crop to 256x256 from (100,100).
processor.crop(100, 100, 356, 356)
```

REMEMBER

Any of the preceding lines that starts with `processor` will alter images you've specified in your input directory and subdirectories (if you set `recursion` to `True`). If you don't want to use any operation, simply comment out the line you don't want to use by preceding the line with a # symbol. You don't have to do all the operations that the script offers every time you run the script.

TIP

After the code runs, you'll find processed images in a subfolder named `processed_images` in the same folders as the original images, specified in the `input_directory` in the `main()` function.

Converting Image File Types

This automation script converts *raster images* (images made up of pixels, such as BMP, JPEG, PNG, or WebP) into other raster image formats. The original files are preserved. The converted images keep the same filenames as the originals, but they use the appropriate filename extension for the new format. Here's the script:

```
# convert_images.py
# Requires: pip install Pillow
from pathlib import Path
from PIL import Image
import os

def convert_images(input_dir, file_patterns, output_format, recursive=True):
    try:
        # Validate input directory.
        input_path = Path(input_dir)
        if not input_path.exists():
            print(f"Input directory does not exist: {input_dir}")
            return
        if not input_path.is_dir():
            print(f"Path is not a directory: {input_dir}")
            return
```

```
        # Create a list of paths matching the specified patterns.
        paths = []
        for pattern in file_patterns:
            if recursive:
                paths.extend(input_path.rglob(pattern))
            else:
                paths.extend(input_path.glob(pattern))

        if not paths:
            print("No matching files found.")
            return

        for file_path in paths:
            try:
                # Verify file is accessible.
                if not os.access(file_path, os.R_OK):
                    print(f"Cannot read file {file_path}: Permission denied")
                    continue

                # Open and convert the image.
                with Image.open(file_path) as img:
                    # Ensure image is in RGB mode for formats that don't
support RGBA.
                    if output_format.lower() in ['jpeg', 'jpg', 'jfif']:
                        if img.mode in ('RGBA', 'LA'):
                            img = img.convert('RGB')

                    # Create the output file path.
                    output_path = file_path.with_suffix(f".{output_format}")

                    # Save the image in the new format.
                    img.save(output_path, quality=100)
                    print(f"Converted {file_path} to {output_path}")

            except Exception as e:
                print(f"Failed to convert {file_path}: {str(e)}")

    except PermissionError as pe:
        print(f"Permission error encountered: {pe}")
    except Exception as e:
        print(f"An unexpected error occurred: {e}")
```

```
def main():
    # Replace with your directory path.
    input_directory = r"C:\Users\Alan\Documents\Practice\Convert Rasters"
    # Mac path example
    #input_directory = "/Users/alan/Practice/Convert Rasters"
    # Raster image file types to convert
    file_types_to_convert = ["*.jpg", "*.jpeg", "*.png"]
    # Raster image output format
    output_file_type = "webp"
    # Change to False if you don't want to walk directories recursively.
    is_recursive = True


    # Call the function to convert images.
    convert_images(input_directory, file_types_to_convert, output_file_type,
    is_recursive)

if __name__ == "__main__":
    main()
```

As with other automation scripts, it looks like a heck of a lot of code. But as usual, much of the code is for walking the directory tree and handling exceptions. The bulk of the work is done with minimal code, which I explain in the following sections.

Converting files with Python

In this script, the actual conversion for one image starts with the code that reads with `Image.open(file_path)` as `img`.

Most raster image file types — including BMP, GIF, PNG, TGA, TIFF, and WebP — support transparency. However, JPEG, JPG, and JFIF do not. Let's focus on the following section of the script:

```
if output_format.lower() in ['jpeg', 'jpg', 'jfif']:
    if img.mode in ('RGBA', 'LA'):
        img = img.convert('RGB')
```

The second line looks to see if the current image color mode is RGBA or LA (both of which support transparency) and is being converted to a format that doesn't support transparency. If the target file type doesn't support transparency, then the third line converts the image to RGB, which is compatible with JPEG and other files that don't support transparency. That third line is necessary to avoid an error that would prevent the file from being converted. The transparent color will be changed to white in the converted image.

The next lines of code define the path and filename for the converted file. Everything but the extension remains the same as the original; the extension is changed to match the new format. The `.save()` method performs the actual conversion and writes the file. The `print()` statement provides feedback onscreen when the conversion and save are successful.

```python
# Create the output file path
output_path = file_path.with_suffix(f".{output_format}")


# Save the image in the new format.
img.save(output_path, quality=100)
print(f"Converted {file_path} to {output_path}")
```

TIP

The `quality=100` setting in the preceding code saves the image at maximum quality with no compression. If you need smaller files, you can lower the number. For example, setting `quality=90` typically reduces the file size by 20 percent to 40 percent (depending on the image resolution, size, and color complexity), but at the cost of a 10 percent reduction in image quality — slightly less detail, color precision, and overall clarity.

Personalizing the conversion script

To use the image conversion script, set your parameters in the `main()` function as shown here:

```python
# Replace with your directory path.
input_directory = r"C:\Users\Alan\Documents\Practice\Convert Rasters"
```

```
# Mac path example
#input_directory = "/Users/alan/Practice/Convert Rasters"
# Raster image file types to convert
file_types_to_convert = ["*.jpg", "*.jpeg", "*.png"]
# Raster image output format
output_file_type = "webp"
# Change to False if you don't want to walk directories recursively.
is_recursive = True
```

REMEMBER

Make sure you specify the path to the starting folder in the `input_directory` variable using the correct format for your operating system. I used a Windows path, but I included a commented-out macOS path as a reminder of the syntax that macOS requires.

Set the `file_types_to_convert` variable to a list of the types of files you want to convert, enclosed in square brackets, separated by commas, with each file type enclosed in quotation marks, as shown in the code.

Set the `output_file_type` to the type of file to which you want to convert by indicating its filename extension without the leading dot.

WARNING

To avoid errors, make sure your `output_file_type` is set to a valid raster format, such as `"bmp"`, `"dib"`, `"exr"`, `"gif"`, `"heic"`, `"heif"`, `"ico"`, `"jfif"`, `"jpeg"`, `"jpg"`, `"pbm"`, `"pgm"`, `"png"`, `"ppm"`, `"psd"`, `"raw"`, `"tga"`, `"tif"`, `"tiff"`, or `"webp"`.

Finally, set `is_recursive` to `True` to convert files in subdirectories; otherwise, set it to `False` to convert only images in the input directory and none of its subdirectories.

Extracting Frames from Video Files

Our next automation can extract individual frames from a video file at any time interval and save each frame as in image file. This allows you to create a lot of photos from any one video file without dredging through the video one frame at a time with a video editor.

I'll start by showing you the script in its entirety:

```
# extract_video_frames.py
from pathlib import Path
```

```python
# Need to pip install opencv-python.
import cv2

def extract_frames(video_path, interval):
    try:
        input_file = Path(video_path)
        if not input_file.exists():
            raise FileNotFoundError(f"Error: The provided video file '{video_path}' does not exist.")

        # Create output directory.
        output_dir = f"{input_file.with_suffix('')}_frames"
        output_path = Path(output_dir)
        output_path.mkdir(parents=True, exist_ok=True)

        # Open the video file.
        cap = cv2.VideoCapture(video_path)
        if not cap.isOpened():
            raise RuntimeError("Error: Could not open video file.")

        # Get video properties and calculate the frame interval (in
        frame count).
        fps = cap.get(cv2.CAP_PROP_FPS)
        frame_interval = int(fps * interval)

        saved_count = 0
        for ret, frame in iter(lambda: cap.read(), (False, None)):

            if cap.get(cv2.CAP_PROP_POS_FRAMES) % frame_interval == 0:
                saved_count += 1
                frame_filename = output_path / f"frame_{saved_count:06d}.png"

                cv2.imwrite(str(frame_filename), frame)
                print(f"Saved frame {saved_count:06d}")

        # Release resources.
        cap.release()
        print(f"Extracted {saved_count} frames to '{output_dir}'\n")

    except FileNotFoundError as e:
        print(e)
    except PermissionError as e:
        print(f"Error: Missing write permissions - {e}")
```

```
        except Exception as e:
            print(f"Unexpected error: {e}")


def main():
    # Replace with the path to your video file.
    video_path = r"C:\Users\Alan\Documents\Practice\Extract Frames\example.mp4"
    # Replace with the desired interval in seconds.
    interval = 10.0  # Interval in seconds


    # Call the function to extract frames.
    extract_frames(video_path, interval)


if __name__ == "__main__":
    main()
```

Like our other scripts, this one contains exception handling to exit the script gracefully with an error message if the script doesn't have sufficient permissions to save images, or some other unforeseen problem occurs.

The bulk of the work is handled by the script named `extract_frames()`, defined in the following line:

```
def extract_frames(video_path, interval):
```

The `video_path` parameter should be the path to the video file from which you want to extract frames (not a folder). The interval should be expressed in seconds, such as 0.5 to extract one frame per half-second of video, or 10 to extract one frame every 10 seconds.

Videos protected by digital rights management (DRM) systems are encrypted to prevent unauthorized access or copying. Attempting to open such a video with OpenCV will likely generate an error, to protect the copyrighted material.

Importing modules for video extraction

This script uses OpenCV (short for Open Source Computer Vision Library), which is a free, open-source software library for computer vision and image processing used across a variety of languages. The import statement shows as simply `import cv2`. But that's misleading. For this script to work, you'll need to create and activate your virtual environment. Then use this command in the Terminal to import the OpenCV library for Python:

```
pip install opencv-python
```

When you run the script, extracted images are stored in a subfolder in the same folder as the initial video. That subfolder's name will be the same as the video's filename, without the filename extension and with the word _frames appended. For example, if you extract frames from a video named example.mp4, images will be in a subfolder named example_frames as shown in Figure 6-1.

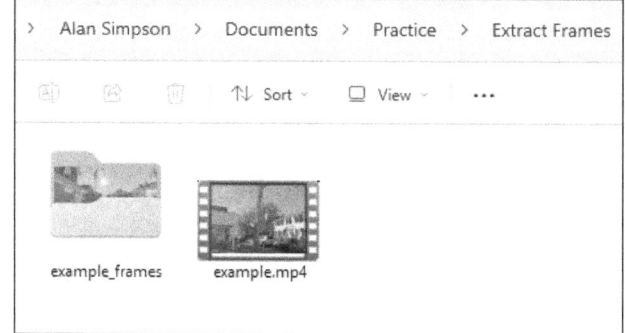

FIGURE 6-1:
Images extracted
from example.
mp4 are
in example_
frames.

The code to open the video is:

```
cap = cv2.VideoCapture(video_path)
```

Subsequent code then gets the videos frames per second (fps) from the video's properties and calculates a frame interval for extractions using this code. The saved_count variable is initialized to zero and is used to count saved frames, and ensure each has a unique filename (for example, 0001.png, 0002.png, and so forth):

```
fps = cap.get(cv2.CAP_PROP_FPS)
frame_interval = int(fps * interval)

saved_count = 0
```

Looping through a video

The main action for the frame extraction starts with a loop that goes through each frame. The loop doesn't stop until it hits the end of the video. That loop is defined by the following code:

```
for ret, frame in iter(lambda: cap.read(), (False, None)):
```

That's quite a mouthful and not your typical for loop. The ret variable remains True each time the loop reads a frame. When the loop reaches the end of the video, ret returns False and ends the loop. The frame variable is the actual frame that was read.

The line that reads lambda: cap.read() keeps calling an anonymous function named read(), as long as there are still frames to read. The (False, None) at the end of that line causes the loop to stop when ret becomes False, and frame becomes None, because there are no more frames in the video.

TECHNICAL
STUFF

Anonymous functions are occasionally used in Python where functions are passed as arguments to simplify syntax and make calls *inline* (within a line of other Python code).

Inside the loop, the following if statement determines whether the current frame is at the specified time interval:

```
if cap.get(cv2.CAP_PROP_POS_FRAMES) % frame_interval == 0:
    saved_count += 1
    frame_filename = output_path / f"frame_{saved_count:06d}.png"
```

If the condition is True, saved_count is incremented, and the frame is given an output path and filename based on that count.

TIP

The .png extension in the code saves each frame as a .png file. You can change that to save in other formats, including .bmp, .jpeg, .jpg, .tif, .tiff, and .webp.

Finally, these two lines actually save the image file, and also provide some feedback onscreen so you can see the progress as the script is running:

```
cv2.imwrite(str(frame_filename), frame)
print(f"Saved frame {saved_count:06d}")
```

When the loop reaches the end of the video, the following lines are executed.

```
# Release resources
cap.release()
print(f"Extracted {saved_count} frames to '{output_dir}'\n")
```

The cap.release() closes the video stream and frees up resources being used by the video. Then the print() statement shows a completion message onscreen.

Tweaking the video conversion script

To use the video extraction script, you just need to define two parameters in the `main()` function, as follows:

```
def main():
    # Replace with the path to your video file.
    video_path = r"C:\Users\Alan\Documents\Practice\Extract Frames\example.mp4"
    # Replace with the desired interval in seconds.
    interval = 10.0  # Interval in seconds
```

Set the `video_path` variable to the video file from which you want to extract frames. Unlike other scripts, this one doesn't walk directories, because you could conceivably extract thousands of frames from one on video. Working with one video at a time is your safest bet.

TIP

OpenCV supports most video types, including `.avi`, `.flv`, `.mkv`, `.mov`, `.mp4`, `.mpeg`, `.webm`, and `.wmv`. You can use a file with any of those extensions in your `video_path` variable.

Keep in mind that every second of video contains about 30 individual frames (images). A one-minute video contains about 1,800 frames. A ten-minute video, about 18,000 frames! When specifying your `interval` variable, you can use whole numbers or decimal numbers. For example, setting `interval` to 1 takes images at one-second intervals. Setting `interval` to 0.5 takes one image every half-second. Setting `interval` to 1.5 takes an image every 1.5 seconds.

WARNING

Keep in mind that the shorter the interval, the more frames you'll generate. Each frame you generate could easily be an image file that's 3MB or more in size. For example, if you capture a frame every second in a ten-minute video, you'll generate 600 image files!

Chapter **7**

Automating Mouse and Keyboard

I n this chapter, you investigate techniques for automating the mouse and keyboard. These techniques allow you to simulate human input for tasks like graphical user interface (GUI) testing, data entry, or repetitive workflows where you need to type the same thing over and over.

PyAutoGUI (short for Python Automation for Graphical User Interfaces) is the main library we'll use for these scripts. It's not part of the standard library. You'll need to `pip install` it yourself. I suggest you create a folder for the script (or all scripts that use PyAutoGUI); then create a virtual environment and activate that virtual environment (see Chapter 2). Then make sure you enter this command at the VS Code Terminal:

```
pip install pyautogui
```

If you want to try out all the scripts in this chapter, you can create each one in that same sample folder to share the PyAutoGUI module.

Granting Permissions on a Mac

By default, Mac computers generally won't allow apps to take control of your mouse or keyboard. On macOS, the first time you try to run a script in this chapter, a permission error may display onscreen, saying the app doesn't have sufficient permissions. Or you may see that the script is running in the VS Code Terminal, but the mouse isn't moving onscreen.

WARNING

For mouse and keyboard operations to work on a Mac, you may need to give accessibility permissions to your code editor. Click the Apple icon in the upper-left corner of your screen and choose System Settings; in System Settings, click Privacy & Security, and then click Accessibility. Set the slider next to your code editor's name to On. In Figure 7-1, I granted permission to Visual Studio Code, since I'm using VS Code as my editor. Enter your password or use Touch ID to make changes if prompted. If you're using a different editor, you may need to grant permission to that editor.

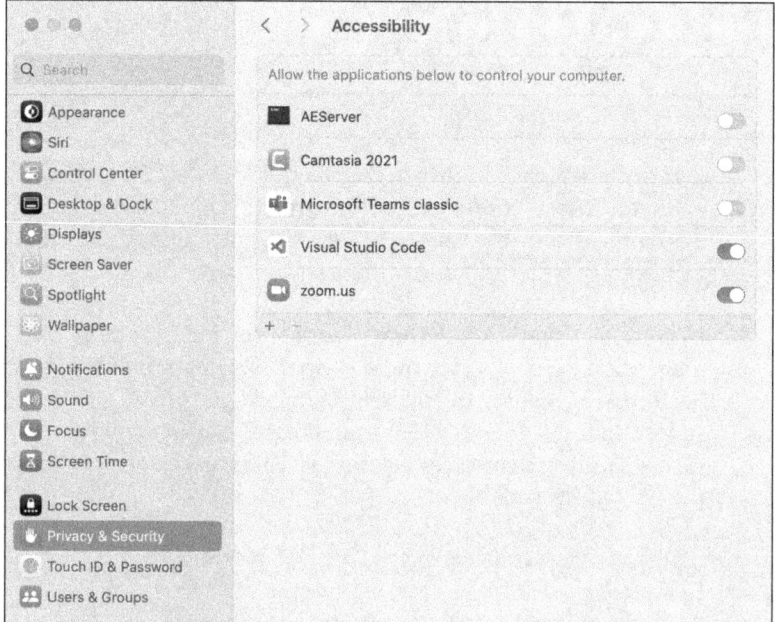

FIGURE 7-1:
Allowing VS Code to control the mouse.

Moving the Mouse, Clicking, Dragging, and Scrolling

Python can take control of your mouse and do anything you'd otherwise do by hand. That includes moving the mouse pointer, clicking, double-clicking, right-clicking, dragging, and scrolling. The library that grants you these powers is PyAutoGUI.

As I mention at the start of this chapter, PyAutoGUI isn't included in the Python standard library. So, make sure you create and activate a virtual environment for this script (if you haven't already done so), and then enter the following command in the Terminal:

```
pip install pyautogui
```

Understanding screen coordinates

PyAutoGUI lets you move the mouse pointer to any location on the screen based on X, Y coordinates, where X is the distance from the left side of the screen, and Y is the distance from the top. The unit of measure is the *pixel*, where each pixel is one tiny lighted dot on your screen.

TECHNICAL STUFF

The word *pixel* is short for *picture element.* A computer screen that's 1,980 x 1,280 is 1,930 pixels across and 1,280 pixels tall.

The very upper-left corner of the screen is position 0,0. The lower-right corner of the screen is whatever your screen resolution happens to be, minus 1 for each coordinate (because the counting starts at 0). So, if you have a 2K QHD computer monitor with a resolution of 2,560 x 1,440, the lower-right corner of your screen is 2559,1439.

Controlling the mouse speed

PyAutoGUI can move the mouse at a very high rate of speed. That can work against you if the mouse starts doing crazy things that you don't want. To slow things down, you can specify how long any operation takes. That way you can see what's going on and keep an eye on things. You do so by adding a duration= parameter to your move command. Here's the syntax:

```
pyautogui.move (x, y, duration= duration)
```

Replace *duration* in the preceding line with the number of seconds the action should take.

In the move(x, y) method, x is the distance from the left side of the screen, in pixels, to move the mouse pointer; y is the distance from the top, in pixels, to move the mouse pointer.

In the following code, the first line moves the mouse pointer to coordinates 1,1 near the upper-left corner of the screen and takes about half a second to do so. The second line moves the mouse pointer down, and to the right, 900 pixels, and takes 1 second to do so:

```
pyautogui.moveTo(1, 1, 0.5)
pyautogui.moveTo(900, 900, 1)
```

Stopping a wild mouse

If PyAutoGUI ever starts doing something that you don't want, you can stop it immediately by grabbing the mouse and moving the mouse pointer yourself to any corner of the screen.

WARNING

PyAutoGUI itself will trigger that instant fail-safe stop, even when it moves the mouse pointer to any corner of the screen. You always want to make sure you don't do that unintentionally in your code. In the sample code earlier, I started by moving the mouse pointer to 1,1 rather than 0,0 to avoid triggering that fail-safe condition.

The fail-safe feature is enabled automatically whenever you use PyAutoGUI in a script. You can disable it by setting pyautogui.FAILSAFE to False, but doing so is risky because it prevents you from stopping the script if the mouse pointer starts doing things you didn't intend.

Finding the screen locations of things

If you want to use PyAutoGUI to control the action in a specific app, you need to know exactly where everything is on the screen in that app. You'll also want to make sure you always maximize the app window, so the screen coordinates are always the same whenever finding the locations of items and when running the script.

To locate coordinates of elements onscreen, use the PyAutoGUI MouseInfo app. To run it, make sure you're in a virtual environment where you've already installed

PyAutoGUI, and create a script named `pyautogui_mouseinfo.py` (or something similar that doesn't conflict with any imports), and add the following code:

```
# pyautogui_mouseinfo.py
# Make sure you pip install pyautogui.
import pyautogui
# Open the MouseInfo window.
pyautogui.mouseInfo()
```

Comments in code are always optional. The comments in the preceding code are just there for reminders.

Run that script using the Run Python File button in VS Code, as usual. You should see a window that looks like Figure 7-2 on your screen. As you move the mouse pointer around the screen, the XY Position field shows the XY coordinates at the tip of the mouse pointer.

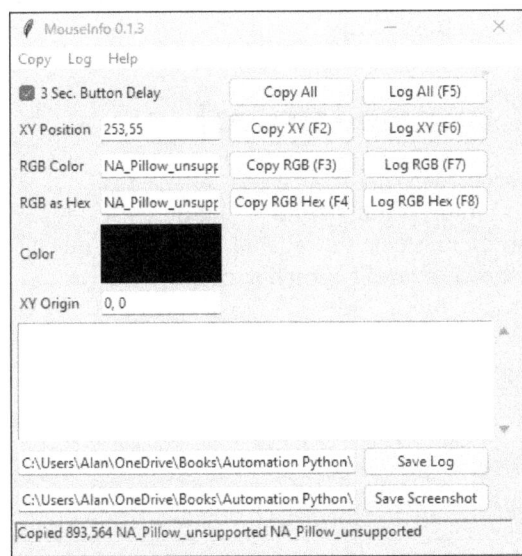

FIGURE 7-2: The MouseInfo app included with PyAutoGUI.

You can jot down the name and X, Y coordinate of whatever the mouse pointer is touching as you go along. Optionally, you can click Log XY in the MouseInfo app, and then, within 3 seconds, move the mouse pointer to the position you want to measure. A log file will record the X, Y coordinate for you. However, there won't be any descriptive text, so you'll probably want to jot that down as you go along.

When you've finished measuring, click Save Log in the MouseInfo app. By default, the file will be named `mouseInfoLog.txt` and likely saved in the same folder as your `pyautogui_mouseinfo.py` script. In VS Code, you can see the contents of that folder just by clicking the `mouseInfoLog.txt`.

Using mouse control with a specific app

The automated mouse action you get from PyAutoGUI always runs in the *active window* (whatever app is in the forefront on the screen). Any time you want to use PyAutoGUI in a specific app, first open that app and maximize its window, to ensure the *X*, *Y* coordinates of elements on the screen are consistent.

When your app is open, you can open VS Code (or whatever code editor you're using) and start your Python script. You can give yourself a couple seconds to bring the other app to the screen by using a timer to pause the Python script before it takes control of the mouse, so you have time to bring the app of interest back onto the screen by clicking its Dock or Taskbar icon.

TIP

Later in this chapter, I show you how to use a command like `time(5)` to pause the Python script in the example script.

Trying out mouse control

There is no universal screen we can all access for me to use as an example to illustrate a practical example of mouse control. But here's a sample script with lots of comments to illustrate methods for moving the mouse and clicking on the screen no matter what's showing on the screen at the moment:

```python
# move_mouse.py
# Must pip install pyautogui.
import pyautogui
import time


# FailSafe is True by default, set here for clarity.
pyautogui.FAILSAFE = True
# Add a 2-second pause after each pyautogui command.
pyautogui.PAUSE = 2

def mouse_operations():
    try:
        # Get screen size for reference.
        screen_width, screen_height = pyautogui.size()
        print(f"Screen size: {screen_width}x{screen_height}")
```

```python
# Get center of screen.
center_x, center_y = screen_width // 2, screen_height // 2
print(f"Center of screen: ({center_x}, {center_y})")

# Moving the mouse
print("Moving mouse pointer to center of screen...")
pyautogui.moveTo(center_x, center_y, duration=1)

# Move in a square to 90 percent of the screen.
print("Moving the mouse pointer in a square...")
pyautogui.moveTo(.1*screen_width,.1*screen_height)
pyautogui.moveTo(.9*screen_width,.1*screen_height, duration=1)
pyautogui.moveTo(.9*screen_width,.9*screen_height, duration=1)
pyautogui.moveTo(.1*screen_width,.9*screen_height, duration=1)
pyautogui.moveTo(.1*screen_width,.1*screen_height, duration=1)

# Move to the center of the screen.
print("Moving back to center of the screen...")
pyautogui.moveTo(center_x, center_y, duration=1)

# Move relative to current position.
print("Moving mouse pointer 300 pixels left and 100 pixels up...")
pyautogui.moveRel(-300, -100, duration=1)

# Clicking
print("Performing a left click...")
pyautogui.click()
pyautogui.press('esc')
time.sleep(1)

# Double-clicking
print("Performing a double click...")
pyautogui.doubleClick()
pyautogui.press('esc')
time.sleep(1)

# Right-clicking
print("Performing a right click...")
pyautogui.rightClick()
time.sleep(1)

# Pressing keys
print("Pressing Escape to close any context menu...")
pyautogui.press('esc')
```

```
        # Scrolling (not universally supported)
        print("Scrolling toward bottom...")
        pyautogui.scroll(-2000)
        time.sleep(3)

        print("Scrolling toward top...")
        pyautogui.scroll(4000)
        time.sleep(3)

        print("All operations completed successfully!\n")

    except pyautogui.FailSafeException:
        print("\nScript aborted by moving mouse to corner.\n")
    except Exception as e:
        print(f"An error occurred: {e}")

if __name__ == "__main__":
    message = "Script will start in 5 seconds.\n"
    message += "To cancel, move the mouse pointer to any corner."
    print(f"\n\n{message}")

    # Pause for 5 seconds before calling the function.
    time.sleep(5)
    mouse_operations()
```

TIP

Near the top of that script, the line that reads import time allows you to set timers to delay execution of the next line of code. The time module is in the standard library, so you don't need to pip install it. Near the bottom of the script, the line that reads time.sleep(5) pauses execution for five seconds, giving you a few seconds to prepare the screen when you want to run a script on a specific app or document on the screen.

Typing Text with Python

PyAutoGUI can simulate human keyboard input by typing text and pressing shortcut keys. It types at the current cursor position in the active window, just like when you type yourself. That will likely be VS Code if you run a script from VS Code. If you don't want PyAutoGUI to type inside your Python script, here's a way you can test it safely:

1. **Open Microsoft Word or any other app in which you normally type (Pages, Google Docs, Notepad, TextEdit), and leave that window open.**

2. **Open VS Code if you haven't already.**

3. **In your script, set a timer to pause code execution before the script runs, to give yourself time to switch windows.**

   For example, `time.sleep(5)` pauses for five seconds.

4. **Run your script in the usual manner in VS Code.**

5. **Switch to the window in which you want the script to type.**

   If the script will be typing into a form, click inside the first form field.

TIP

When using a script to fill in a form, it's best to use the Tab key to move from one field to the next. That way, you don't need to know the exact screen position of each field in which you want to type.

Controlling the typing speed

To type text with PyAutoGUI, use the `.write()` method. The text will type at lightning speed. Here's an example:

```
pyautogui.write("Hello World")
```

If you need to slow down the typing, add an `interval=` parameter and the number of seconds to pause between each typed character. For example, if you want to delay by half a second, type the code like this:

```
pyautogui.write("Hello World", interval=0.5)
```

Typing long passages of text

If you want to type long passages of text with line breaks and such, your best bet it to put that text in a variable first. Then put the name of the variable between the parentheses, without quotation marks.

REMEMBER

Python allows you to put long passages of text with line breaks inside triple quotation makes. Although it's often used for lengthy comments, you can also store long passages of text with line breaks using triple quotation marks. You can use either double quotation marks, like " " " or single quotation marks like ' ' '. Just make sure you use the same type to start and end the text.

For example, here's a long passage of text that contains line breaks, stored in a variable named long_message. The pyautogui.write() statement types the text with a tenth of a second delay between each character:

```
long_message = """Enclose longer passages of text like this,
with line breaks if you like, inside triple quotation marks.
Then to have Python type the text, put the variable
name inside the parentheses of .write()."""
pyautogui.write(long_message, interval=0.1)
```

Pressing special keys

To type special keys, like Enter or Tab, use pyautogui.press() with the name of the key to press, in quotation marks, inside the parentheses. The key names include "enter", "tab", "space", "backspace", "delete", "esc", "win", "up", "down", "left", "right", "f1", "f2", "f3", "f4", "f5", "f6", "f7", "f8", "f9", "f10", "f11", "f12", "home", "end", "pageup", and "pagedown".

As an example, here's some code to type some text, press Enter, press Tab, type some more text, press Enter, and type one more line of text:

```
pyautogui.write("This is a line of text.")
pyautogui.press("enter")
pyautogui.press("tab")
pyautogui.write("This line is indented.")
pyautogui.press("enter")
pyautogui.write("One final line of text.")
```

The output is three lines of text with the middle line indented, like this:

```
This is a line of text.
    This line is indented.
One final line of text.
```

Pressing hotkeys

PyAutoGUI offers a hotkeys() method for typing shortcut keys that often involve two or more key presses. That includes the Shift, Ctrl, Alt, and Windows keys in Windows (typed as "shift", "ctrl", "alt", and "win" in PyAutoGUI). On macOS, you can use the Command, Option, and Control keys (typed as "command", "option", and "ctrl" on a Mac).

As you probably know, in Windows, you press Ctrl+C to copy text. To do that in PyAutoGUI, use the command `pyautogui.hotkey('ctrl', 'c')`. On macOS, use ⌘+C to copy text. In PyAutoGUI the command is `pyautogui.hotkey('command', 'c')`.

PyAutoGUI also lets you hold down one key for as long as you need, via the `.keyDown()` method. To release the key, use the `.keyUp()` method.

```
pyautogui.keyDown('shift')
# Keep it held for 2 seconds.
time.sleep(2)
# Release the Shift key.
pyautogui.keyUp('shift')
```

Detecting the operating system

If you ever want to write an app that presses shortcut keys correctly both on Windows and on macOS, you can use the `platform` module with `.system` to detect on which operating system the script is running. You don't need to `pip install` that module — just import it into your script. For example, here's some code that uses Ctrl+*key* shortcuts when running on Windows, and Command+*key* shortcuts when running on macOS.

TECHNICAL STUFF

The code refers to macOS as Darwin because the platform module prioritizes the kernel name over the operating system name. macOS is a Unix-like operating system, which, at its core, uses a kernel named Darwin to handle interaction between hardware and software.

```
import pyautogui
import platform

pyautogui.FAILSAFE = True
pyautogui.PAUSE = 0.1

# Select, copy, and paste the text on a Mac.
if platform.system() == 'Darwin':
    # Select all in current document.
    pyautogui.hotkey('command', 'a')
    # Copy selected text.
    pyautogui.hotkey('command', 'c')
    # Move to the end of the document.
    pyautogui.hotkey('command', 'down')
    # Move to the next line.
```

```
    pyautogui.press('enter')
    # Paste the copied text.
    pyautogui.hotkey('command', 'v')
# Select, copy, and paste the text on Windows.
elif platform.system() == 'Windows':
    # Select all in current document.
    pyautogui.hotkey('ctrl', 'a')
    # Copy selected text.
    pyautogui.hotkey('ctrl', 'c')
    # Move to end of document.
    pyautogui.hotkey('ctrl', 'end')
    # Move to the next line.
    pyautogui.press('enter')
    # Paste the copied text.
    pyautogui.hotkey('ctrl', 'v')
```

TIP The shortcut keys for Linux generally duplicate those for Windows. If you want to support Linux, you can probably get away with changing `elif platform.system() == 'Windows':` to `else:` to cover both Windows and Linux. There are multiple GUIs for Linux, including GNOME, KDE Plasma, XFCE, Cinnamon, and others. You may want to test things out on whichever GUI you're using, just to be sure.

Detecting Keystrokes

Whenever you're running a Python script in VS Code, you can press Ctrl+C to stop code execution, but only if VS Code (or whatever editor/Terminal you're using) is in the active window. If you're using Python to automate other apps, you may want to be able to detect keystrokes from other windows. The pynput module lets Python detect keystrokes on the operating system level. In other words, pynput can detect keystrokes from windows other than the window from which you launched your Python script.

The pynput module isn't part of the standard library. Make sure you pip install pynput to your virtual environment before creating scripts that import that module.

WARNING As with PyAutoGUI used in this chapter, you'll need to enable Accessibility features on a Mac for pynput to work. See "Granting Permissions on a Mac," earlier in this chapter, for details.

To illustrate how pynput works, the following script will stop the currently running Python script from any open window in Linux, macOS, or Windows when the user presses the Escape key (esc in the code):

```
# listen_esc.py
# You must pip install pynput for this to work.
from pynput import keyboard
import sys

def on_press(key):
    # Check if the Esc key is pressed.
    if key == keyboard.Key.esc:
        print(f'Esc key detected! Stopping the script...')
        # Stop the listener and exit the script
        sys.exit(0)

# Set up the keyboard listener.
print(f'Press Esc in any window to stop')
with keyboard.Listener(on_press=on_press) as listener:
    listener.join()
```

Notice the function named on_press(key). Whenever the preceding script is running, the key parameter in parentheses receives the last key pressed on the keyboard, no matter what window you're in. The line that reads if key == keyboard.Key.esc is True when you press Esc, so the function simply prints a little feedback and stops script execution with sys.exit(0).

The most complicated code is probably with keyboard.Listener(on_press=on_press), which creates a pynput listener that can detect every key pressed at the keyboard. The on_press=on_press bit says to call the function names on_press every time a key is pressed. Whatever key was pressed is then passes to that function as the key parameter.

The as listener part simply names that keyboard listener listener. The listener.join() activates the listener by temporarily blocking the Python script from being the only one listening for keystrokes, so the listener can monitor keystrokes globally, across all open windows. That listener stays in effect until sys.exit(0) terminates the Python script, which also terminates the listener.

Creating Your Own Keyboard Shortcuts

If you want to create custom shortcut keys that you can call from any app or window, you can use pynput (described earlier) to listen for the key combinations. Try not to replace commonly used shortcuts, like Ctrl+C or ⌘+C for Copy in Windows or Mac, respectively, or things could become very confusing when you're calling your Python script rather than doing the shortcut key's original task!

TIP

If you're targeting a specific app for your shortcut key action, you can ask artificial intelligence (AI) whether the shortcut key you're planning to use already has some role in that app.

WARNING

For unknown reasons, pynput doesn't always play nicely with Microsoft Word. If you're looking to create shortcut keys for Windows, consider using a macro in Word instead. If you don't know how, just ask any AI.

In this next script, we'll use pynput to listen for the shortcut key. We'll also allow you to end the script by pressing the Escape key. So basically, after you start the script, you can go to any other app and use the shortcut key to type your text, as long as the script is running. Press Escape to end the script and stop listening for the shortcut key.

First, I'll show you the entire script; then I'll explain how it works.

```
# shortcut_key.py
# pip install pynput and pyautogui
from pynput import keyboard
import pyautogui
import sys
import platform
import time


# Define hotkeys for typing boilerplate text.
windows_hotkey = '<ctrl>+<alt>+t'
mac_hotkey = '<cmd>+<shift>+t'
# Define boilerplate text and hotkeys for Windows, Mac.
boilerplate_text = """Hello, this text was typed by pynput!
    You can make this any length and any number of lines."""

def type_boilerplate():
    time.sleep(0.5)
    pyautogui.write(boilerplate_text, interval=0.05)

def exit_script():
    print("Esc pressed. Exiting...")
    sys.exit(0)

def main():
    # Set up the hotkey based on the operating system.
    system = platform.system()
    # Mac shortcut key
```

```
    if system == 'Darwin':
        hotkey = mac_hotkey
    else:
        # Windows/Linux shortcut key
        hotkey = windows_hotkey

    # Set up the hotkeys dictionary and what each calls.
    hotkeys = {
        hotkey: type_boilerplate,
        '<esc>': exit_script
    }
    # Start listening.
    print(f"Listening for {hotkey}. Press Esc to end...")
    with keyboard.GlobalHotKeys(hotkeys) as listener:
        listener.join()

if __name__ == '__main__':
    try:
        main()
    except KeyboardInterrupt:
        print("\nExiting...")
        sys.exit(0)
```

The following block of code is where you define your hotkeys. You can define as many hotkeys as you want. I've done two — one for typing boilerplate text and one for exiting the script. If you want to support both macOS and Windows, you'll have to define hotkeys for each, as I've done here:

```
# Define hotkeys for typing boilerplate text.
windows_hotkey = '<ctrl>+<alt>+t'
mac_hotkey = '<cmd>+<shift>+t'
```

I've set up Ctrl+Alt+T for the Windows hotkey and ⌘+Shift+T for the Mac. That key combination isn't used for anything important, as far as I know. So, I'm not replacing some commonly used shortcut key with my own.

The syntax requires that the modifier keys ctr, alt, and cmd (command) be enclosed in angle brackets, while the regular letter t isn't in angle brackets.

For my example, I'm going to have the shortcut key type some text into whatever app I happen to be using. Frequently typed text is sometimes called *boilerplate text,* so I've used the variable name boilerplate_text to hold mine. You can type any text you want, and any number of lines of text, between the triple quotation marks when writing your own code.

```
# Define boilerplate text and hotkeys for Windows, Mac.
boilerplate_text = """Hello, this text was typed by pynput!
    You can make this any length and any number of lines."""
```

Define the action that you want the shortcut key to perform in a function. In my case, I've created a function named `type_boilerplate()`, as shown next. The `time.sleep()` line provides a half-second delay before typing, to allow a little time for the cursor to get into position before the typing begins:

```
def type_boilerplate():
    time.sleep(0.5)
    pyautogui.write(boilerplate_text, interval=0.05)
```

I'll pair that function with the hotkey a little later in the code. But let me briefly explain the rest. This next function, when called, simply exits the script. I'll pair that with the Escape key later. Because that's not a combination keystroke and is the same on Windows and macOS, you don't need to define it as a "special key."

```
def exit_script():
    print("Esc pressed. Exiting...")
    sys.exit(0)
```

Next, we need to define the hotkey the script will use, depending on whether the script is running on macOS, Windows, or Linux (which generally uses the same keys as Windows). That's done in this block of code, where the variable named `hotkey` gets the appropriate key combination for the current operating system:

```
def main():
    # Set up the hotkey based on the operating system.
    system = platform.system()
    # Mac shortcut key
    if system == 'Darwin':
        hotkey = mac_hotkey
    else:
        # Windows/Linux shortcut key
        hotkey = windows_hotkey
```

Next, we can pair keys with functions we defined earlier. Here's a dictionary named `hotkeys` that pairs `hotkey` with the `type_boilerplate` function, and the Escape key (`<esc>`) with the `exit_script` function:

```
# Set up the hotkeys dictionary and what each calls.
hotkeys = {
    hotkey: type_boilerplate,
    '<esc>': exit_script
}
```

Finally, the `main()` function tells the script to print a little text identifying which keys the script is listening for. Then it sets up the listener to listen for the keys defined in the `hotkeys` dictionary:

```
print(f"Listening for {hotkey}. Press Esc to end...")
with keyboard.GlobalHotKeys(hotkeys) as listener:
    listener.join()
```

The rest of the code runs the `main()` function to activate the hotkeys when you run the script. The `try` block detects when the script was ended by pressing Escape, and prints a friendly `Exiting...` message in the Terminal instead of just stopping the script abruptly with no additional feedback.

Automating Screenshots

Taking screenshots is easy, thanks to the Snipping Tool in Windows and the Screenshot app on macOS. But what if you want to take screenshots automatically during some long-running process? Well, you can do that, too, with Python, thanks to PyAutoGUI. As with other apps in this chapter, you'll need to grant accessibility rights on a Mac, as discussed near the start of this chapter.

WARNING

One caveat to taking screenshots is that the script needs access to `pyscreeze`, which is a component of the Pillow library. So, even though you don't see Pillow in the script's imports, you do need to install that into your virtual environment for the script to work. This script also requires PyAutoGUI so make sure you install both by entering this command at the Terminal when you're in your virtual environment:

```
pip install pillow pyautogui
```

I'll start by showing you the entire script for automatic screenshots next. Then I'll point out key features and personalization in the following sections. Here's the script in its entirety:

```
# auto_screenshots.py
# pip install pillow pyautogui for this script
```

```python
import pyautogui
import time
from datetime import datetime
from pathlib import Path
pyautogui.PAUSE = 0.1


def take_screenshot(save_path: Path):
    # Get current timestamp for filename.
    timestamp = datetime.now().strftime("%Y%m%d_%H%M%S")
    filename = f"screenshot_{timestamp}.png"
    full_path = save_path / filename

    try:
        # Take screenshot and save it.
        screenshot = pyautogui.screenshot()
        screenshot.save(full_path)
        print(f"Screenshot saved to {full_path}")
        return full_path
    except Exception as e:
        print(f"Error taking screenshot: {e}")
        return None


def start_recording(save_path: Path, time_delay):
    # Create screenshots directory if it doesn't exist.
    if not save_path.exists():
        save_path.mkdir(parents=True, exist_ok=True)
    try:
        while True:
            take_screenshot(save_path)
            time.sleep(time_delay)
    except KeyboardInterrupt:
        return False


def main():
    # Where to save screenshots
    save_path = Path(R"C:\Users\Alan\Documents\Practice\Auto Screenshots")
    # For macOS/Linux, make sure to change the path to a valid one with write
    #           permissions.
    # save_path = Path("/Users/alan/Practice/Auto Screenshots")
    # How many seconds between each screenshot
    time_delay = 5  # seconds
```

```
# Start the screenshot recording.
print("\nTaking Screenshots.\nPress Ctrl+C here to stop the recording.\n")
recording = start_recording(save_path, time_delay)
# Message shown when recording was stopped with Ctrl+C
if not recording:
    print("\nRecording stopped")


if __name__ == "__main__":
    main()
```

Taking screenshots with Python

The `take_screenshot()` function in the screenshots script does the work of taking the screenshot and saving screenshots. When called, it generates a filename using `datetime.now()`. Then it appends that to the path to which the file should be saved using the following code:

```
def take_screenshot(save_path: Path):
    # Get current timestamp for filename.
    timestamp = datetime.now().strftime("%Y%m%d_%H%M%S")
    filename = f"screenshot_{timestamp}.png"
    full_path = save_path / filename
```

The actual screenshot is taken using `screenshot = pyautogui.screenshot()` and saved using the `screenshot.save(full_path)` line:

```
# Take screenshot and save it.
screenshot = pyautogui.screenshot()
screenshot.save(full_path)
```

TIP

The rest of the code provides printed feedback in the Terminal while the script is running.

The automation part happens in the `start_recording()` script, which first creates the folder (if it doesn't already exist) to which the screenshots are saved. Then the script uses a simple `while True` loop to keep calling `take_screenshot()` until you press Ctrl+C in the Terminal window to stop the script.

```
def start_recording(save_path: Path, time_delay):
    # Create screenshots directory if it doesn't exist.
    if not save_path.exists():
        save_path.mkdir(parents=True, exist_ok=True)
```

```
try:
    while True:
        take_screenshot(save_path)
        time.sleep(time_delay)
except KeyboardInterrupt:
    return False
```

Personalizing the auto screenshot script

The auto screenshot script is ready to go on any operating system. To make it your own, just set the save_path variable to the path to which you want to save the screenshots using the syntax shown in the main() function. Use the time_delay variable to specify how many seconds to pause between each screenshot.

```
def main():
    # Where to save screenshots
    save_path = Path(R"C:\Users\Alan\Documents\Practice\Auto Screenshots")
    # For macOS/Linux, make sure to change the path to a valid one with write
    permissions.
    # save_path = Path("/Users/alan/Practice/Auto Screenshots")
    # How many seconds between each screenshot
    time_delay = 5  # seconds
```

Make sure you specify a folder to which Python has write permissions, so the script can save files without generating an error.

WARNING

Chapter **8**

Automating the Office

I n this chapter, you automate common office apps and tasks, particularly Microsoft Word, Microsoft Excel, and PDFs. You find techniques for creating new files, opening existing files, and adding content to files. I also show you a script that can add a watermark image to every page of a PDF.

Automating Microsoft Word

You can create, open, add content to, and save Word documents with Python. If you find yourself doing any of those tasks repetitively, you'll appreciate the first script in this chapter, which does all those things.

For our first script, we'll use the python-docx module to create, open, add content to, and save a Word document. In the code, you'll see a line that reads from docx import Document, but that's a little misleading. The actual name of the module is python-docx. To use this script, make sure you activate your virtual environment and enter the following command in the Terminal:

```
pip install python-docx
```

Here's the script in its entirety:

```
# create_open_word.py
# You must pip install python-docx.
from docx import Document
```

```python
from pathlib import Path
import os
import sys


# Here is where you define what you want to put into the document.
def add_content(doc: Document) -> None:
    try:
        doc.add_heading('Sample Document', level=1)
        doc.add_paragraph('This is a sample paragraph added to the document.')
        doc.add_paragraph('Created using python-docx on Windows or macOS.')
        print("Content added to the document.")
    except Exception as e:
        print(f"Error adding content to document: {e}")
        raise


# Create the folder path if it doesn't exist.
def ensure_path_exists(folder_path: str) -> Path:
    try:
        path = Path(folder_path).resolve()
        path.mkdir(parents=True, exist_ok=True)
        return path
    except OSError as e:
        print(f"Error creating directory {folder_path}: {e}")
        raise


# Ensure the filename has a .docx extension.
def validate_file_name(file_name: str) -> str:
    if not file_name.lower().endswith('.docx'):
        file_name += '.docx'
    return file_name


# Open an existing .docx file or create a new one.
def open_or_create_docx(folder_path: Path, file_name: str) -> Document:
    file_path = folder_path / file_name
    # Returns the Document object.
    try:
        if file_path.exists():
            print(f"Opening existing document: {file_path}")
            return Document(file_path)
        else:
            print(f"Creating new document: {file_path}")
            doc = Document()
            doc.save(file_path)  # Initialize the file
            return doc
```

```python
    except Exception as e:
        print(f"Error opening or creating document {file_path}: {e}")
        raise


# Save the document to the specified path.
def save_document(doc: Document, file_path: Path) -> None:
    try:
        doc.save(file_path)
        print(f"Document saved successfully: {file_path}")
    except Exception as e:
        print(f"Error saving document {file_path}: {e}")
        raise


# Open the file in the default application on Windows or macOS.
def open_file(file_path: Path) -> None:
    try:
        if sys.platform.startswith('win'):
            os.startfile(str(file_path))
        elif sys.platform.startswith('darwin'):
            # Use os.system instead of subprocess to open the file on macOS
            os.system(f'open "{file_path}"')
        else:
            print("Unsupported OS for auto opening the file. Please open
                  manually:", file_path)
    except Exception as e:
        print(f"Error opening the file {file_path}: {e}")
        raise


# Uses all the preceding functions to create or open a Word document and
  add content
def process_document(folder_path: str, file_name: str) -> None:
    try:
        path = ensure_path_exists(folder_path)
        file_name = validate_file_name(file_name)
        file_path = path / file_name
        doc = open_or_create_docx(path, file_name)
        add_content(doc)
        save_document(doc, file_path)
        open_file(file_path)
    except Exception as e:
        print(f"Failed to process document: {e}")
        raise
```

```
# Specify your path and filename here.
def main():
    # Windows path
    folder_path = R"C:\Users\Alan\Documents\Practice\Word Docs"
    # macOS path
    # folder_path="/Users/alan/Documents/Practice/Word Docs"
    file_name = "Sample Generated.docx"

    # Create or open the document and add content.
    process_document(folder_path, file_name)

if __name__ == "__main__":
    main()
```

The script is organized into several functions, with exception handling to handle any unforeseen problems like insufficient permissions for creating or saving documents. Making the script your own is mostly about defining the location and name of the Word document you want to create or modify, as well as the content you want to put into the document.

Naming your Word document

The main() function is where you specify the filename and location of your Word document. If you specify a folder or document that doesn't exist, the script creates the folder and document for you. If you specify an existing Word document, the script opens that document and adds your content to that document. Use the main() function to specify your path and filename:

```
# Specify your path and filename here.
def main():
    # Windows path
    folder_path = R"C:\Users\Alan\Documents\Practice\Word Docs"
    # macOS path
    # folder_path="/Users/alan/Documents/Practice/Word Docs"
    file_name = "Sample Generated.docx"
```

WARNING

I've included both Windows and macOS paths as example code. Be sure to use the right syntax for your operating system, as well as a folder for which you have write permissions.

Defining your Word content

The `add_content()` function is where you add code to define the content you want to type into the Word document. I've presented a simple example adding a heading with `doc.add.heading()`, and a couple of paragraphs with `doc.add.paragraph()`:

```
# Here is where you define what you want to put into the document.
def add_content(doc: Document) -> None:
    try:
        doc.add_heading('Sample Document', level=1)
        doc.add_paragraph('This is a sample paragraph added to the document.')
        doc.add_paragraph('Created using python-docx on Windows or macOS.')
        print("Content added to the document.")
    except Exception as e:
        print(f"Error adding content to document: {e}")
        raise
```

TIP

I've intentionally added minimal text in this example so as not to overcomplicate the code, but you can add any element type to any Word document using similar code. For the full range of possibilities, check out the `python-docx` code at `https://python-docx.readthedocs.io`.

Here are some of the things you can do with `python-docx` in Word documents:

» Add, change, or delete paragraphs.

» Change the alignment, indentation, or line spacing of paragraphs.

» Insert text formatting like bold and italic.

» Add, change, or remove headings.

» Create tables with a specified number of rows and columns.

» Populate table cells with text or other content.

» Edit cell content, merge cells, or adjust table properties.

» Insert, replace, or resize images.

» Create bulleted or numbered lists.

» Add content to headers and footers, including text or images.

» Insert page breaks to start a new page.

» Change font properties including size, color, and typeface.

» Apply or modify paragraph styles (for example, Normal or Title).

REMEMBER

Just about anything you can do in Word you can automate with Python and python-docx. Most artificial intelligence (AI) can easily write the code for you as well. Start your AI prompt with "Write Python python-docx code to . . . " and describe exactly what you want the code to do.

Automating Microsoft Excel

Just as you can create and edit Word documents with Python, you can do the same with Excel. You'll need the openpyxl module, which isn't part of the standard library. So, after you create and activate your virtual environment, enter the following command in the Terminal:

```
pip install openpyxl
```

This is a sample script to automate Excel. It has capabilities similar to those for automating Word. You can use it to create a new Excel workbook or open and modify an existing workbook. This script is organized into functions that perform specific tasks, like creating necessary folders, catching exceptions, and entering content into a workbook. Here's the entire script:

```
# create_open_excel.py
# You must pip install openpyxl.
from openpyxl import Workbook, load_workbook
from pathlib import Path
import os
import sys

# Here is where you define what you want to put into the workbook.
def add_content(wb) -> None:
    try:
        ws = wb.active
        ws.title = "Sample Data"
        # Add header row.
        ws.append(["ID", "Name", "Value"])
        # Add sample rows.
        ws.append([1, "Sample Item 1", 123])
        ws.append([2, "Sample Item 2", 456])
        ws.append([3, "Sample Item 3", 789])
        print("Content added to the workbook.")
    except Exception as e:
        print(f"Error adding content to workbook: {e}")
        raise
```

```python
# Create the folder path if it doesn't exist.
def ensure_path_exists(folder_path: str) -> Path:
    try:
        path = Path(folder_path).resolve()
        path.mkdir(parents=True, exist_ok=True)
        return path
    except OSError as e:
        print(f"Error creating directory {folder_path}: {e}")
        raise


# Ensure the filename has a .xlsx extension.
def validate_file_name(file_name: str) -> str:
    if not file_name.lower().endswith('.xlsx'):
        file_name += '.xlsx'
    return file_name


# Open an existing .xlsx file or create a new one.
def open_or_create_workbook(folder_path: Path, file_name: str):
    file_path = folder_path / file_name
    try:
        if file_path.exists():
            print(f"Opening existing workbook: {file_path}")
            return load_workbook(file_path)
        else:
            print(f"Creating new workbook: {file_path}")
            wb = Workbook()
            wb.save(file_path)  # Initialize the file.
            return wb
    except Exception as e:
        print(f"Error opening or creating workbook {file_path}: {e}")
        raise


# Save the workbook to the specified path.
def save_workbook(wb, file_path: Path) -> None:
    try:
        wb.save(file_path)
        print(f"Workbook saved successfully: {file_path}")
    except Exception as e:
        print(f"Error saving workbook {file_path}: {e}")
        raise
```

```python
# Open the file in the default application on Windows or macOS.
def open_file(file_path: Path) -> None:
    try:
        if sys.platform.startswith('win'):
            os.startfile(str(file_path))
        elif sys.platform.startswith('darwin'):
            os.system(f'open "{file_path}"')
        else:
            print("Unsupported OS for auto opening the file. Please open
    manually:", file_path)
    except Exception as e:
        print(f"Error opening the file {file_path}: {e}")
        raise


# Uses all the preceding functions to create or open an Excel workbook and
    add content.
def process_workbook(folder_path: str, file_name: str) -> None:
    try:
        path = ensure_path_exists(folder_path)
        file_name = validate_file_name(file_name)
        file_path = path / file_name
        wb = open_or_create_workbook(path, file_name)
        add_content(wb)
        save_workbook(wb, file_path)
        open_file(file_path)
    except Exception as e:
        print(f"Failed to process workbook: {e}")
        raise


# Specify your path and file name here.
def main():
    # Windows path example
    # folder_path = r"C:\Users\Alan\Documents\Practice\Excel Files"
    # macOS path example
    folder_path = "/Users/alan/Practice/Excel Files"
    file_name = "Sample Generated.xlsx"
    process_workbook(folder_path, file_name)


if __name__ == "__main__":
    main()
```

The key functions in this script are main() and add_content(), which I describe
in the next two sections.

Specifying your workbook

The `main()` function lets you use the script to create a new workbook or open an existing workbook. Use the `folder_path` variable to define the location of the workbook. If you specify a folder that doesn't exist, the script will create a folder for you.

As always, make sure you use proper syntax for your path depending on whether you're using Windows or macOS.

```
# Specify your path and filename here.
def main():
    # Windows path example
    folder_path = r"C:\Users\Alan\Documents\Practice\Excel Files"
    # Mac path example
    # folder_path = "/Users/alan/Practice/Excel Files"
```

Use the `file_name` variable to indicate the filename of the workbook. If the file doesn't exist, the script will create and open a workbook with that filename. If the file already exists, the script will open it. Either way, the script will add whatever content you specify into that open workbook.

```
file_name = "Sample Generated.xlsx"
```

Defining content for your workbook

Use the `add_content()` function to specify what you want to put into the workbook. In the example script, I added some generic sample content to keep things relatively simple:

```
# Here is where you define what you want to put into the workbook.
def add_content(wb) -> None:
    try:
        ws = wb.active
        ws.title = "Sample Data"
        # Add header row
        ws.append(["ID", "Name", "Value"])
        # Add sample rows
        ws.append([1, "Sample Item 1", 123])
        ws.append([2, "Sample Item 2", 456])
        ws.append([3, "Sample Item 3", 789])
        print("Content added to the workbook.")
```

```
except Exception as e:
    print(f"Error adding content to workbook: {e}")
    raise
```

The wb parameter refers to the current open workbook, which is passed in by other functions after the workbook is opened. The line that reads ws=wb.active defines that open workbook as the active workbook, and subsequent lines use ws to add content to that active workbook.

TIP

The openpyxl module allows you to do just about anything in a workbook that you can do manually, including the following:

>> Insert and delete rows and columns.

>> Iterate over rows and columns.

>> Append rows.

>> Insert formulas using ranges and read formula results.

>> Apply conditional formatting.

>> Insert charts and images.

>> Format cells using fonts, alignment, colors, borders, number formats, and more.

>> Adjust row heights and column widths.

For the full range of openpyxl capabilities, check out the documentation at https://openpyxl.readthedocs.io.

TECHNICAL
STUFF

If you're an advanced Python user, you may be glad to know that openpyxl can allow export data to and import data from Pandas DataFrames.

Creating and Opening PDFs

Portable Document Format (PDF) is a popular format for sharing documents online, largely because the document always looks the same, whether you view it on a PC or Mac. PDF readers, like Adobe Acrobat Reader, are free and plentiful. These days, most web browsers can open and display PDFs.

In this section, I show you how to create new PDFs, open existing PDFs, and add content to any PDF. We'll use the PyPDF2 and reportlab modules. Neither of these modules is part of the Python standard library, so after creating and activating your virtual environment, enter the following command in the Terminal to install them:

```
pip install reportlab PyPDF2
```

This script uses PyPDF2 mainly for file-level tasks like opening and reading existing PDFs. It uses reportlab to add content to a page, because reportlab is generally preferred for that part of the job.

As with other scripts in this book, I show you the complete script first. Then I show you how to adapt it to your own needs. Here's the script:

```
# create_open_pdf.py
# pip install reportlab PyPDF2
import os
import sys
from pathlib import Path
from io import BytesIO
from reportlab.lib.pagesizes import letter
from reportlab.pdfgen import canvas
from reportlab.lib.units import inch
from PyPDF2 import PdfReader, PdfWriter


# This is where you define the content to put into the PDF.
def add_content(c: canvas.Canvas) -> None:
    # Define the content to be added to the PDF.
    c.setFont("Helvetica", 16)
    c.drawString(1 * inch, 10 * inch, "Sample PDF Report")
    c.setFont("Helvetica", 12)
    c.drawString(1 * inch, 9.5 * inch, "Generated with Python, ReportLab
    and PyPDF2")
    c.line(1 * inch, 9.3 * inch, 7.5 * inch, 9.3 * inch)


    # Add the additional paragraph.
    textobject = c.beginText()
    textobject.setTextOrigin(1 * inch, 8.7 * inch)
    textobject.setFont("Helvetica", 10)
    textobject.textLine("Use the canvas in reportlab to add content to
    the PDF page.")
    textobject.textLine("See the reportlab documentation at https://docs.
    reportlab.com for more.")
    c.drawText(textobject)
```

```python
def ensure_path_exists(folder_path: str) -> Path:
    # Create the folder path if it doesn't exist.
    try:
        path = Path(folder_path).resolve()
        path.mkdir(parents=True, exist_ok=True)
        return path
    except Exception as e:
        print(f"Error creating directory: {e}")
        raise


def validate_file_name(file_name: str) -> str:
    # Ensure the filename has a .pdf extension.
    if not file_name.lower().endswith('.pdf'):
        file_name += '.pdf'
    return file_name


def create_new_page_pdf() -> BytesIO:
    # Create a new PDF with content using ReportLab.
    buffer = BytesIO()
    c = canvas.Canvas(buffer, pagesize=letter)
    add_content(c)
    c.showPage()
    c.save()
    buffer.seek(0)
    return buffer


def open_file(file_path: Path) -> None:
    # Open the PDf in the default application.
    try:
        if sys.platform.startswith('win'):
            os.startfile(str(file_path))
        elif sys.platform.startswith('darwin'):
            os.system(f'open "{file_path}"')
        else:
            print(f"Unsupported OS for automatic opening: {file_path}")
    except Exception as e:
        print(f"Error opening file {file_path}: {e}")


def process_pdf(folder_path: str, file_name: str) -> None:
    # If the PDF doesn't exist, create it.
    # Otherwise, open it and append a new page.
```

```python
    try:
        path = ensure_path_exists(folder_path)
        file_name = validate_file_name(file_name)
        pdf_path = path / file_name

        writer = PdfWriter()
        # If the PDF exists, load its pages.
        if pdf_path.exists():
            print(f"\nOpening existing PDF: {pdf_path}")
            reader = PdfReader(str(pdf_path))
            for page in reader.pages:
                writer.add_page(page)
        else:
            print(f"\nCreating new PDF: {pdf_path}")

            # Create a new content page and add it.
            new_page_buffer = create_new_page_pdf()
            new_reader = PdfReader(new_page_buffer)
            writer.add_page(new_reader.pages[0])
            print("Added new content page.")

            # Write the updated PDF content to the file.
            with open(pdf_path, "wb") as f:
                writer.write(f)
            print(f"PDF processed and saved successfully: {pdf_path}\n")

            # Open the file using the default application.
            open_file(pdf_path)

    except Exception as e:
        print(f"Failed to process PDF: {e}")
        raise


def main():
    # Where to put (or open) the PDF file.
    # Windows example:
    folder_path = r"C:\Users\Alan\Documents\Practice\PDFs"
    # macOS/Linux example:
    # folder_path = "/Users/alan/Documents/Practice/PDFs"
    # Filename of PDF
    file_name = "Sample Generated.pdf"
```

```
        # Create or open the PDF and add content.
        process_pdf(folder_path, file_name)

if __name__ == "__main__":
    main()
```

All the code for creating a new PDF or opening an existing PDF is already contained in the script. The script contains exception handling to catch possible errors and display error messages for unforeseen exceptions. You don't need to do anything in the script for all of that to work. But it's up to you to determine what you want to put into the PDF, as I explain next.

Defining content for your PDF

The code for defining what you want to put into your PDF is contained within the add_content() function in the script. Unfortunately, you can't just type what you want there. You must use the syntax specified by reportlab. The script shows examples of using textobject and the .setFont, .drawString, and .line methods of reportlab. See the reportlab documentation at https://docs. reportlab.com for more information.

Identifying your PDF

In the main() function, specify the path and filename for your PDF. As with other automation scripts in this book, if you specify a PDF that already exists, the script will open that PDF and your content to that file. If you want to create a new PDF from scratch, make up a new file with a .pdf extension.

REMEMBER

As always, make sure to use a valid path for Windows or macOS/Linux. In the following example, I use Windows, and I comment out the macOS/Linux path. I've included that path only as a reminder of the proper syntax for those paths.

```
def main():
    # Where to put (or open) the PDF
    # Windows example:
    folder_path = r"C:\Users\Alan\Documents\Practice\PDFs"
    # macOS/Linux example:
    # folder_path = "/Users/alan/Documents/Practice/PDFs"
    # Filename of PDF
    file_name = "Sample Generated.pdf"
```

The `file_name` variable must be the name of the PDF you want to create or modify. If you specify a path and filename to an existing PDF, the script appends a new page to that PDF and inserts the content on that page.

Watermarking PDFs

Watermarking PDFs is a common procedure, sometimes done to protect intellectual property, establish ownership, and prevent misuse by deterring unauthorized copying, distribution, or alteration, particularly of sensitive or confidential materials.

TIP

Watermarks also serve branding purposes by embedding logos or names, reinforce document status with labels like *Draft* or *Confidential,* and enable tracking of distribution through unique identifiers to trace leaks or unauthorized sharing, providing a visible layer of security and control while maintaining the document's content.

In this section, you create a script that can open any existing PDF and add a watermark to each page of the document. The script saves the watermarked file with the original filename with _watermarked appended to the filename, so you retain your original document.

The script uses `reportlab` and `PyPDF2` to manage the PDF, and `Pillow` to get the dimensions of your image. After you create and activate your virtual environment, make sure to enter this command at the Terminal to install those modules (if they're not already installed):

```
pip install reportlab PyPDF2 Pillow
```

First, let me show you the entire script. I explain how to adapt it to your own needs in the sections that follow.

```
# watermark_pdf.py
# pip install reportlab PyPDF2 Pillow
import os
import sys
from pathlib import Path
from io import BytesIO
from PIL import Image
from reportlab.pdfgen import canvas
from PyPDF2 import PdfReader, PdfWriter
```

```python
def create_watermark_pdf(page_width, page_height, watermark_path, magnification):
    # Center the watermark vertically and horizontally.
    try:
        # Open the watermark image to get its dimensions.
        with Image.open(watermark_path) as img:
            img_width, img_height = img.size

            # Scale the image dimensions by the magnification percentage.
            scaled_width = img_width * magnification / 100
            scaled_height = img_height * magnification / 100

            # Compute the centered position using scaled dimensions.
            x = (page_width - scaled_width) / 2
            y = (page_height - scaled_height) / 2

            buffer = BytesIO()
            c = canvas.Canvas(buffer, pagesize=(page_width, page_height))
            # Draw the image with scaled dimensions.
            c.drawImage(str(watermark_path), x, y, width=scaled_width,
                height=scaled_height, mask='auto')
            c.showPage()
            c.save()
            buffer.seek(0)
            return buffer
    except Exception as e:
        print(f"Error creating watermark PDF: {e}")
        raise


def add_watermark_to_pdf(pdf_path: Path, watermark_path: Path, magnification:
    int) -> None:
    # Opens the given PDF file and adds a watermark to every page
    try:
        reader = PdfReader(str(pdf_path))
        writer = PdfWriter()

        for page in reader.pages:
            # Get page dimensions from the media box.
            page_width = float(page.mediabox.width)
            page_height = float(page.mediabox.height)

            # Create the watermark page for the current page dimensions using
        the provided magnification.
            watermark_buffer = create_watermark_pdf(page_width, page_height,
        watermark_path, magnification)
            watermark_reader = PdfReader(watermark_buffer)
```

```python
            watermark_page = watermark_reader.pages[0]

            # Merge the watermark page with the current page.
            page.merge_page(watermark_page)
            writer.add_page(page)

        # Save the watermarked PDF to a new file, keeping the original intact.
        output_pdf = pdf_path.with_name(f"{pdf_path.stem}_watermarked.pdf")
        with open(output_pdf, "wb") as f_out:
            writer.write(f_out)
        print(f"Watermarked PDF saved as: {output_pdf}")
    except Exception as e:
        print(f"Error processing PDF file: {e}")
        raise


def main():
    try:
        # Path to your existing PDF to which you'll add watermarks
        pdf_file_path = R"C:\Users\Alan\Documents\Practice\PDFs\practice.pdf"
        #pdf_file_path = "/Users/alan/Practice/PDFs/practice.pdf"
        # Path to your watermark image file
        watermark_image_path = R"C:\Users\Alan\Documents\Practice\PDFs\
    watermark.png"
        #watermark_image_path = "/Users/alan/Practice/PDFs/watermark.png"

        # Set magnification value (for example, 80 for 80 percent).
        magnification = 100

        # Resolve the paths to pathlib Paths.
        pdf_path = Path(pdf_file_path).resolve()
        watermark_path = Path(watermark_image_path).resolve()

        # Validate the existence of files.
        if not pdf_path.exists() or not pdf_path.is_file():
            raise FileNotFoundError(f"PDF file not found: {pdf_path}")
        if not watermark_path.exists() or not watermark_path.is_file():
            raise FileNotFoundError(f"Watermark image not found:
    {watermark_path}")

        add_watermark_to_pdf(pdf_path, watermark_path, magnification)
    except Exception as e:
        print(f"An error occurred: {e}")


if __name__ == "__main__":
    main()
```

Creating your watermark image

TIP

To prevent your watermark image from obscuring content in your document, use very light colors in the image. Ideally, ensure the image has a transparent background. You can remove the background from an image using Preview on macOS computers or Photos on Windows. Optionally, use any free AI tool that allows you to remove image backgrounds.

TECHNICAL STUFF

If the watermark is obscuring text, you may also want to reduce the opacity of the image foreground. If you don't have a graphics editor with that capability, you can use the free Photopea editor at www.photopea.com. These are the steps:

1. **Open your image in Photopea.**

2. **Click the image layer in Photopea.**

   If you just opened the image, the image layer is labeled Background in the layers list.

3. **Set the Opacity to 30%, as shown in Figure 8-1.**

4. **To save the image, choose File ⇨ Export As ⇨ PNG.**

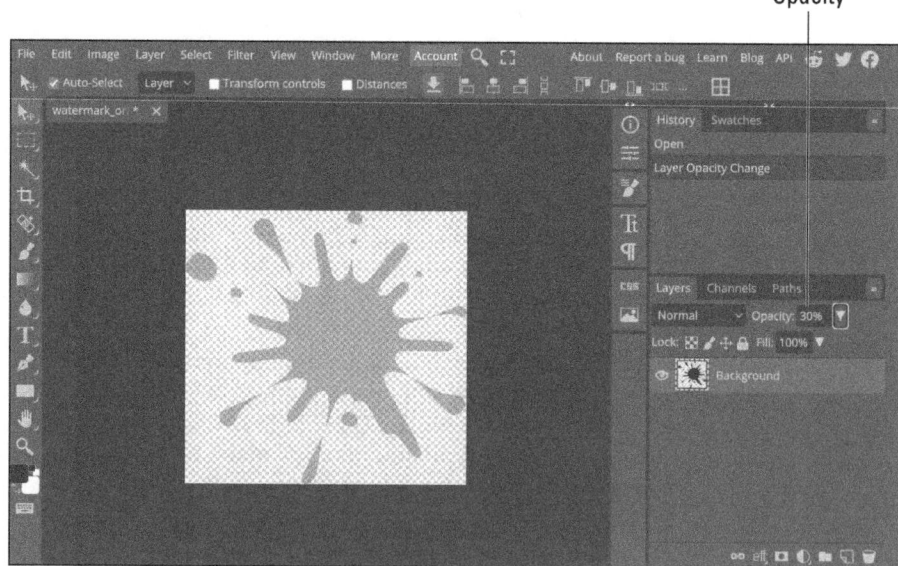

FIGURE 8-1:
Reducing an image's opacity in Photopea.

TIP

You may want to experiment with a few different opacities to determine what works best for you. Consider saving different opacities with different filenames, such as Watermark 20pct.png for an image with 20 percent opacity, so you can try out different images and see what works best for your document.

Adapting the script to your needs

To adapt this script to your own needs, set paths to your PDF and watermark image in the main() function. As always, remember to use the correct syntax for your operating system. Here are examples using Windows paths.

```
# Path to your existing PDF to which you'll add watermarks
pdf_file_path = R"C:\Users\Alan\Documents\Practice\PDFs\practice.pdf"
# Path to your watermark image file
watermark_image_path = R"C:\Users\Alan\Documents\Practice\PDFs\watermark.png"
# Set magnification value (for example, 80 for 80 percent)
magnification = 100
```

TIP

If the watermark image is too large or too small, when placed in the PDF, use the magnification variable to adjust the size. For example, setting the magnification variable to 50 will shrink the image to 50 percent its size. Setting magnification to 200 doubles the size of the watermark image.

3

Automating the Internet

IN THIS PART . . .

Master application programming interfaces (APIs) and JavaScript Object Notation (JSON) for online interaction.

Automate web browsers.

Scrape web pages for code and content.

Automate email and Short Message Service (SMS) text messages.

Automate social media contents and metrics.

Chapter **9**

Interacting with APIs

M uch of the interaction between your Python scripts and internet content will take place through an application programming interface (API). To gain access to an API, you typically have to sign up with the API provider and obtain an API key, which is a unique code provided by an API provider to identify you and your app. Keys are strings of characters and numbers, 20 to 50 characters in length.

In this chapter, I show you how to obtain API keys, store them safely, and use them with Python to take advantage of internet API services. I also show you how to use JSON to format data when interacting with APIs.

Obtaining API Keys

To obtain an API key, you typically need to sign up with the API provider and request access. The steps are usually something like this:

1. **Go to the website of the API provider, and create a user account or sign into your existing account.**

2. **Navigate to the API section of the provider's website.**

    It's often under a heading like Developer Portal or API Dashboard.

3. **Follow the onscreen instructions to generate an API key.**

   You may need to create a project or application on the site.

4. **Agree to the API's Terms of Service.**

   After it's generated, your unique API key will be displayed on the screen.

5. **Copy the API key and store it a secure place on your own computer.**

WARNING

It may take a couple of hours or more for a new API key to be activated for use. Check the documentation on the site where you got the key. Watch for any email messages about how long to wait before testing the key.

WARNING

Don't share your API key with others or expose the key to the public. Doing so could allow others to access the API under your identity to abuse or misuse the service. If you're paying for an API service, others using the service on your dime could end up costing you a lot of money. (See the next section for tips on safely storing your API keys.)

REMEMBER

Not all API keys are free. In this chapter, I focus on APIs that were free at the time of this writing, because I know people don't always want to set up a paid account when they're just trying to learn. But things change, so I apologize in advance if I unwittingly send you someplace that asks for payment.

Safely Storing API Keys

It's important to keep your API keys private, because they identify your account. You don't want imposters misusing an API under your identity. If you ever do start using paid services, you don't want to be paying for other people to use your account either.

Using a .env file is a common way to use API keys without putting the key in your Python code. A .env file is just a simple text file with the name .env and no extension. In that file, you can give the key a variable name of your own choosing. That way, you can show only the variable name, not the actual key, in your code. So, if you share your code with others, your key is still hidden.

As you may know, a variable whose value never changes is referred to as a *constant* in Python and other programming languages. Because your API key won't change as your script is running, it's actually a constant in your code. Though not required, it's customary to show constant names in all uppercase letters (to distinguish constants from variables). So, if you decide on a name like Weather_API_Key for your variable name, you could actually type the name in all uppercase letters, like this:

WEATHER_API_KEY=8c21435c4317367221435aac09bf4c1d

You can put as many API keys as you like into a .env file. Just make sure each has a unique name. Here are the steps for adding an API key to a Python project in Visual Studio Code (VS Code):

1. **Open your Python project folder in VS Code.**

2. **Create and activate a virtual environment if you haven't already done so.**

   See Chapter 2 for complete instructions.

3. **Touch the mouse pointer to the project folder name at the top of the Explorer pane and click New File, or choose File ⇨ New File from the menu bar.**

4. **Name the file** .env.

   Don't use any spaces or a filename extension — just type the name as shown.

5. **With the file open in the editor, type a name for the key (usually in all uppercase letters) followed by an equal sign (=) and the API key.**

   Figure 9-1 shows an example.

6. **Close and save the** .env **file.**

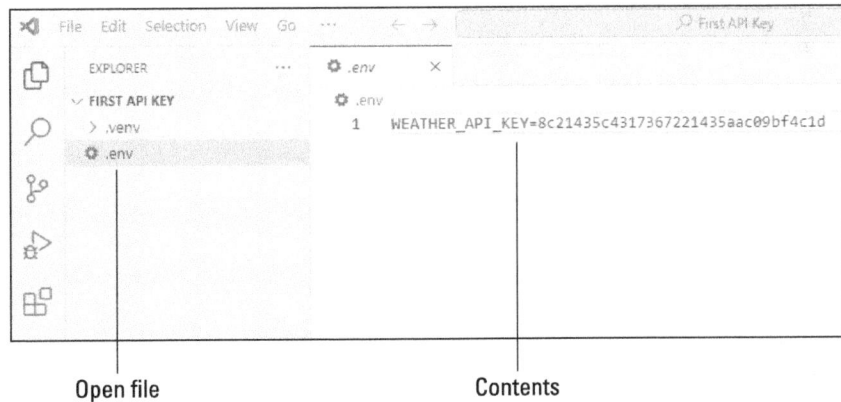

FIGURE 9-1:
A .env file with an API name and key.

Open file   Contents

REMEMBER

The API key must be a valid key that you got from the provider. The one shown in Figure 9-1 is just an example and won't work in real life. Make sure you use your own API key.

Creating a .gitignore file

If there is any chance you'll upload the project to GitHub, be sure to include a .gitignore file with .env included in it to prevent your key from being shared with your Python code. You can also include the .venv filename in that .gitignore file, so users can create their own virtual environment for their own system after they download your code.

TIP

I cover virtual environments and the .venv file in Chapter 2.

Adding a .gitignore file to a VS Code project is the same as adding any other file. Just create a new file, as you did with .env, but name this one .gitignore with no spaces and no filename extension. When the file is open in the editor, just type in .env and .venv, each on its own line, as shown in Figure 9-2.

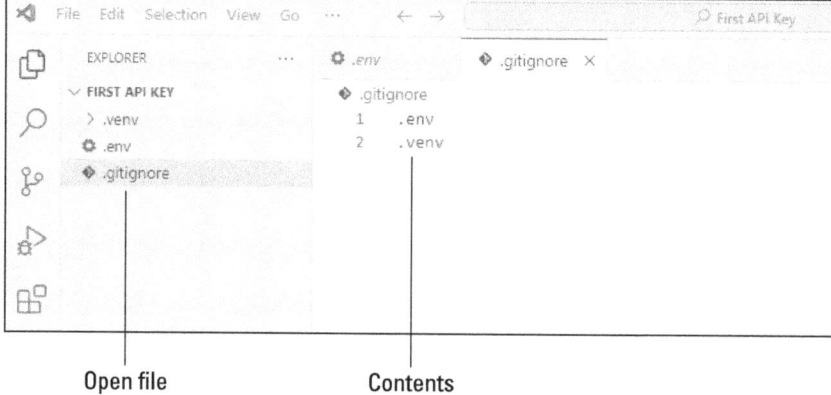

FIGURE 9-2:
A .gitignore file protecting .env and the .venv folder.

Open file   Contents

TIP

Adding a `.gitignore` file to your project won't affect how your Python code works. The `.gitignore` file just prevents any files or folders listed in its contents from being pushed to a GitHub repository if you decide to share your Python code with the world using GitHub.

Using an API key in your script

To use the API from the `.env` file in your code, you need to `pip install hon-dotenv` into your virtual environment. Then include all the following lines near the top of your Python script:

```
from dotenv import load_dotenv
import os

# Load the .env file
load_dotenv()

# Get the API key
api_key = os.getenv("SAMPLE_API_KEY")
```

TIP

The variable to the left of `= os.getenv` can be any valid Python variable name you like, but make sure the name inside the parentheses and quotation marks after `os.getenv` exactly matches the name you gave to the API key inside the `.env` file.

Throughout the rest of your code, use the variable name at the left side of that line (`api_key` in the example) anywhere you need to provide your API key. You'll see an example in the "Making API requests" section in this chapter.

Handling JSON Data

JavaScript Object Notation (JSON) is a data format used for storing and exchanging data. The *JavaScript* part of the name is just because its syntax resembles Java-Script, which uses lots of curly braces ({}). JSON is widely supported across programming languages and platforms, and it's commonly used in APIs, as well as for configuration files and data storage.

Like a Python data dictionary, JSON consists of key–value pairs where each item of data has a name and a value. The value can be a string, a number, a Boolean, an array (list), an object, or null. Each key–value pair is enclosed in curly braces.

```
{
  "username": "Alice",
  "age": 25,
  "is_student": true,
  "hobbies": ["reading", "hiking"],
  "address": {
    "street": "123 Main St",
    "city": "Boston"
  }
}
```

Each name in this example ("username", "age", "is_student", "hobbies", and "address") is a *key*. Each key has a *value* to the right of the colon. Here's some information about each key in that example:

>> The "username" key contains a string.

>> The "age" key contains a number.

>> The "hobbies" key contains an *array* (list).

>> The "address" key contains an object.

TECHNICAL
STUFF

Because the entire block of JSON data is sometimes referred to as a JSON object, the "address" key may also be referred to as a *nested object* (because it's contained with the larger JSON object). The address is unique in that it's a dictionary object in its own right, containing two keys of its own, one named "street" and the other named "city". Each of the other keys only contains one value (like age, which contains the value 18).

Python doesn't have a JSON data type, so JSON data in Python code is often stored as a string. When defining such strings, it's important to use single-quotes (') to enclose the entire string, because each key name inside that string must be enclosed in double quotation marks for JSON. A JSON string containing just two key–value pairs in Python looks like this:

```
json_string = '{"username": "Alice", "age": 25}'
```

Parsing and serializing JSON data

In Python, the dictionary (dict) data type is better suited to dealing with name–value pairs than the string (str) data type. So Python includes a built-in json module, which simplifies converting between dictionaries and JSON strings. The json module is built in, so you just need to include import json near the top of your code to use the module. No need to pip install the module.

The json module contains methods to *parse* and *serialize* JSON data. Let's start by defining those two buzzwords:

» **Parsing JSON:** Parsing refers to the process of converting a JSON string into a Python object, such as a dict, list, str, int, float, bool, or None.

» **Serializing JSON:** Serializing is the process of converting a Python object (for example, a dict, list, str, int, float, bool, or None) into a JSON-formatted string or writing it to a file as JSON data.

Four methods are contained within the json module for parsing and serializing JSON data:

Method	What It Does
json.loads()	Parses a JSON-formatted string into a Python object (for example, dict or list)
json.dumps()	Converts a Python object into a JSON-formatted string
json.load()	Reads JSON data from a file into a Python object
json.dump()	Writes a Python object to a file as JSON

The first two methods, .loads and .dumps, allow you to work with JSON strings. Here's an example of using json.loads() to parse a JSON string into a Python object:

```
import json
# Create a JSON string.
json_string = '{"username": "Alice", "age": 25}'
print(json_string)
print(type(json_string))

# Parse JSON string to Python object
python_obj = json.loads(json_string)

print(python_obj)  # Output: {'name': 'Alice', 'age': 25}
print(type(python_obj))  # Output: <class 'dict'>
```

Running that code produces the following output in the Terminal:

```
{"username": "Alice", "age": 25}
<class 'str'>
{'username': 'Alice', 'age': 25}
<class 'dict'>
```

The output tells you that the first item is a string (`<class 'str'>`) in Python. The second item is a Python dictionary (`<class 'dict'>`) because the `.loads` method converted the original string to a Python dictionary.

This next code does the opposite — it serializes a Python dictionary object into a Python string:

```
import json

# Create a Python dictionary object
python_obj = {"username": "Alice", "age": 25}
print(python_obj)
print(type(python_obj))

# Serialize the Python dictionary to a JSON string
json_string = json.dumps(python_obj)

print(json_string)
print(type(json_string))
```

Reading and writing JSON files

Python makes quick work of saving dictionary data to data files via the `.dump` method of the `json` module. In your Python code, you can start with a `dict` object, which is the preferred object type for storing name–value pairs. The syntax for using `.dump` is as follows:

```
with open("filename", "w") as file:
    json.dump(dictionary, file)
```

Replace `filename` with the name of the file in which you want to store the JSON object. Use a `.json` filename extension to best identify the file type. If you don't specify a path, the file will be created in the same folder as the code in which you're running Python. Here's an example of a complete script:

```
import json
# Create a Python dictionary object
python_dictionary = {
    "username": "Alice",
    "age": 25,
    "is_student": True,
    "hobbies": ["reading", "hiking"],
    "address": {
        "street": "123 Main St",
        "city": "Boston"
    }
}

# Serialize to a JSON file
with open("data.json", "w") as file:
    json.dump(python_dictionary, file))
```

The script starts by creating a Python dictionary that contains several key–value pairs and data types. Then it stores that dictionary data serialized into JSON format in a file named data.json. That file contains the same data as a JSON object, as shown in Figure 9-3.

```
{} data.json   ×

{} data.json > ...
    1    {"username": "Alice", "age": 25, "is_student":
         true, "hobbies": ["reading", "hiking"],
         "address": {"street": "123 Main St", "city":
         "Boston"}}
```

Next, let's look at a script that does the opposite of the preceding script in that it reads the data.json file and imports its data into a Python dictionary. To make it realistic, I've included some exception handling for bad or missing files. I've also included some code to display each item from the dictionary on a separate line in the Terminal:

```
import json

# Step 1: Open and read the JSON file
try:
    with open("data.json", "r") as file:
        # Step 2: Parse JSON file into a Python dictionary using json.load()
        user_data = json.load(file)
```

```
# Step 3: Print the data type and contents to verify
print("Type of data:", type(user_data))
print("Username:", user_data["username"])
print("Age:", user_data["age"])
print("Is Student:", user_data["is_student"])
print("Hobbies:", user_data["hobbies"])
print("City:", user_data["address"]["city"])

except FileNotFoundError:
    print("Error: The file 'data.json' was not found.")
except json.JSONDecodeError as e:
    print("Error: Invalid JSON format in 'data.json' -", e)
except KeyError as e:
    print("Error: Missing key in dictionary -", e)
```

Assuming the data.json file exists and is the one shown in Figure 9-3, the output from that code is as follows:

```
Type of data: <class 'dict'>
Username: Alice
Age: 25
Is Student: True
Hobbies: ['reading', 'hiking']
City: Boston
```

The <class 'dict'> in the output tells you that the data read from the file is in a Python dictionary. Subsequent print statements display individual items of data from the dictionary.

Understanding REST APIs

Most modern APIs today are Representational State Transfer (REST) APIs, all of which follow the same standards and rules for accessing information via the internet. REST APIs use the Hypertext Transfer Protocol (HTTP), the same as all websites, to allow a *client* (your Python script or any other app) to access another app on a server on the internet, which can provide useful information.

REST is a stateless API, meaning there is no open connection between the client and the server during a transaction. Your app sends a request to an endpoint — typically, a web Uniform Resource Locator (URL) that starts with https://. The server sends back a response containing the information you requested. That response is typically data in JSON format, discussed in the previous section.

Amazon, Google, Meta, Microsoft, PayPal, Salesforce, Shopify, Stripe, Twilio, and X (formerly Twitter) are just a few of the major tech companies offering REST APIs to developers. Many of those companies offer REST APIs specifically for AI. Major players in the AI world offering REST APIs include Anthropic, DeepSeek, Hugging Face, OpenAI, Stability AI, xAI, and others.

WARNING

Not all REST APIs are free. However, many offer a free tier so you can learn and test your code for free.

Any script that interacts with a REST API is likely to use the requests library. That's not part of the standard library. When you're writing Python code to interact with a REST API, make sure to create and activate a virtual environment. Enter a pip install requests command in the Terminal. Include an import requests command in your code.

Making API requests

A REST API request happens when your Python code requests information from a REST API on the internet. Each request gets a response that includes a status code to indicate whether the request succeeded or failed.

You can make five main types of requests:

Type of Request	What It Does
GET	Retrieves data from a server. GET is used to fetch information only. This is the most common type of request when you're interacting with AI. It returns status code 200 (OK) on success.
POST	Sends data to the server to create a new resource. POST is typically used with databases to insert a new record into a database table. It returns status code 201 (Created) on success.
PUT	Updates an existing resource with new data. PUT is typically used to change a record in a database table. It returns 200 (OK) or 204 (No Content) on success.
DELETE	Removes a resource from the server. DELETE is typically used to delete a record from a database. It returns 204 (No Content) on success.
PATCH	Partially updates a resource, such as a single field in a database record. It returns 200 (OK) or 204 (No Content) on success.

TECHNICAL STUFF

Don't worry if you're not already familiar with database terminology like tables and records. That knowledge isn't required for Python or Python automation.

There is no hard-and-fast rule that applies to every REST API request, but most include at least some of the following components:

» **URL/endpoint:** The URL to which the request is sent (for example, `https://api.example.com/data`).

» **Headers (optional):** A `dict` of metadata sent with the request, which may include things like authentication tokens or API keys.

» **Query parameters (optional):** Key–value pairs appended to the URL or passed as a dictionary (for example, `params={"key": "value"}`).

» **Response handling:** Code that processes the server's response (for example, `.json()` to parse JSON or `response.status_code` to check for success).

The documentation for the REST API will tell you the URL/endpoint to which you'll send your request. For example, to get the current weather for any location, use the URL `https://api.openweathermap.org/data/2.5/weather`.

You must include your API key in a parameter named `appid`. You can send numerous optional parameters. For example, if you want to get the weather for a city in the United States, and you want the temperature expressed in degrees Fahrenheit, use the `q` parameter to specify the city and state and use the `units` parameter with the value `"imperial"` for Fahrenheit.

Specify the URL to which you'll send the request (as specified in the OpenWeatherMap API documentation). In this example, let's assume you have the key in the `.env` file, as shown in the "Making API requests section, earlier in this chapter, assigned to the name `WEATHER_API_KEY` as follows:

```
WEATHER_API_KEY=8c21435c4317367221435aac09bf4c1d
```

REMEMBER

The API key shown in the example isn't a valid one — it's just an example. Make sure to get your own API key from `https://openweathermap.org` and use that key to try out the code.

Here is a more complete example that includes the `import os` and `load_dotenv` code needed to access the `.env` file, followed by a complete REST API request for OpenWeatherMap, with lots of comments to explain what's going on:

```
from dotenv import load_dotenv
import os

# Load the .env file
load_dotenv()
```

```
# Retrieve the API key from the environment variable
API_KEY = os.getenv("WEATHER_API_KEY")

# OpenWeatherMap API endpoint for current weather data
url = "https://api.openweathermap.org/data/2.5/weather"

# Put parameters in a dictionary.
params = {
    "appid": API_KEY,
    "q": "San Diego, CA USA",
    "units": "imperial"  # Change to "metric" if Celsius is preferred
}

# Send a GET request to the API endpoint with the defined parameters
response = requests.get(url, params=params)
```

That last line sends the actual API request. The response from the API will be placed in the variable named response.

Parsing API responses

After you send an API request, the server sends a response, usually within a few seconds, depending on what you've requested. In the code in the preceding section, that response is stored in a variable named response. Let's assume I follow that line of code with two print statements — one to print the data type of the response and the other to print the actual response, like this:

```
response = requests.get(url, params=params)
print(type(response))
print(response)
```

Running the script, and assuming you get a valid response, displays the following in the Terminal:

```
<class 'requests.models.Response'>
<Response [200]>
```

The data type, requests.models.Response, indicates that the response is a Response object from the requests library. The 200 is the status code, indicating that the transaction was successful. Perhaps you're now wondering where the actual data, the weather in the requested city, is located.

A more realistic way to handle the data would be to use an `if` statement to verify that the transaction was successful first. If it was, use `response.json()`, a method of the `requests` library, to convert the response to a Python dictionary. Then print the data type and contents of the response, as follows:

```python
response = requests.get(url, params=params)
# Check if the request was successful
if response.status_code == 200:
    # Parse the response JSON into a Python dictionary
    data = response.json()
    print(type(data))
    print(data)
```

In the Terminal, the output looks like this:

```
<class 'dict'>
{'coord': {'lon': -117.1573, 'lat': 32.7153}, 'weather': [{'id': 804, 'main':
    'Clouds', 'description': 'overcast clouds', 'icon': '04n'}], 'base':
    'stations', 'main': {'temp': 59.02, 'feels_like': 58.28, 'temp_min': 57.29,
    'temp_max': 60.6, 'pressure': 1014, 'humidity': 78, 'sea_level': 1014, 'grnd_
    level': 1010}, 'visibility': 10000, 'wind': {'speed': 5.75, 'deg': 320},
    'clouds': {'all': 100}, 'dt': 1746187856, 'sys': {'type': 2, 'id': 2095167,
    'country': 'US', 'sunrise': 1746190812, 'sunset': 1746239447}, 'timezone':
    -25200, 'id': 5391811, 'name': 'San Diego', 'cod': 200}
```

The `<class 'dict'>` tells you that the data variable contains a Python dictionary. The second line is all the data received from the OpenWeatherMap REST API, which includes much more information than just the temperature. For example, `'lon'` is the longitude, `'lat'` is the latitude, and `'temp'` is the current temperature. There's also visibility, clouds, humidity, sunrise, sunset . . . all kinds of information. You can refer to the OpenWeatherMap API documentation for anything you don't understand.

Realistically, you're probably going to want to display the information in a more user-friendly way. But I wanted to show you how you can "inspect" the true nature of the response from the REST API, so that, in your own code, you can figure out how to retrieve information from a REST API, pick apart the response, and then choose what you want to show and how to show it.

Reviewing a Complete REST API Script

Throughout this chapter, I mainly show you bits and pieces of code for interacting with a REST API. In this section, I show you a complete working script with all the pieces in place.

This is a complete script for querying the OpenWeatherMap REST API. It includes code to load an API key from a .env file, handle exceptions, and display the weather in a user-friendly format. I've included lots of comments to explain everything that's going on in the code.

```python
# openweathermap.py
# pip install python-dotenv requests
import os
# For making HTTP requests to a REST API.
import requests
# For loading variables from the .env file
from dotenv import load_dotenv

# Load environment variables from the .env file
load_dotenv()

# Retrieve the API key from the environment variable
API_KEY = os.getenv("WEATHER_API_KEY")
# If the API key doesn't exist, print an error message and exit
if not API_KEY:
    print("ERROR: WEATHER_API_KEY not found in .env file.")
    exit(1)

# OpenWeatherMap API endpoint for current weather data
url = "https://api.openweathermap.org/data/2.5/weather"

# Define the parameters to send with the request:
# - q: the city to search for weather data
# - appid: your API key for authentication
# - units: "imperial" for Fahrenheit, "metric" for Celsius
params = {
    "q": "San Diego, CA USA",
    "appid": API_KEY,
    "units": "imperial"
}

# Send a GET request to the API endpoint with the defined parameters
response = requests.get(url, params=params)

# Check if the request was successful
if response.status_code == 200:
    # Parse the response JSON into a Python dictionary
    data = response.json()
    # Extract the city, temperature, and description.
```

```
    city = data["name"]
    temperature = data["main"]["temp"]
    description = data["weather"][0]["description"]

    # Print the weather information
    print(f"\nWeather in {city}: {temperature}°F, {description}\n")
else:
    # If request failed, print the status code and the error message.
    print(f"Error {response.status_code}: {response.text}")
```

When you run that code successfully, the output is a simple line of text in the Terminal that reads something like this:

```
Weather in San Diego: 59.05°F, overcast clouds
```

That's an awful lot of bother to go through, just to get the weather in some city. But the point is, there are thousands of REST APIs in the world, capable of returning all kinds of data. What you've learned in this chapter should apply to virtually every one of those APIs. So, you could use that last script as a general model for any Python script you use to access a REST API.

REMEMBER

You always have the option to ask any AI to write the script for you. For example, tell AI to "Write a script that gets the S&P 500 index price from a free Alpha Vantage REST API account," so you get some code to work with. You'll still need to get your own API key. The code the AI generates for you won't look exactly like the example I provide. But you should be able to understand and modify that code, as needed, based on everything I explain in this chapter.

TIP

You can also ask AI for help finding APIs for different domains. For example, ask AI, "Where can I find free APIs for AI chatbots?" or "Where can I find free REST APIs for AI image generation?"

Chapter **10**

Automating the Web

This chapter is all about automating web browsers. You'll learn techniques to open a web page, find and fill text boxes, and submit the form data, exactly as you would do yourself using a mouse and keyboard. In this chapter, you make Python do all that for you.

Automating Web Browsers

If you're looking for a way to automate opening a web page and filling one or more text boxes with known information, selenium is your best bet. Two key modules that you can import into your Python scripts are named selenium and webdriver-manager. They aren't part of the Python standard library, so when you plan to use them in a script, make sure to create and activate your virtual environment. Then enter the following command at the Terminal:

```
pip install selenium webdriver-manager
```

The selenium module provides the ability to automatically control the browser and interact with controls on a web page. The webdriver-manager module allows you to use different web browsers, such as Apple Safari, Google Chrome, and Microsoft Edge, without manually downloading and installing drivers for each browser yourself and adding them to your system PATH.

Loading drivers for your browser

One of the first steps to creating a script to interact with a web page is to import the correct drivers for that browser. I'll provide a few simple scripts that you can try out yourself, to illustrate the syntax. But be aware that each script only opens the browser, navigates to www.google.com, and then holds the browser window open until you press Enter on VS Code's Terminal window.

You can only use a web browser that's installed on your computer. You can't simulate an uninstalled browser using selenium.

Here's a script that loads the correct drivers for Chrome, which you can try if you have Chrome installed on your computer.

```
# pip install selenium webdriver-manager
from selenium import webdriver
from selenium.webdriver.chrome.service import Service
from webdriver_manager.chrome import ChromeDriverManager

# Set up the Chrome WebDriver.
driver = webdriver.Chrome(service=Service(ChromeDriverManager().install()))

# Open https://www.google.com in Chrome.
driver.get("https://www.google.com")

# Keep the browser open until the user presses Enter.
input("Press Enter to close the browser...")
driver.quit()
```

Here's the same script, but this one uses Edge as the browser:

```
# pip install selenium webdriver-manager
from selenium import webdriver
from selenium.webdriver.edge.service import Service
from webdriver_manager.microsoft import EdgeChromiumDriverManager

# Set up the Microsoft Edge WebDriver.
driver =webdriver.Edge(service=Service(EdgeChromiumDriverManager().install()))

# Open https://www.google.com in Edge.
driver.get("https://www.google.com")
```

```
# Keep the browser open until the user presses Enter.
input("Press Enter to close the browser...")
driver.quit()
```

If you're using Safari on a Mac, you'll need to enable remote automation in Safari Settings in order for any automation script to work. Here's how:

1. **Open Safari and choose Safari ⇨ Settings.**

   The Settings dialog box appears.

2. **Click the Advanced tab.**

3. **Select the Show Features for Web Developers check box at the bottom of the dialog box.**

   The Settings dialog box should change to display a Developer tab. If it doesn't, close the Settings dialog box, close and reopen Safari, and choose Develop ⇨ Developer Settings.

4. **Click the Developer tab.**

   If you had to close and reopen Safari and choose Develop ⇨ Developer Settings, you're already there.

5. **Select the Allow Remote Automation check box, as shown in Figure 10-1.**

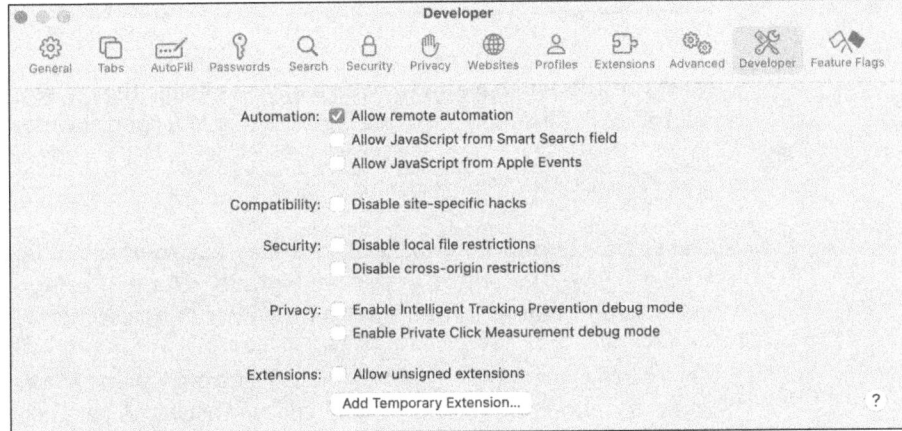

FIGURE 10-1:
Allowing remote
automation
in Safari.

6. **Close the dialog box.**

7. **Close Safari.**

After you've enabled remote automation, you should be able to run the script to open Safari, navigate to www.google.com, and keep the browser window open until you press Enter in VS Code's Terminal window to end the script.

Finding text boxes to fill

On web pages, controls like text boxes are defined in Hypertext Markup Language (HTML) using tags like those shown in Table 10-1.

TABLE 10-1 **Common HTML Tags for Controls on Web Pages**

HTML Tag	Control Type
`<input type="text">`	Text box
`<input type="search>`	Text box used for searches
`<textarea>`	Multiline text box
`<select>`	Drop-down list
`<input type="radio">`	Radio button
`<input type="checkbox">`	Check box
`<input type="submit">`	Submit button for a form

Most controls will have an id, which appears inside the tag as id= followed by the identifier. For example, here's a tag for a text box control with an id of "prompt":

```
<input type="text" id="prompt">
```

The Submit button for a form may or may not have an id. But its tab is always `<input type="submit">`, so you can typically refer to it using syntax that identifies a Submit button, as you'll see a little later in this section.

The id of a control isn't usually obvious just from looking at a web page. Typically, you can right-click the control and choose Inspect. A panel opens the HTML tag for the control highlighted, as shown in Figure 10-2. In this example, I right-clicked the Search box on Wikipedia's page. The highlighted tag includes id="searchInput", which shows that the control's id is "searchInput".

TIP

If you can't find the id of a control using your current web browser, try visiting the same page with Edge or Chrome to see if you get better results.

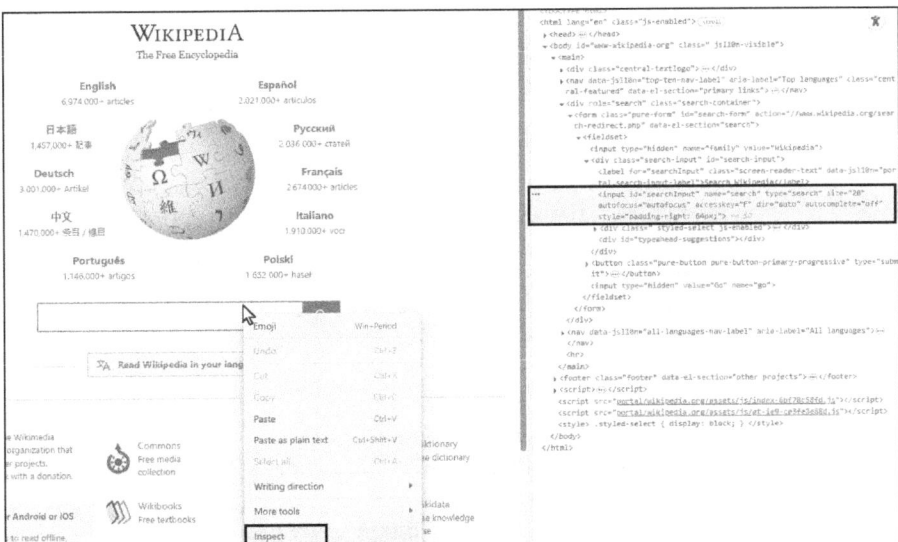

That box also contains type="search", and there is no Submit button on the page. There is a magnifying glass next to the text box. If you can type a word or phrase into the Search box, press Enter, and the search is performed, that tells you there is no need to click a Submit button. In your automation code, you can fill the searchInput box and have the script press Enter — that's sufficient.

On larger forms with multiple controls, where pressing Enter doesn't submit the form automatically, your Python script will need to click the Submit button. I show you examples of both in the following sections.

Automating Filling Forms Online

So far, all we've done with code is get the browser open and onto a page. Next, we need to talk about having Python put the cursor into a specific control on an open page and typing text there. Doing so requires two additional imports from selenium; a class named By that helps you find a control based on its id, name, or other characteristic; and a class named Keys that can simulate pressing special keys like Return (Keys.RETURN) and Tab (Keys.TAB) on the keyboard.

Following is a script to open the page at www.wikipedia.org, type the text *Blue whale* in the Search box, and then press Enter, so you can see a more complete example. This script uses Chrome as the browser, as evidenced by code near the stop of the script:

```python
# fill_form_one.py
# pip install selenium webdriver-manager
from selenium import webdriver
from selenium.webdriver.common.by import By
from selenium.webdriver.common.keys import Keys
from selenium.webdriver.chrome.service import Service
from webdriver_manager.chrome import ChromeDriverManager
import time

def open_page(url, search_box_id, search_term, click_submit):
    # Set up the Chrome WebDriver, requires import Service above
    driver = webdriver.Chrome(service=Service(ChromeDriverManager().install()))
    driver.get(url)

    # Find the search input field and fill it with the search term.
    # The following line requires you to import By, as shown earlier.
    search_box = driver.find_element(By.ID, search_box_id)
    # The following line requires you to import Keys, as shown earlier.
    search_box.send_keys(search_term)
    # Optional; wait to see input before submitting.
    time.sleep(2)

    # Click Submit or press Enter depending on the click_submit flag.
    if click_submit:
        submit_button = driver.find_element(By.XPATH, "//button
[@type='submit']")
        submit_button.click()
    else:
        search_box.send_keys(Keys.RETURN)
    return driver

def main():
    # Define the page URL.
    site_url = "https://www.wikipedia.org/"
    # The ID of the text box to fill
    search_box_id = "searchInput"
    # What to type into the Search box
    search_term = "Blue whale"
    # Set to True if you want to click Submit at end.
```

```
    # Otherwise, set to False to just press Enter.
    click_submit = False

    # Open the page and perform the search, with exception handling
    try:
        driver = open_page(site_url, search_box_id, search_term, click_submit)
    except Exception as e:
        print(f"An error occurred: {e}")
    finally:
        print("\nScript completed; browser remains open.")
        input("Press Enter or ^C to exit the script and close the browser\n")
        driver.quit()

if __name__ == "__main__":
    main()
```

In the following sections, I focus on the code in this script that finds and fills the searchInput box.

Finding a control

A key element in the script is the code that finds and fills the Search box. The script stores the id of that control, searchInput for Wikipedia, in a variable named search_box_id in this line:

```
search_box_id = "searchInput"
```

The following code then finds that control and uses send_keys to type the search term, which is stored in a variable named search_term, into that text box. Then it pauses for two seconds so you can see in the browser that the text has been placed into the text box:

```
# Find the search input field and fill it with the search term.
# The following line requires you to import By, as shown earlier.
search_box = driver.find_element(By.ID, search_box_id)
# The following line requires you to import Keys, as shown earlier.
search_box.send_keys(search_term)
# Optional; wait to see input before submitting.
time.sleep(2)
```

To complete the process, the script needs to submit the search term, as described in the following section.

Submitting a form with Enter

In addition to typing text into text boxes, you typically want your script to submit the text. On page with multiple controls, you generally do this by clicking a Submit button. However, just pressing Enter after typing your text often works, too, especially with pages that offer a single text box like search engines and artificial intelligence (AI) chatbots.

The Wikipedia site used in the previous script has no Submit button. To search the site, you can type your search prompt and press Enter. The script uses the following line of code to press Enter while the cursor is still in the Search box:

```
search_box.send_keys(Keys.RETURN)
```

To use the script with another website, first make sure you're using Chrome as your browser, or adjust the imports and set the `driver` variable near the top of the script to your preferred browser. Then use the `main()` function shown next to specify your web page and the `id` of the text box you want to fill, by setting the `site_url` and `search_box_id` variables to the appropriate values. If the page has a Submit button, and you want the script to click that instead of pressing Enter, set the `click_submit` variable to True.

```
def main():
    # Define the page URL.
    site_url = "https://www.wikipedia.org/"
    # The ID of the text box to fill
    search_box_id = "searchInput"
    # What to type into the Search box
    search_term = "Blue whale"
    # Set to True if you want to click Submit at end.
    # Otherwise, set to False to just press Enter.
    click_submit = False
```

I show you how to write a script that clicks Submit to submit a form later in this chapter. That's more likely to happen on pages with multiple input controls, so I'll start by looking at a script that fills multiple text boxes.

Filling Multiple Text Boxes

Let's talk about filling multiple text boxes on a web page. Here's an example HTML form with several text boxes, each with an `id` that starts with `"tb"` (short for *text box*). The form also includes a Submit button. The specific `id` names on a real site can vary, but I'll use this as a working example for the next script.

```
<form>
    <input type="text" id="tbFirstName"><br>
    <input type="text" id="tbLastName"><br>
    <input type="text" id="tbUserName"><br>
    <input type="tel" id="tbCellPhone"><br>
    <button type="submit" id="submit_button">Submit</button>
</form>
```

Following is a script that can type text into each text box and then click the Submit button. Most of the code is the same as the previous example, but it's adapted to fill multiple fields and then click Submit.

```
# fill_form_multi.py
# pip install selenium webdriver-manager
from selenium import webdriver
from selenium.webdriver.common.by import By
from selenium.webdriver.common.keys import Keys
from selenium.webdriver.chrome.service import Service
from webdriver_manager.chrome import ChromeDriverManager

def open_and_fill_page(site_url, sample_data, click_submit):
    # Initialize Chrome WebDriver with automatic driver management.
    service = Service(ChromeDriverManager().install())
    driver = webdriver.Chrome(service=service)

    try:
        # Open the form page.
        driver.get(site_url)

        # Fill in the text boxes using their IDs from sample_data dictionary.
        for control_id, value in sample_data.items():
            driver.find_element(By.ID, control_id).send_keys(value)

        if click_submit:
            submit_button = driver.find_element(By.XPATH, "//button[@
type='submit']")
            submit_button.click()
        else:
            # Get the last control ID from sample_data dictionary.
            last_control_id = list(sample_data.keys())[-1]
            driver.find_element(By.ID, last_control_id).send_keys(Keys.RETURN)
```

```
                print("Form filled successfully!")

            except Exception as e:
                print(f"An error occurred: {e}")

            finally:
                # Keep the browser open for inspection.
                print("Script completed; browser remains open.")
                input("Press Enter to exit the script and close the browser...")
                driver.quit()

def main():
    # Define site URL.
    site_url = "https://replace_with_your_url.com/form.html"
    # Each key should be the ID of the control to fill in the HTML form.
    sample_data = {
        "tbFirstName": "John",
        "tbLastName": "Doe",
        "tbUserName": "johndoe123",
        "tbCellPhone": "123-456-7890"
    }
    # Set to True to click the Submit button; otherwise, set to False.
    click_submit = True

    # Open the page, fill the controls, and optionally click Submit.
    open_and_fill_page(site_url, sample_data, click_submit)

if __name__ == "__main__":
    main()
```

In this script, the job of finding each control on the page to be filled, and then typing in the desired text, is handled by the following loop:

```
# Fill in the text boxes using their IDs from sample_data dictionary.
for control_id, value in sample_data.items():
    driver.find_element(By.ID, control_id).send_keys(value)
```

The loop goes through each `control_id` and `value` in `sample_data`. For each pair, `driver.find_element(By.ID, control_id)` locates the text box by its `id`, and `.send_keys(value)` types the value associated with that `control_id`. A slick trick, indeed, that `selenium` makes it so easy to copy text into text boxes, for any number of controls, just using a couple of lines of code.

Clicking a form's Submit button

After the loop has completed the task of typing text into all the text boxes on the form, the following lines click the Submit button to submit the form:

```
submit_button = driver.find_element(By.XPATH, "//button[@type='submit']")
submit_button.click()
```

That syntax is, admittedly, a bit strange looking. The word `driver` refers to the Selenium WebDriver instance that's currently controlling the browser. The `.find_element()` method tells the driver to locate a specific element on the page. `By.XPATH` specifies the method to locate the element, which is what Selenium uses to locate tags in HTML documents. Then the crazy-looking `"//button[@type='submit']"` expression starts with `//`, which tells XPath to search the entire page to look for a button that has a `type="submit"` attribute. That line simply finds the button; the following line actually clicks it:

```
submit_button.click()
```

I've tried to make the script as generic as possible, even though no two web pages are exactly alike in terms of URL or controls on a page. In the following section, I explain how to adapt it to your own use case.

Adapting the script to your needs

To adapt this script to your own needs, set the variables in the `main()` function. Be sure to set the `site_url` to the URL of the page that contains your form. The `sample_data` variable must be a dictionary with the ID of each text box to fill, followed by a colon and the text to type into that text box. Here, you can see that the dictionary keys match the IDs of the sample HTML form I show you near the start of this section:

```
# Each key should be the ID of the control to fill in the HTML form.
sample_data = {
    "tbFirstName": "John",
    "tbLastName": "Doe",
    "tbUserName": "johndoe123",
    "tbCellPhone": "123-456-7890"
}
```

If the form requires clicking Submit, make sure to set `click_submit` to `True` in your code.

Inside the `open_and_fill_page()` function, the following loop handles the job of filling each text box with appropriate data from the `sample_data` variable, which contains the dictionary defined in the `main()` function:

```
# Fill in the text boxes using their IDs from sample_data dictionary.
for control_id, value in sample_data.items():
    driver.find_element(By.ID, control_id).send_keys(value)
```

When you set `click_submit` to `True` in `Main()`, the following code executes to click Submit after all the text fields have been filled:

```
if click_submit:
    submit_button = driver.find_element(By.XPATH, "//button[@type='submit']")
    submit_button.click()
```

Filling Text Boxes from a File

In this section, you take what you've learned so far one step further. Let's say you have quite a bit of data put into a form, stored in a JavaScript Object Notation (JSON) file, and you want to put all the data into the form. For the sake of example, let's say that file is named `data.json`, and it's stored in the same folder as your Python code. Here are the file's contents:

```
[
    {
        "tbFirstName": "Alice",
        "tbLastName": "Smith",
        "tbUserName": "alicesmith456",
        "tbCellPhone": "234-567-8901"
    },
    {
        "tbFirstName": "Bob",
        "tbLastName": "Johnson",
        "tbUserName": "bobjohnson789",
        "tbCellPhone": "345-678-9012"
    },
    {
        "tbFirstName": "Carol",
        "tbLastName": "Williams",
```

```
        "tbUserName": "carolw123",
        "tbCellPhone": "456-789-0123"
    },
    {

        "tbFirstName": "David",
        "tbLastName": "Brown",
        "tbUserName": "davidb456",
        "tbCellPhone": "567-890-1234"

    }
]
```

For this to work, the code needs to open the data.json file. Then in a loop, it converts each JSON object into a data dictionary, types the text into the text boxes, and clicks Submit each time it fills a form. Here's a complete script that does exactly that:

```python
# fill_form_from_file.py
# pip install selenium webdriver-manager
import json
import time
from selenium import webdriver
from selenium.webdriver.common.by import By
from selenium.webdriver.common.keys import Keys
from selenium.webdriver.chrome.service import Service
from webdriver_manager.chrome import ChromeDriverManager


def open_and_fill_page(driver, sample_data, click_submit):
    try:
        # Fill in the text boxes using their IDs from the sample_data
    dictionary.
        for control_id, value in sample_data.items():
            # Locate each element, clear any existing text, and then send keys.
            element = driver.find_element(By.ID, control_id)
            element.clear()
            element.send_keys(value)


        # Pause before clicking Submit.
        time.sleep(2)
        if click_submit:
            submit_button = driver.find_element(By.XPATH, "//button
    [@type='submit']")
            submit_button.click()
```

```python
        else:
            # Get the last control ID from sample_data dictionary and simulate
    pressing Enter.
            last_control_id = list(sample_data.keys())[-1]
            driver.find_element(By.ID, last_control_id).send_keys(Keys.RETURN)

        print("Form filled and submitted successfully!")

    except Exception as e:
        print(f"An error occurred while processing data: {e}")

    finally:
        # Pause for two seconds after processing each form.
        time.sleep(2)

def main():
    # Define site URL.
    site_url = "https://your_url_here.com/form.html"

    # Initialize Chrome WebDriver (opened only once).
    service = Service(ChromeDriverManager().install())
    driver = webdriver.Chrome(service=service)

    # Open the form page.
    driver.get(site_url)

    # Load JSON data from file.
    with open("data.json", "r") as f:
        data_list = json.load(f)

    # Process each JSON object to fill and submit the form.
    for sample_data in data_list:
        open_and_fill_page(driver, sample_data, click_submit=True)

    print("All forms submitted successfully!")
    # Keep the browser open until the user presses Enter.
    input("Press Enter to close the browser...")
    driver.quit()

if __name__ == "__main__":
    main()
```

As with other scripts in this section, fill in the `site_url` variable with the link to the page in which the script will be filling the data. This script already assumes that it needs to click Submit after filling each form, so there is no need to set a variable for that.

TIP

If your data is in a CSV file, you should be able to just copy its data into any AI and tell the AI to "convert this CSV data into JSON" to create your JSON file.

The code assumes the data file is a JSON file named `data.json` in the same folder as the code. If you need to change that, do so in the code directly here:

```
with open("data.json", "r") as f:
```

The rest of the code is much like the two previous examples. The only real difference is that each dictionary object being typed into the form is stored in a JSON file.

Chapter **11**

Scraping Web Pages

n the previous chapter, you automated the web browser to fill out forms. The star of that show was the Selenium library. In this chapter, you automate the browser to extract data from websites instead of entering it.

The technique you'll use is sometimes called *web scraping.* It's also sometimes called *screen scraping,* because it seems as though the code is pulling content right from the screen. In reality, the content is pulled from the web page .html or .htm file. So, you can extract Hypertext Markup Language (HTML) tags along with any other content on the page.

Picking the Right Tools for Web Scraping

The most widely used module for web scraping is BeautifulSoup, from the bs4 package. An optional secondary tool, lxml, offers some speed advantages over html.parser, which is part of the Python standard library, for extracting content from the web page.

BeautifulSoup is also often used with the requests library, used for making web requests from Python. Before writing a script that uses BeautifulSoup, create and activate your virtual environment; then import all three modules by entering the following commands in the Terminal:

```
pip install beautifulsoup4 lxml requests
```

To provide a relatively simple example, I'll show you how to extract the URLs from all the links on a web page. This technique can be used to extract all the URLs for any given topic. You may use those links to explore web pages about any topic, or to curate your own links to recommend to your own followers or website visitors.

Scraping Links from a Web Page

The basic idea behind Beautiful Soup and web scraping is to download a web page from some location, defined by its URL. The page is downloaded into an object in your code, which you can then parse for any information you need. Here's a relatively simple page that extracts the URLs from all the links on a web page. This script illustrates some code and basic concepts of all Python web-scraping scripts:

```python
# scrape_links.py
# pip install requests beautifulsoup4 lxml
import requests
from bs4 import BeautifulSoup

def get_links(page_url):
    # Headers to mimic a browser
    headers = {
        "User-Agent": "Mozilla/5.0 (Macintosh; Intel Mac OS X 10_15_7) "
                      "AppleWebKit/537.36 (KHTML, like Gecko) "
                      "Chrome/95.0.4638.69 Safari/537.36"
    }
    try:
        # Send HTTP request and get the page content.
        response = requests.get(page_url, headers=headers)
        response.raise_for_status()  # Check for request errors

        # Parse the page content with BeautifulSoup.
        soup = BeautifulSoup(response.content, "lxml")
        # Optional; use html.parser; doesn't require lxml.
        # soup = BeautifulSoup(response.content, "html.parser")
```

```
        # Find all <a> tags and extract href attributes.
        links = soup.find_all("a")

        # Print each link's href (if it exists).
        for link in links:
            href = link.get("href")
            if href and href.startswith("https://"):
                print(href)

    except requests.RequestException as e:
        print(f"Error fetching the page: {e}")

def main():
    # URL of the web page to scrape.
    page_url = "https://en.wikipedia.org/wiki/Platypus"

    get_links(page_url)

if __name__ == "__main__":
    main()
```

I'll step through this script and discuss key components. The imports at the top of the page load the `requests` module (for accessing a web page) and bs4 from BeautifulSoup. BeautifulSoup is a library of code, and bs4 is a core component for parsing web pages.

TECHNICAL STUFF

Even though you `pip install lxml`, you don't need an `import lxml` statement in your script to use it. BeautifulSoup will use `lxml`, when needed, as long as it's available because you installed it.

Sending a browser header

When you browse the web using a web browser, your browser identifies itself with a User-Agent header. This sometimes includes text that identifies the browser and the operating system you're using.

When you access a site using an automation script, no such header is sent. Some sites may reject or limit access to pages on the assumption that the script is a search engine indexer or an advertising-related bot that adds a lot of traffic to the site.

When you're simply scraping data from pages and not putting a huge load on the server, you can have your script send a User-Agent header to appear as a browser for low-volume web scraping. That's what this line in the sample code offers:

```
headers = {
    "User-Agent": "Mozilla/5.0 (Macintosh; Intel Mac OS X 10_15_7) "
                  "AppleWebKit/537.36 (KHTML, like Gecko) "
                  "Chrome/95.0.4638.69 Safari/537.36"
}
```

You don't have to change that code in your own script — just use it exactly as shown. When you make your request for a web page, use the same syntax as in the sample script:

```
response = requests.get(page_url, headers=headers)
```

response is just a variable that stores the page you requested. page_url is the URL of the web page you're requesting. As you may have guessed, the argument header=headers passes the User-Agent header (defined in the headers variable) to the web server, telling the server to return the page exactly as if a web browser had made the request.

Parsing a web page

The response object that receives the requested web page can't be parsed directly. You need to copy that web page to a BeautifulSoup object for parsing. The following code does exactly that:

```
soup = BeautifulSoup(response.content, "lxml")
```

In this example, I've specified the faster, more modern lxml parser for parsing the soup object. If you have any trouble with that one and prefer to use the older html.parser, you can write your code as follows instead:

```
# soup = BeautifulSoup(response.content, "html.parser")
```

I've included that line of code in the script, commented out so it's not executed. I just put it there as a syntax example. If you prefer to use it, you can comment out the line that uses the lxml parser and remove the # from the front of the line that uses html.parser.

After the page has been loaded into a BeautifulSoup object, (soup in the working example), you can loop through HTML elements by their tag — for example "p" for paragraphs (`<p>`...`</p>` in HTML) or "li" for list items (`<li>`...`</li>`). Here, you loop through all links (`<a>`...`</a>`) on the page:

```
links = soup.find_all("a")
```

After that line executes, the `links` variable contains all the `<a>`...`</a>` tags in the page. Links always contain an `href=` attribute that identifies the target of the link. This next bit of code then loops through all the links, and for any link that has an `href=` value that starts with `https://` (meaning it points to a page outside the current page), it prints that URL:

```
for link in links:
    href = link.get("href")
    if href and href.startswith("https://"):
        print(href)
```

To personalize the script for your own use, set the `page_url` variable to the URL of the page from which you want to extract links:

```
page_url = "https://en.wikipedia.org/wiki/Platypus"
```

You can use this script to create an extensive list of web pages related to any topic by scraping links from different pages related to the topic of interest (the mighty platypus, in this example).

Extracting Data from a Web Page

Web scraping isn't limited to extracting HTML elements from a page. You can also extract specific items of data, so long as you can find some way of identifying the data to extract. In some cases, you may be able to use the HTML `id` attribute, as when filling text boxes. But there may be times when you need to rely on some other identifier.

TIP

Often, the easiest way to find unique identifiers is simply to ask artificial intelligence (AI) to "Write a python script to extract *data* from the page at *URL* using `BeautifulSoup`." Replace *data* with a description of the fields from which you want to extract data, and replace *URL* with the URL of the web page.

For a working example, I'll use the Books to Scrape website (`https://books.toscrape.com`), which is a website pretending to sell books, offering easy access to people learning how to scrape and access data automatically, like we're doing right now. Each book at the site has a cover image, a rating, a title, a price in British pounds (GBP), and more, as shown in Figure 11-1.

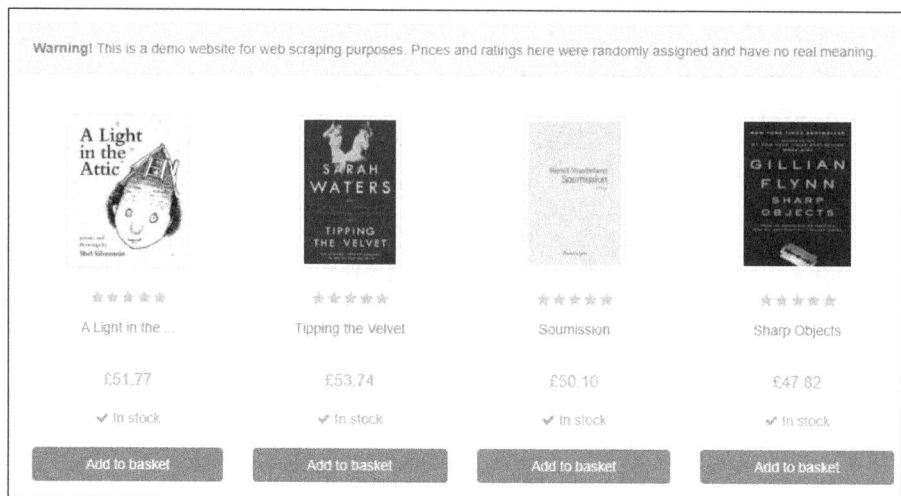

FIGURE 11-1: One row of data from Books to Scrape.

> Warning! This is a demo website for web scraping purposes. Prices and ratings here were randomly assigned and have no real meaning.

Finding elements to scrape

You need to look at the HTML code of a page to find a way to identify the elements you want to scrape from the page. The easiest way to do that is to right-click the item in your browser and choose Inspect. In this example, you would discover that each book is enclosed in ⟨article⟩...⟨/article⟩ tags with a Cascading Style Sheets (CSS) class of "product_pod", like this:

```
<article class="product_pod">...</article>
```

Within those tags, the title of the book is enclosed in ⟨a⟩...⟨/a⟩ tags after a title= attribute inside the ⟨a⟩...⟨/a⟩ tags:

```
<a href="catalogue/tipping-the-velvet_999/index.html" title="Tipping the
    Velvet">Tipping the Velvet</a>
```

The price of the book is inside a paragraph with a style class of price_color:

```
<p class="price_color">£53.74</p>
```

Books to Scrape contains 50 pages of sample books you can access and scrape data from. So, how do you get through all 50 pages and scrape just the book titles and prices? The following script does exactly that. I'll show you the whole script first, with lots of comments. In the following sections, I focus on key elements of the script for scraping data from each page:

```
# scrape_books.py
# pip install requests bs4 lxml
import requests
```

218   PART 3 Automating the Internet

```
from bs4 import BeautifulSoup
import time


page_url = "https://books.toscrape.com/catalogue/page-{}.html"
headers = {
    "User-Agent": "Mozilla/5.0 (Macintosh; Intel Mac OS X 10_15_7) "
                  "AppleWebKit/537.36 (KHTML, like Gecko) "
                  "Chrome/95.0.4638.69 Safari/537.36"
}
# Exchange rate to convert GBP to USD
exchange_rate = 1.3  # 1 GBP = 1.3 USD


def get_soup(url):
    # Fetch the page content and return a BeautifulSoup object.
    try:
        response = requests.get(url, headers=headers, timeout=10)
        response.raise_for_status()
        return BeautifulSoup(response.content, 'lxml')
    except requests.RequestException as e:
        print(f"Error fetching {url}: {e}")
        return None


def scrape_books():
    page = 1
    all_books = []
    # There are 50 pages of books on the site.
    while page <= 50:
        # Copy one page to a BeautifulSoup object.
        url = page_url.format(page)
        soup = get_soup(url)
        if not soup:
            break  # Stop if the page could not be loaded.
        # Selects all articles that are books
        books = soup.select('article.product_pod')
        # If no books are found, break the loop.
        if not books:
            break
        # Loop through each book and extract the title and price.
        for book in books:
            try:
                # Extract the title.
                title = book.h3.a['title']
                # Extract the price.
                price_text = book.select_one('p.price_color').text
                # Convert the price to a float no currency symbol.
```

```
                    price_str = price_text.lstrip('£').strip()
                    price_gbp = float(price_str)
                except (AttributeError, ValueError):
                    continue  # Skip any book with missing/invalid data.
                # Convert GBP to USD (optional)
                price_usd = price_gbp * exchange_rate
                all_books.append((title, price_usd))

        print(f"Scraped page {page}")
        page += 1
        time.sleep(0.5)

    return all_books

def main():
    # Set max_price to a USD value to filter books based on price.
    # Example: Only show books with a price at or below US$20.
    max_price = 20.0
    # For no limit set to None
    # max_price = None

    # Scrape the books.
    books = scrape_books()

    # If there are books, list them with their prices.
    if books:
        print(f"\nBooks with converted USD prices:")
        for title, price in books:
            # Filter books based on max_price if set.
            if max_price is None or price <= max_price:
                print(f"{title} - ${price:.2f}")
    else:
        print("No books found.")

if __name__ == "__main__":
    main()
```

The script needs to access one page at a time in order to scrape book data. Notice the URL defined in this line of code:

```
page_url = https://books.toscrape.com/catalogue/page-{}.html
```

The square brackets are just a placeholder. Each page is actually numbered, such as page-1.html, page-2.html, page-3.html, and so forth.

In the script, the code to go through each page of the site is near the top of the `scrape_books()` function:

```
def scrape_books():
    page = 1
    all_books = []
    # There are 50 pages of books on the site.
    while page <= 50:
```

The `page` variable is the current page number (we start at 1). `all_books` is an empty list that will grow as we get books from each page. The loop will keep looping until `page` is less than or equal to 50, so all 50 pages of the site are visited.

Near the end of that loop are the following lines of code:

```
print(f"Scraped page {page}")
page += 1
time.sleep(0.5)
```

The `print` statement simply provides some feedback in the Terminal as to which page was processed. The `page+=1` line then increments the page counter by 1. The `time.sleep` line just pauses execution for a moment. When web scraping, it's a good idea to pause for half a second to a second when performing a repetitive task. If you try to go too fast, you risk overloading the server.

WARNING

Scraping a web page too fast can also trigger web server security algorithms that watch for bots that are extracting large amounts of data from the site. If your script is being blocked by a server at high speed, try adding some `time.sleep()` code to slow down processing.

Scraping data from the page

Next, let's take a look at how we access one book at a time, and grab the title and unit price from each book. First, the code selects all the `article.product_pod` elements from the `BeautifulSoup` object (`soup`):

```
books = soup.select('article.product_pod')
```

In other words, that line grabs every element that starts with `<article class="product_pod">` and ends with `</article>` and puts each into a list named `books`.

Then the line for book in books processes one book at a time from that list. Inside that loop, the following line grabs the book title, which is stored as the title= attribute inside <a>...</a> tags inside <h3>...</h3> tags:

```
title = book.h3.a['title']
```

The next line grabs the price from between the <p class= "price_color"> ... </p> tags.

```
price_text = book.select_one('p.price_color').text
```

Subsequent code removes the currency symbol from the price and converts it from a string to a quote. The rest of the code just displays the script's progress through the pages, handles exceptions, and lists all the book titles at the end of the script.

TIP

If you're not familiar with HTML and CSS, identifying elements to scrape can be especially daunting. I've had good luck with AI being able to isolate data from web pages for me. Just make sure you word your prompt something like "Write a Python script that scrapes *data* from *URL* using BeautifulSoup," and replace *data* with the elements you want to scrape and replace *URL* with the URL of the web page to scrape.

There isn't much I can do to make this particular script generic, because there are countless web pages and data elements. However, I did put this line into the main() function:

```
max_price = 20.0
```

You can change that line to limit the output to books at or under a price point in US dollars. For example, setting max_price to 20 lists only books that cost $20 or less. If you don't want to set a price limit, you can set max_price to None like this:

```
max_price = None
```

Automating Data Extraction

Let's take data extraction a step further, and say you want a script that automatically extracts data every one minute or so from a live site, but only during business hours when the data is changing. In this section, I show you a script that does just that, by extracting index prices every minute from the US stock market while the market is open.

I'll start by showing you the entire script, below. Then I'll follow by pointing out key elements that are unique to this script.

```python
# scrape_stocks_auto.py
# pip install requests beautifulsoup4 tzdata holidays
import requests
from bs4 import BeautifulSoup
import time
from datetime import date, datetime
from zoneinfo import ZoneInfo
import holidays


# Is today a weekday and not a holiday?
def is_business_day():
    # Get current date.
    today = date.today()
    # Create US holidays object.
    us_holidays = holidays.US()
    # Check if today is a weekday (Monday=0, Sunday=6).
    is_weekday = today.weekday() < 5
    # Check if today is a US federal holiday.
    is_not_holiday = today not in us_holidays
    return is_weekday and is_not_holiday


# Stock market open hours
def is_market_open(now):
    # Stock market open hours are 9:30 AM to 4:00 PM EST.
    open_time = now.replace(hour=9, minute=30, second=0, microsecond=0)
    close_time = now.replace(hour=16, minute=0, second=0, microsecond=0)
    return is_business_day() and open_time <= now < close_time


# Get one index price (DOW, S&P 500, or Nasdaq).
def get_index_price(url, symbol):
    headers = {
        "User-Agent": "Mozilla/5.0 (Macintosh; Intel Mac OS X 10_15_7) "
                      "AppleWebKit/537.36 (KHTML, like Gecko) "
                      "Chrome/95.0.4638.69 Safari/537.36"
    }
    try:
        response = requests.get(url, headers=headers)
        response.raise_for_status()
    except Exception as e:
        print(f"Failed to retrieve data from {url}: {e}")
        return None
```

```python
    # Put page into a soup object and parse for index price.
    soup = BeautifulSoup(response.text, "html.parser")
    # Look for the fin-streamer tag with both the regularMarketPrice field and
    matching symbol.
    price_tag = soup.find("fin-streamer", {"data-field": "regularMarketPrice",
    "data-symbol": symbol})
    if price_tag:
        return price_tag.text.strip()
    else:
        print(f"Unable to find the price for symbol {symbol}.")
        return None

def main():
    # Dictionary now contains tuples of (url, symbol).
    indices = {
        "Dow Jones": ("https://finance.yahoo.com/quote/%5EDJI", "^DJI"),
        "S&P 500": ("https://finance.yahoo.com/quote/%5EGSPC", "^GSPC"),
        "Nasdaq": ("https://finance.yahoo.com/quote/%5EIXIC", "^IXIC")
    }

    # Time zone for US Eastern time
    eastern_tz = ZoneInfo("America/New_York")

    # Current time in time zone
    now = datetime.now(eastern_tz)

    # If not open, don't run the rest of the code.
    if not is_market_open(now):
        print("\nUS Stock Market is Closed\n")
        return

    # Print the opening message and index prices.
    print("\nUS Stock Market Open")
    print("Initial US Index Prices:")
    for index_name, (url, symbol) in indices.items():
        price = get_index_price(url, symbol)
        if price:
            print(f"{index_name} Index Price: {price}")
        else:
            print(f"{index_name}: Price not found.")
```

```
    # Loop to update prices every minute while the market is open.
    while is_market_open(datetime.now(eastern_tz)):
        current_time = datetime.now(eastern_tz).strftime('%Y-%m-%d %H:%M:%S')
        print(f"\n------ Updated Prices at {current_time} ------")
        for index_name, (url, symbol) in indices.items():
            price = get_index_price(url, symbol)
            if price:
                print(f"{index_name} Index Price: {price}")
            else:
                print(f"{index_name}: Price not found.")
        time.sleep(60)  # Update every 1 minute

    print("\nMarket update complete.")

if __name__ == "__main__":
    main()
```

In the next section, I explain how this script determines whether the stock market is currently open.

Determining whether a business is open

This script shows how you can limit your automation script to run only on certain days and times. To help with that, this script requires two modules that aren't part of the standard Python library: tzdata (which helps with time zones) and holidays (which lists US holidays).

Because this is a web scraping script, it also requires the requests and BeautifulSoup modules. So, to use this script, make sure you create and activate your virtual environment. Then enter the following command in the Terminal:

```
pip install requests beautifulsoup4 tzdata holidays
```

Now let's take a look at two functions that allow this script to determine whether the US stock market is currently open. The first is the function named is_business_day():

```
# Is today a weekday and not a holiday?
def is_business_day():
    # Get current date.
    today = date.today()
    # Create US holidays object.
```

```
    us_holidays = holidays.US()
    # Check if today is a weekday (Monday=0, Sunday=6).
    is_weekday = today.weekday() < 5
    # Check if today is a US federal holiday.
    is_not_holiday = today not in us_holidays
    return is_weekday and is_not_holiday
```

The function is pretty simple. The today variable gets the current date. Then the variable is_weekday is set to True if the current day is a weekday (day 0 to 5), and that date is not in the list of US holidays. In other words, the function returns True only if the current day is a weekday and not a holiday.

The US stock market is open from 9:30 AM to 4:00 PM. Here's the function that determines whether the current time is between those hours:

```
# Stock market open hours
def is_market_open(now):
    # Stock market open hours are 9:30 AM to 4:00 PM EST
    open_time = now.replace(hour=9, minute=30, second=0, microsecond=0)
    close_time = now.replace(hour=16, minute=0, second=0, microsecond=0)
    return is_business_day() and open_time <= now < close_time
```

Notice that the is_market_open(now) function returns True, only if is_business_day() is True, open_time is less than (earlier than) or equal to the current time, and the current time is less than the close time. Subsequent code can determine whether the stock market is currently closed using the simple if statement:

```
# If not open, don't run the rest of the code.
if not is_market_open(now):
    print("\nUS Stock Market is Closed\n")
    return
```

When you run the script, you see a message that the stock market is closed. The script won't keep checking every minute.

If the stock market is open, the following while loop scrapes the index prices from the screen every 60 seconds:

```
# Loop to update prices every minute while the market is open.
while is_market_open(datetime.now(eastern_tz)):
    current_time = datetime.now(eastern_tz).strftime('%Y-%m-%d %H:%M:%S')
    print(f"\n------- Updated Prices at {current_time} -------")
    for index_name, (url, symbol) in indices.items():
        price = get_index_price(url, symbol)
```

```
        if price:
            print(f"{index_name} Index Price: {price}")
        else:
            print(f"{index_name}: Price not found.")
    time.sleep(60)  # Update every 1 minute
```

Inside that loop, the line that reads `price = get_index_price(url, symbol)` uses the `get_index_price()` function to scrape the index price for a stock symbol when called. In the next section, I explain how that part works.

Scraping stock market data

The script I'm discussing here scrapes the current index price for the Dow, S&P 500, and Nasdaq from the following pages at Yahoo! Finance:

>> https://finance.yahoo.com/quote/%5EDJI

>> https://finance.yahoo.com/quote/%5EGSPC

>> https://finance.yahoo.com/quote/%5EIXIC

The HTML tags in which prices are contained look like this in the page's HTML code (I've summarized a bit so you can see key items):

```
<fin-streamer data-symbol="^IXIC" data-field="regularMarketPrice">
    18,708.34
</fin-streamer>
```

REMEMBER

Using DevTools in a browser to find data to scrape can be challenging. Consider asking AI to write your entire script for you first. I've had great luck with that in the past.

The loop that accesses each page loops through this dictionary that uses the common name of an index as a key, followed by the URL of the page where the price can be found, and the Yahoo! ticker symbol, such as ^DJI for the Dow, ^GSPC for the S&P 500, and ^IXIC for the Nasdaq.

```
# Dictionary now contains tuples of (url, symbol).
indices = {
    "Dow Jones": ("https://finance.yahoo.com/quote/%5EDJI", "^DJI"),
    "S&P 500": ("https://finance.yahoo.com/quote/%5EGSPC", "^GSPC"),
    "Nasdaq": ("https://finance.yahoo.com/quote/%5EIXIC", "^IXIC")
}
```

TECHNICAL STUFF

In the `indices` dictionary, the `%5E` at the end of each URL represents the caret symbol (^), which can't be typed directly into a URL due to web standards. For example `%5EDJI` represents ^DJI, the Yahoo! ticker symbol for the Dow.

The `get_index_price()` function uses the request module to send a page request for one URL at a time to the web server. The page is returned to a variable named `response`, as in other examples in this chapter.

```
# Get one index price (DOW, S&P 500, or Nasdaq).
def get_index_price(url, symbol):
    headers = {
        "User-Agent": "Mozilla/5.0 (Macintosh; Intel Mac OS X 10_15_7) "
                      "AppleWebKit/537.36 (KHTML, like Gecko) "
                      "Chrome/95.0.4638.69 Safari/537.36"
    }
    try:
        response = requests.get(url, headers=headers)
        response.raise_for_status()
    except Exception as e:
        print(f"Failed to retrieve data from {url}: {e}")
        return None
```

Assuming there were no problems accessing the page, the next lines put the page into a `BeautifulSoup` object named `soup` in the following code. Then the price is pulled from the `<fin-streamer>` tag and returned by the function. As usual, the code contains exception handling to prevent the script from crashing if some unforeseen problem prevents successful scraping of the data:

```
# Put page into a soup object and parse for index price
soup = BeautifulSoup(response.text, "html.parser")
# Look for the fin-streamer tag with both the regularMarketPrice field and
  matching symbol
price_tag = soup.find("fin-streamer", {"data-field": "regularMarketPrice",
    "data-symbol": symbol})
if price_tag:
    return price_tag.text.strip()
else:
    print(f"Unable to find the price for symbol {symbol}.")
    return None
```

Chapter **12**

Automating Email and Text Messages

I n this chapter, you explore Python automation for email and text messages. You can use these scripts to automate marking emails, send newsletters, remind people of upcoming appointments, and more.

For sending email messages, you'll need an email account and the built-in `smtp` module. You can send plain-text messages or messages formatted with HTML. If your email recipient addresses are in an app, you can export them to a simple text file and have Python send an email to every address in that file.

For text messaging, you'll need an account with the ability to send Short Message Service (SMS) messages, which you'll access through an application programming interface (API). I take you through all the necessary steps using the popular Twilio service for sending bulk text messages. That service includes a free tier, so you can learn without spending any additional money.

Sending Bulk Email Automatically

Sending email can be a great way to keep in touch with subscribers, customers, followers, or any other group of people for whom you've acquired email addresses. You can send reminders, newsletters, invitations, product announcements, or whatever works for your business or organization. To get started, you'll need to gather some information about your email account.

Collecting account information

To send emails automatically, you'll need some technical information about your email account. Typically, you can find this by logging into your email account via a web browser and searching its documentation or settings or by asking AI. To set up an automation script for your own email, you'll need the following information about your email account and service provider:

>> **Username:** The username you use to log into your email account

>> **Password:** The password you use to log into your email account

>> **Email address:** Could be the same as your username

>> **Simple Mail Transfer Protocol (SMTP) server address:** A URL for sending email messages (typically something like `smtp.gmail.com` or `smtp-mail.outlook.com`)

>> **SMTP port:** Typically 587 for Transport Layer Security (TLS) or 465 for Secure Sockets Layer (SSL)

SMTP is a standard protocol used for sending emails across the internet. It's used by popular email services, including Gmail, Microsoft Outlook, Proton Mail, Yahoo! Mail, and many others.

TECHNICAL
STUFF

TLS is a newer, more secure protocol for internet encryption. It uses port 587. SSL is older and less secure and uses port 465.

Creating a .env file

REMEMBER

Putting passwords and other sensitive data directly into your Python code risks exposing that information to others, if you share your code or post it to GitHub. You're better off putting that information in a `.env` file in the same folder as your code, and not sharing it with your source code.

To create a `.env` file, first create your project folder normally. Create and activate a virtual environment. Enter the following command in the Terminal to install the `dotenv` module:

```
pip install python-dotenv
```

If you're using VS Code, create the `.env` file the same way you'd create a new script. But don't use a `.py` extension. Instead, just name the file `.env` with no extension. You can then create variables and values for your account information like the example shown in Figure 12-1.

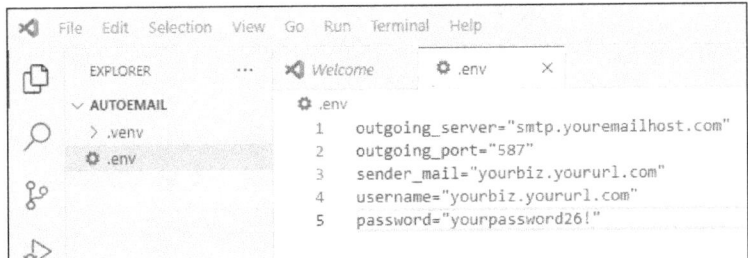

FIGURE 12-1:
A .env file
for Python
SMTP email
automation.

WARNING

The values shown in Figure 12-1 are just hypothetical and won't work if you try them. You must provide the actual information for your own email account.

If there's any chance you'll be sharing your code on GitHub, also create a .gitignore file and include both .env and .venv in that file (see Chapter 9 for more information).

Creating your email-sending script

I'll show you an entire script for sending a plain-text email to multiple addresses automatically. Then I'll discuss key features and ways to adapt the script to your own needs.

```python
# email_send.py
# pip install python-dotenv
import os
import smtplib
from email.mime.text import MIMEText
from email.mime.multipart import MIMEMultipart
from dotenv import load_dotenv

# Load environment variables from .env file.
load_dotenv()

def send_bulk_email(subject, body, recipients):
    # Get email credentials and server settings from the .env file.
    outgoing_server = os.getenv("outgoing_server")
    # Change 587 to match port number in your .env file.
    outgoing_port = int(os.getenv("outgoing_port", 587))
    sender_email = os.getenv("sender_mail")
    username = os.getenv("username")
    password = os.getenv("password")
```

```
        if not (sender_email and username and password and outgoing_server):
            print("Missing required environment variables.")
            return

        # Create the email message.
        msg = MIMEMultipart()
        msg["From"] = sender_email
        msg["Subject"] = subject
        # Set the email body as plain text.
        msg.attach(MIMEText(body, "plain"))

        try:
            # Connect to the SMTP server.
            server = smtplib.SMTP(outgoing_server, outgoing_port)
            server.ehlo()
            # The next two lines are only needed for port 587.
            server.starttls()
            server.ehlo()
            # Log in with the provided credentials.
            server.login(username, password)

            # Send email to each recipient.
            for recipient in recipients:
                msg["To"] = recipient
                server.sendmail(sender_email, recipient, msg.as_string())
                print(f"Email sent to {recipient}")

            server.quit()
            print("All emails sent successfully!")

        except Exception as e:
            print(f"An error occurred: {str(e)}")

def main():
    # List of recipient email addresses
    recipients = [
        "someone@somewhere.com",
        "customerjow@gmail.com"
        # Add more email addresses as needed
    ]
    # Email subject and body
    subject = "Test Email"
    body = """
    Hello,
```

```
      This is a test email sent from a Python script.
      Thank you for your attention!

      Best regards,
      Your Name Here
      """

      # Call the function to send emails
      send_bulk_email(subject, body, recipients)

if __name__ == "__main__":
    main()
```

This script assumes you're using the TLS protocol and port 587. If you're using SSL and port 465, just change the 587 in the following line to 465 after `outgoing_port=`, as shown here:

```
outgoing_port = int(os.getenv("outgoing_port", 465))
```

In the code where the script connects to the server, change `SMTP` to `SMTP_SSL`. Then remove the `server.starttls()` `server.ehlo()` right below that line, so the code looks like this:

```
# Connect to the SMTP server.
server = smtplib.SMTP_SSL(outgoing_server, outgoing_port)
server.ehlo()
# Log in with the provided credentials.
server.login(username, password)
```

In case you're wondering, `ehlo` stands for *Extended Hello.* It's a standard command sent to SMTP servers to initiate a connection.

TECHNICAL STUFF

To configure the script for a specific audience and message, look to the `main()` function. Change the fake email addresses to your own email addresses shown to your actual audience. For initial testing, you may just want to test the script by sending messages to yourself. But when you're comfortable that everything is working correctly, you can list as many email addresses as you like. Put each email address in quotation marks, and follow each address (except the lest one), with a comma, as shown in the example list:

```
# List of recipient email addresses
recipients = [
    "someone@somewhere.com",
    "customerjow@gmail.com"
    # Add more email addresses as needed
]
```

Also, in the `main()` function, replace the sample subject with the Subject line for your own email message. Type the body of the email between the triple quotation marks.

```
# Email subject and body
subject = "Test Email"
body = """
Hello,

This is a test email sent from a Python script.
Thank you for your attention!

Best regards,
Your Name Here
"""
```

To test the script, run it as you would any other script. Make sure to send a copy of the email message to yourself, so you can verify that the script worked.

Sending HTML mail

If you prefer to send HTML mail rather than plain-text messages, find the word `plain` in the following line:

```
msg.attach(MIMEText(body, "plain"))
```

And change it to `html`, like this:

```
msg.attach(MIMEText(body, "html"))
```

Then mark up your email message with HTML and inline CSS as in the following example:

```
body = """
<div style="font:14pt Arial, Helvetica, sans-serif; color:#333;">
<h1>Hello!</h1>

<p>This is a <b>test email</b> sent from a Python script.
Thank you for your attention! Visit our
<a href="https://example.com">website</a> for more details.</p>
<p>Best regards,<br>Your Name Here</p>
</div>
"""
```

TIP

If you're not familiar with using HTML and CSS with email, you can search the web for tutorials. Or ask any AI questions like "How do I mark up email body text with HTML and CSS when sending with Python SMTP?" or "How do I include images in email sent by Python SMTP?"

Putting email recipient addresses in a file

If you have a large number of email recipient addresses in a database or spreadsheet, and you'd rather send from there, you can export the addresses to a simple text file. You don't need quotation marks or commas or anything else. Just export so that each address is on its own line, like this:

```
john.doe@example.com
sarah.smith@fakeemail.com
mike.jones@samplemail.com
emily.brown@mockemail.com
david.wilson@testemail.com
```

In this example, I name the file that contains those addresses `email_recipients.txt` and put that file in the same folder as my Python code.

To use the email addresses in the file, rather than a list in code, remove the code that defines the list of addresses, shown here, in the `main()` function:

```
# List of recipient email addresses
recipients = [
    "someone@somewhere.com",
    "customerjow@gmail.com"
    # Add more email addresses as needed
]
```

Replace that code with the following code to build the list from the addresses in the file. Make sure to provide the correct path and filename of the file. In my case, I named the file `email_recipients.txt` and put it in the same folder as the Python script. So, the following code will work fine with that setup:

```
# Load recipient email addresses from email_recipients.txt
recipients = load_recipients("email_recipients.txt")
```

Some SMTP providers limit the rate at which you can send email messages, or the number of emails you can send per day, to avoid overuse and excessive spamming. If you need to slow down the script so it doesn't send at too high a rate, you can add a delay after each email is sent. Add a `time.sleep()` to the code in the script, after each message is sent, as in the following example:

```
# Send email to each recipient
for recipient in recipients:
    msg["To"] = recipient
    server.sendmail(sender_email, recipient, msg.as_string())
    print(f"Email sent to {recipient}")
    time.sleep(1)
```

If the problem is the number of emails you're sending each day, you may need to sign up for a service that has fewer restrictions, such as Amazon Simple Email Service (`https://aws.amazon.com/ses`), Mailgun (`www.mailgun.com`), or SendGrid (`https://sendgrid.com`). But you may have to pay for the service, depending on how much email you intend to send. Feel free to ask AI for help by asking, "How can I deal with throttling problems when sending email with Python SMTP?"

Automatically Sending Text Messages

You've probably done some texting on your phone, where you send and receive short text messages via phone numbers. Sending text messages (also known as SMS messages) to customers is a great way to give them appointment reminders, announce new events or products, thank them for something, and so on. With Python and an online service, you can send such messages in bulk automatically, not just one at a time.

TECHNICAL STUFF

SMS is the technology behind the day-to-day texts you probably send and receive on your phone.

Twilio (`www.twilio.com`) is a popular service for sending texts through Python automation. As of this writing, they offer a free tier that lets you send a limited number of texts, so you have time to write and test your code before spending any money. Visit the Twilio website for more information and to set up your free account.

TIP

ClickSend (www.clicksend.com), Courier (www.courier.com), Plivo (www.plivo.com), SendGrid (https://sendgrid.com), Sinch (https://sinch.com), Telnyx (https://telnyx.com), and Vonage (www.vonage.com) are other online services that allow you to send text messages from Python.

Storing SMS account information

To send SMS messages, you'll need an account with Twilio or a similar service provider. Doing so will get you an account string identifier (SID), an authorization token, and a Twilio phone number from which your messages will be sent.

REMEMBER

You should store such information in a .env file rather than in your code (see Chapter 9).

Create a folder for your project as usual. Create and activate your virtual environment. Then enter the following command in the Terminal to install the Python dotenv module, which you'll use later in your code to retrieve account information from the .env file:

```
pip install python-dotenv
```

Next, create a .env file in your project (no filename extension). Then enter your Twilio account SID, Twilio authorization token, and Twilio phone number, as shown in Figure 12-2. You can use different variable names if you like. However, the variables in your code must match the variable names in your .env file, so be careful with that. The values shown in the figure are, of course, hypothetical. Those you must replace with your own Twilio account information.

FIGURE 12-2:
A .env file for a hypothetical Twilio account.

After you have all of that squared away, you can write your Python script as shown here. Note that that script uses a couple of hypothetical cellphone numbers to which the sample message will be sent. Replace those with at least one phone (your own) to test the script and verify you got the text.

```python
import os
from twilio.rest import Client
from twilio.base.exceptions import TwilioRestException

# Twilio credentials (set these as environment variables for security)
account_sid = os.environ.get('twilio_account_sid')
auth_token = os.environ.get('twilio_auth_token')
twilio_number = os.environ.get('twilio_phone_number')

# Initialize Twilio client.
client = Client(account_sid, auth_token)

# Function to send text messages
def send_text_messages(numbers, message, from_number):
    for number in numbers:
        try:
            message = client.messages.create(
                body=message,
                from_=from_number,
                to=number
            )
            print(f"Message sent to {number}: SID {message.sid}")
        except TwilioRestException as e:
            print(f"Error sending to {number}: {e}")

def main():
    # List of recipient phone numbers with country code
    phone_numbers = [
        '+12345678901',  # Replace with actual phone numbers.
        '+19876543210',
        # Add more numbers as needed.
    ]

    # Message to send
    message_body = "Hello! This is a test message sent from Python."

    # Check if credentials and phone number are set.
    if not account_sid or not auth_token or not twilio_number:
        print("Error: Invalid or missing account information in .env file.")
```

```
    else:
        # Send messages.
        send_text_messages(phone_numbers, message_body, twilio_number)


if __name__ == "__main__":
    main()
```

The function that actually sends text messages is named sent_text_messages, and it starts with the following line of code:

```
def send_text_messages(numbers, message, from_number):
```

As you can see, the function receives as input numbers (the list of phone numbers to which you're texting), message (the text message you're sending), and from_number (the Twilio number from which you're sending texts).

Defining your recipient list and message

To specify phone numbers to which you want to send messages, use the phone_numbers list in the main() function, shown here. Make sure you enclose each number in quotation marks, include the country code at the start of the number (+1 for US), and separate numbers with commas.

```
phone_numbers = [
    '+12345678901',  # Replace with actual phone numbers.
    '+19876543210',
    # Add more numbers as needed.
]
```

Use the message_body variable shown here to set the text of the message you want to send:

```
message_body = "Hello! This is a test message sent from Python."
```

Storing recipient numbers

If you have a large collection of phone numbers to manage, putting them directly into your code may be unwieldy. Feel free to store them in a database, spreadsheet, or text file, if that's easier. Then you can rewrite the script to pull numbers from that file into the phone_numbers list when you run the script.

I can't show you how to do that for every app you may use to store phone numbers, so I'll show you how to retrieve them from a text file. Regardless of what specific app you use to manage numbers, it should be fairly easy to export those numbers to a text file that looks like this, with each number on its own line within the file:

+12025550123

+447911123456

+919876543210

+5511987654321

+61412345678

As a working example, let's assume that file is named sms_numbers.txt and is in the same folder as the Python code. Here's a version of the script that gets the list of phone numbers from that file, with a bit of extra exception handling to deal with unforeseen problems with the text file.

```python
import os
from twilio.rest import Client
from twilio.base.exceptions import TwilioRestException

# Twilio credentials (set these as environment variables for security)
account_sid = os.environ.get('twilio_account_sid')
auth_token = os.environ.get('twilio_auth_token')
twilio_number = os.environ.get('twilio_phone_number')

# Initialize Twilio client
client = Client(account_sid, auth_token)

def load_phone_numbers(filename):
    numbers = []
    try:
        with open(filename, 'r') as f:
            for line in f:
                line = line.strip()
                if line:
                    numbers.append(line)
    except Exception as e:
        print(f"Error loading phone numbers: {e}")
    return numbers
```

```
# Function to send text messages
def send_text_messages(numbers, message, from_number):
    for number in numbers:
        try:
            sms = client.messages.create(
                body=message,
                from_=from_number,
                to=number
            )
            print(f"Message sent to {number}: SID {sms.sid}")
        except TwilioRestException as e:
            print(f"Error sending to {number}: {e}")

def main():
    # Load recipient phone numbers from sms_numbers.txt.
    phone_numbers = load_phone_numbers("sms_numbers.txt")

    # Message to send
    message_body = "Hello! This is a test message sent from Python."

    # Check if credentials and phone number are set.
    if not account_sid or not auth_token or not twilio_number:
        print("Error: Invalid or missing account information in .env file.")
    else:
        # Send messages.
        send_text_messages(phone_numbers, message_body, twilio_number)

if __name__ == "__main__":
    main()
```

Even if you don't use Twilio as your service provider for your text messaging, the basic logic and structure of your Python script should resemble this example.

REMEMBER

AI can be a great help in generating such a script. Make sure you tell AI you're using Python, which service provider you're using (SendGrid, Sinch, or something else), and exactly what you want the script to do. Make sure to create your .env file with the account information for your own account, and you should be good to go.

Chapter **13**

Automating Social Media

I f you regularly use social media to stay in contact with customers or followers, or to track performance metrics, trends, likes, shares, comments, and such, Python automation can be your best friend. Allowing Python automation to handle some of the boring, repetitive, routine grunt work frees up your time for more creative endeavors and personal involvement in your social media presence.

This chapter offers social media automation techniques you can use with most social media services, including Facebook, Instagram, LinkedIn, X, and others. As in previous chapters in this part of the book, much of what you do here will involve interacting with the application programming interfaces (APIs) offered by social media sites. You'll need an API key for any social media platform you intend to automate.

Acquiring API Keys and Modules

The first step to automating anything on a social media site is to get an API key from the site itself. Look around the site for information about obtaining an API key, usually in the site's Developers section.

For Python, you'll want to `pip install` an appropriate module for that site. Here are some examples of modules:

>> **Facebook:** `python-facebook-api`

>> **Instagram:** `Instapy`

>> **Linked-In:** `linkedin-api`

>> **Reddit:** `praw`

>> **X:** `tweepy`

TIP

If you want to post to multiple sites simultaneously, consider setting up an account with Hootsuite (`www.hootsuite.com`). They specialize in multisite social media marketing and management.

In the following sections, I provide examples of automating different sites in different ways. But the basic concepts will apply no matter what website you use.

REMEMBER

You can always start by asking artificial intelligence (AI) to write some code for you. Just make sure to start your AI prompt with "Write a Python automation script to . . ." and then state exactly what you want the script to do and on which social media site.

Automating Posting

Let's say you want to post a simple one-line question, every few hours, to a social media site. These questions can help with social media engagement because they're easy to read and easy to answer.

You could start by creating a simple text file of such questions, which I'll refer to as `questions.txt` in this example. Of course, you can have as many or as few lines in your text file as you like. You can replenish and change it whenever you want.

Here's a list of five questions, as an example, but you can put hundreds of questions in your file if you like:

>> What's the weirdest food combo you've ever tried?

>> If you had one superpower, what would it be and why?

>> What's the last song that got stuck in your head?

>> What's the most random fact you know?

>> What's your go-to comfort movie or TV show?

As a working example, let's assume you want to post these questions to your account at X (https://x.com). You'll need to log into your account at X, go to the X Developer Portal, set up a project, and apply for API access by following the instructions at X. You'll be given the following credentials:

>> API key

>> API secret key

>> Access token

>> Access token secret

TIP

Make sure you set your project to read and write settings while setting up your project, because that's necessary if you want to post content to X.

REMEMBER

Keep your API key and other credentials secret — you don't want to risk other people using your credentials to post to X and possibly violate the terms and conditions of your agreement with X.

Setting up your project

Setting up your social media automation project is similar to setting up any internet-related automation script, but this one has quite a few moving parts, so I'll take it slowly before we get to the actual code. As always, you want to create your project folder, create a virtual environment, and activate that virtual environment.

After you have all your credentials to post to your social media site, put that information in a .env file. For example, if you're posting to X, create a .env file inside of your project folder, and fill in your information as shown in Figure 13-1. Make sure to replace everything to the right of the equal sign (=) with the correct information for your account.

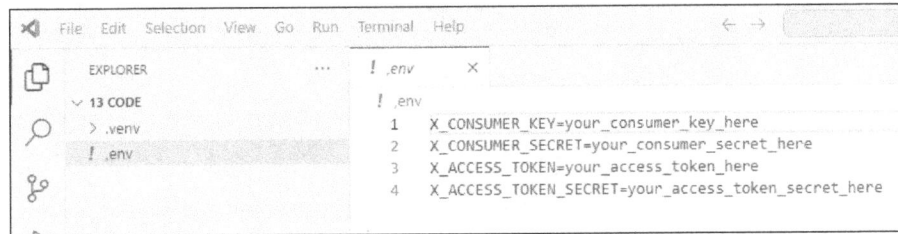

FIGURE 13-1: Structure of a .env file for posting to X.

Next, you'll need to `pip install` three modules that aren't part of the standard Python library: `python-dotenv` to pull data from your `.env` file, `tweepy` to simplify access to X, and `schedule` to simplify posting based on a schedule, such as every four hours. Enter the following command in the Terminal to ensure those modules are installed before running your script:

```
pip install tweepy schedule python-dotenv
```

With all those pieces in place, here's the entire script, which I've named `post_to_x.py`:

```python
# post_to_x.py
# pip install tweepy schedule python-dotenv
import tweepy
import schedule
import time
import os
from dotenv import load_dotenv
from datetime import datetime

# Load environment variables from .env file.
load_dotenv()

# Retrieve X API credentials from .env.
consumer_key = os.getenv("X_CONSUMER_KEY")
consumer_secret = os.getenv("X_CONSUMER_SECRET")
access_token = os.getenv("X_ACCESS_TOKEN")
access_token_secret = os.getenv("X_ACCESS_TOKEN_SECRET")

# Validate environment variables.
if not all([consumer_key, consumer_secret, access_token, access_token_secret]):
    print("Missing one or more environment variables in .env file")
    raise ValueError("The .env file is missing some required credentials.")

# Initialize Tweepy client.
try:
    client = tweepy.Client(
        consumer_key=consumer_key,
        consumer_secret=consumer_secret,
        access_token=access_token,
        access_token_secret=access_token_secret
    )
```

```python
        print("Tweepy client initialized successfully")
except Exception as e:
    print(f"Failed to initialize Tweepy client: {str(e)}")
    raise


def process_file(filename):
    """
    Reads the first line from the specified file, removes it from the file,
    and returns the question along with the count of remaining questions.
    If the file is missing or empty, returns (None, 0).
    """
    try:
        with open(filename, "r") as file:
            lines = file.readlines()
    except FileNotFoundError:
        print(f"Error: {filename} not found.")
        return None, 0

    if not lines:
        print(f"Warning: {filename} is empty before attempting to post.")
        return None, 0

    # Retrieve the first line and remove it from the file.
    question = lines[0].strip()
    remaining_questions = len(lines) - 1

    with open(filename, "w") as file:
        file.writelines(lines[1:])

    return question, remaining_questions

# Function to post to X using the question text from the specified file
def post_to_x(filename):
    question, remaining = process_file(filename)
    if question is None:
        print("No question available for posting.")
        return

    try:
        response = client.create_tweet(text=question)
        print(f"Successfully posted to X: {question}")
        print(f"Posted: {question}")
```

```python
        except tweepy.TweepyException as e:
            print(f"Error posting to X: {str(e)}")
            if "429" in str(e):
                print("Warning: Rate limit reached. Waiting for reset...")
            elif "403" in str(e):
                print("Error: Forbidden. Check app permissions or credentials.")
            elif "401" in str(e):
                print("Error: Unauthorized. Verify API credentials.")
            return

        print(f"Number of questions left in {filename}: {remaining}")

# Main loop to run the scheduler
def main():
    # Define the filename of the file containing questions.
    content_filename = "questions.txt"
    # Define how many hours between each post.
    interval_hours = 4

    # Schedule the post every interval_hours hours.
    schedule.every(interval_hours).hours.do(lambda: post_to_x(content_filename))
    print(f"Scheduled posts every {interval_hours} hour(s) using file:
{content_filename}")

    print("Starting X posting script... Check terminal for details.")
    while True:
        try:
            schedule.run_pending()
            time.sleep(60)  # Check every minute
        except Exception as e:
            print(f"Error in scheduler loop: {str(e)}")
            time.sleep(300)  # Wait 5 minutes before retrying on error.

if __name__ == "__main__":
    try:
        main()
    except KeyboardInterrupt:
        print("Script terminated by user")
    except Exception as e:
        print(f"Unexpected error: {str(e)}")
```

That's a lot of code, but as always, much of it is exception handling, to prevent the script from crashing due to unforeseen problems, like an incomplete .env file or questions.txt file.

Making the script your own

As written, the `post_to_x.py` script posts one line of text at a time from a file named `questions.txt`. Make sure that file is in the same folder as your script and that each line contains one question. To avoid duplication, the script removes the question from the file right after posting. Keep an eye on that file and replenish it with new questions from time to time to keep your content fresh.

If you prefer to name your file something other than `questions.txt`, make sure you change the following line of code in the `main()` function to your chosen filename:

```
content_filename = "questions.txt"
```

As written, the script posts once every four hours, as long as the script is running and there are questions in the `questions.txt` file.

WARNING

Posting too quickly can cause X's bot police to disable your account. Be sure to limit your script to posting 10 or 15 posts an hour.

Creating Content for Your Posts

If you're having trouble coming up with things to write about for your social media, consider the fact that you can always use AI to generate posts for you. You can generate posts on any topic, using any AI chatbot, and store them in a file similar to `questions.txt` to post them automatically using the same code. There's really no need to write a Python script to generate such content — it's probably faster and easier to just do it interactively.

For example, browse to ChatGPT (`https://chatgpt.com`), Grok (`https://x.ai`), or the website of any other chatbot. Type your prompt in a way that specifies what you want your posts to be about and how many posts you want. Use wording like that shown in Figure 13-2 so the text is easily copied to a text file.

FIGURE 13-2: Prompting ChatGPT to write social media posts.

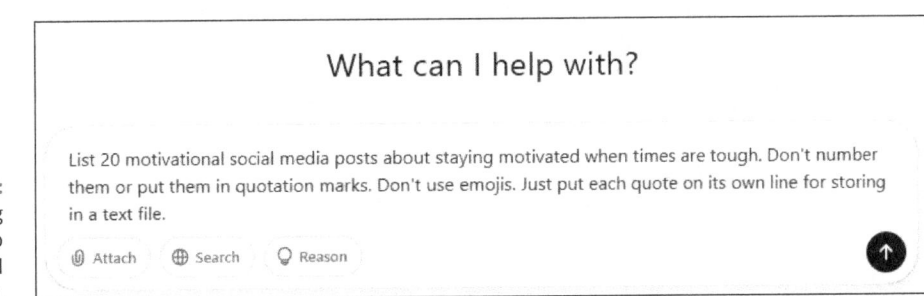

What can I help with?

List 20 motivational social media posts about staying motivated when times are tough. Don't number them or put them in quotation marks. Don't use emojis. Just put each quote on its own line for storing in a text file.

Attach   Search   Reason

After all of your posts have been generated, click the Copy button to copy them all. Typically, the Copy icon looks like two sheets of paper. It may be at the bottom of the generated output, as shown in Figure 13-3, or at the top, depending on which AI chatbot you use to generate your posts.

When everything feels like it's falling apart, remember it's also a chance to rebuild stronger

Tough times don't last, but the strength you build during them will

Keep going—not because it's easy, but because you've come too far to quit

Storms make trees take deeper roots; let challenges deepen your resolve

Every setback is a setup for a stronger comeback

Pain is temporary, but the growth it sparks can last forever

You don't need to see the whole path—just take the next step

Progress isn't always loud—sometimes it's surviving the day

Strength doesn't come from what you can do; it comes from what you overcome

Your future self is already proud of how you're showing up today

Hard days build discipline, and discipline builds success

Even slow progress is progress; keep moving forward

The darkest nights produce the brightest stars

You are allowed to rest, but not to give up

Challenges are the training ground for your future strength

Keep your head up—grit grows when it's tested

You've made it through 100% of your worst days so far

The struggle you're in today is shaping the person you'll be tomorrow

Sometimes courage is simply refusing to quit

When you feel like quitting, remind yourself why you started

FIGURE 13-3: The copy icon at the bottom of ChatGPT output.

Copy

If you already have your automatic posting script written, like the `auto_post.py` script from the previous section, open that project in your code editor (VS Code in our example). Create a new text file in the same folder as the script itself. Name it anything you like. I'll name this one `content.txt`. Paste in the posts you copied from your chatbot. Then close and save the file.

Finally, just make sure your auto-posting script knows to use that file to find your posts. In the `post_to_x.py` script from the previous section, look for this one line of code:

```
content_filename = "questions.txt"
```

Now change it to reflect the name of the file you just created. For example, if you named it `content.txt`, change that line to:

```
content_filename = "content.txt"
```

Tracking Performance Metrics

Using Python automation to track performance metrics helps individuals, businesses, and marketers optimize their social media strategy. Automating performance metrics with Python saves time and eliminates boring repetitive tasks by eliminating the need for manual tracking of data such as user engagement, growth trends, or content performance. Python enables you to collect data daily, hourly, or at any interval you like.

For a working example, I'll show you a script that can collect metrics from Instagram. As with other internet-related scripts, this will involve using an API with your current social media account. The same basic logic can be applied to any social media site. Feel free to use AI to adapt the code to whatever sites you intend to use.

Getting Instagram API access

To best automate Instagram, you should set up a business account. A business account gives you access to the Instagram Graph API, which provides richer data for performance metrics.

TIP If you already have a personal Instagram account, you can convert it to a business account for free. Doing so provides access to Instagram Insights and other performance metrics that aren't available with a personal account.

TIP If you need help converting your account, log into Instagram and use Meta's help resources or Meta AI to find step-by-step instructions.

Next, you'll need an API key. Go to the Meta for Developers website (https://developers.facebook.com) and log in with your Facebook credentials. Create a developer account; then go to the Developer Dashboard and register a new app, selecting Instagram as the product. Choose the Instagram Graph API as the API your app will use.

After you've completed all these steps, you'll receive two keys: an Instagram Business Account ID and an Access Token. Save them in a safe place and keep them private. You'll need them for your Python script (see the next section).

Setting up your script

Create your project folder and create and activate a virtual environment. The script I show you here uses three modules that aren't part of the Python standard library.

So, before you get started writing the script, make sure to enter this command at the command prompt:

```
pip install requests schedule python-dotenv
```

Next, create a .env file in your project folder to store private key information. Then give your business account ID and access tokens each a variable name and assign them the values you got from Instagram. Figure 13-4 shows an example, but make sure you replace the text after the equal sign (=) on each line with your actual key information from Instagram.

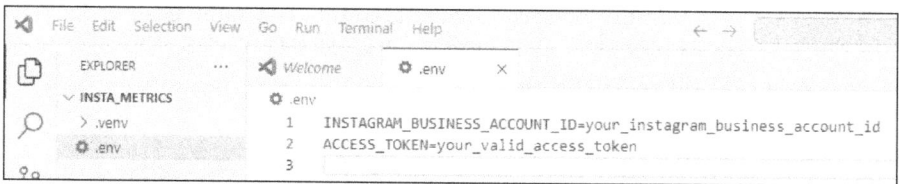

FIGURE 13-4:
Setting up a .env file for Instagram.

Here's the entire Python automation script for accessing Instagram performance metrics:

```
# instagram_metrics.py
# pip install requests schedule python-dotenv
import requests
import os
import schedule
import time
from dotenv import load_dotenv
from datetime import datetime

# Load environment variables from .env file.
load_dotenv()

# Retrieve Instagram API credentials from .env.
INSTAGRAM_BUSINESS_ACCOUNT_ID = os.getenv("INSTAGRAM_BUSINESS_ACCOUNT_ID")
ACCESS_TOKEN = os.getenv("ACCESS_TOKEN")

# Validate required environment variables.
if not INSTAGRAM_BUSINESS_ACCOUNT_ID or not ACCESS_TOKEN:
    print("Missing account ID or access token in .env file.")
    exit(1)
```

```python
def fetch_instagram_metrics(metrics):
    # Fetch daily performance metrics from the Instagram business account.
    url = f"https://graph.facebook.com/v14.0/{INSTAGRAM_BUSINESS_ACCOUNT_
    ID}/insights"
    params = {
        "metric": metrics,
        "period": "day",
        "access_token": ACCESS_TOKEN
    }

    try:
        response = requests.get(url, params=params)
        response.raise_for_status()
        data = response.json()
        print(f"\nMetrics for {datetime.now().strftime('%Y-%m-%d')}:")
        for item in data.get("data", []):
            metric_name = item.get("name")
            values = item.get("values", [])
            if values:
                # Assuming the most recent value is of interest
                value = values[0].get("value")
                print(f"{metric_name}: {value}")
            else:
                print(f"{metric_name}: No data available.")
    except Exception as e:
        print(f"Error fetching metrics: {str(e)}")

def main():
    print("Starting Instagram metrics fetching script...")

    # Define the metrics variable and the scheduled time.
    metrics = "impressions,reach,profile_views"
    # Time of day to run script (00:00 is midnight)
    schedule_time = "00:00"

    # Fetch metrics immediately when the script starts.
    fetch_instagram_metrics(metrics)

    # Schedule to run the metrics fetch every day at the user-defined time with
    the metrics parameter.
    schedule.every().day.at(schedule_time).do(fetch_instagram_metrics, metrics)
    print(f"Metrics fetching scheduled to run daily at {schedule_time}.")
```

```
    while True:
        schedule.run_pending()
        time.sleep(60)  # Wait one minute between checks


if __name__ == "__main__":
    try:
        main()
    except KeyboardInterrupt:
        print("Script terminated by user.")
    except Exception as e:
        print(f"Unexpected error: {str(e)}")
```

The script will gather performance metrics as soon as you run it. If you leave it running, it will grab metrics every day at midnight. You can change which metrics it downloads, and at what time, by modifying the code as discussed next.

Defining your metrics and timeframe

You can personalize the Instagram performance metrics script to your own needs via two variables inside the `main()` function:

```
# Define the metrics variable and the scheduled time.
metrics = "impressions,reach,profile_views"
# Time of day to run script (00:00 is midnight)
schedule_time = "00:00"
```

The `metrics` variable defines the following values from Instagram Insights:

>> **Impressions:** The total number of times your posts, Stories, or Reels have been viewed

>> **Reach:** The number of unique accounts that have seen your posts, Stories, or Reels at least once

>> **Profile views:** The number of times your Instagram profile has been viewed

TECHNICAL
STUFF

Other available metrics are documented at the Meta for Developers site at https://developers.facebook.com. (Search the site for Instagram Insights Metrics.)

When you run the script, the output will look something like this in the Terminal:

```
Metrics for 2026-06-08:
impressions: 1234
reach: 5678
profile_views: 42
```

TIP

The numbers represent the overall daily activity for your Instagram account on the day that you ran the script. For that reason, having the script check automatically at midnight is your best bet for getting the most accurate one-day results.

If you prefer to run the script at a time other than midnight, change the scheduled time from `"00:00"` to something else. For example, to run the script at 6:00 AM, change `schedule_time = "00:00"` to `scheduled_time = "06:00"`. To run it at noon each day, change it to `scheduled_time = "12:00"`.

Analyzing Trends

Analyzing trends over time is a good way to keep your social media content relevant to people's current interests. Google searches provide a quick and easy way to look at trends for various keywords. Python can make quick work of that.

Unlike other scripts in this chapter, you don't need to get access to any APIs (hooray!), but you will need to install some modules. Create your project folder, create and activate your virtual environment, and then run the following command in the Terminal to install the required modules:

```
# pip install pytrends pandas matplotlib
```

Here's the entire script for analyzing trends using Python:

```
# analyze_trends.py
# pip install pytrends pandas matplotlib
from pytrends.request import TrendReq
import pandas as pd
import matplotlib.pyplot as plt

def analyze_trends(keyword_list, timeframe):
    # Connect to Google Trends.
    pytrends = TrendReq(hl='en-US', tz=360)

    # Build payload with the provided keywords and timeframe.
    pytrends.build_payload(keyword_list, cat=0, timeframe=timeframe,
geo='', gprop='')
```

```python
    # Retrieve interest over time data.
    interest_over_time_df = pytrends.interest_over_time()

    if not interest_over_time_df.empty:
        print("See the pop-up chart for results")

        # Remove the "isPartial" column if present.
        if 'isPartial' in interest_over_time_df.columns:
            interest_over_time_df = interest_over_time_df.drop(columns=['
isPartial'])

        # Adjust granularity:
        # If the timeframe indicates a long period, aggregate to monthly data.
        if 'y' in timeframe:
            data_to_plot = interest_over_time_df.resample('M').mean()
        else:
            data_to_plot = interest_over_time_df

        data_to_plot.plot()
        plt.title("Google Trends Interest Over Time")
        plt.xlabel("Date")
        plt.ylabel("Interest")
        plt.legend(loc='upper left')
        plt.tight_layout()
        plt.show()
    else:
        print("No trend data available.")

def main():
    # Define the list of keywords and the timeframe.
    keyword_list = ['AI', 'Python', 'JavaScript']

    # Set the timeframe here (change as desired)
    # timeframe = 'now 7-d'  # One-week timeframe
    # timeframe = 'today 12-m'  # For the last 12 months
    timeframe = 'today 5-y'   # For the last 5 years

    analyze_trends(keyword_list, timeframe)

if __name__ == "__main__":
    main()
```

Viewing the trends

When you run the script as shown, the output will be the trends for the specified keywords (AI, Python, and JavaScript) over the last five years. That will pop up into a chart on your screen that looks something like Figure 13-5. The `matplotlib` module displays the chart.

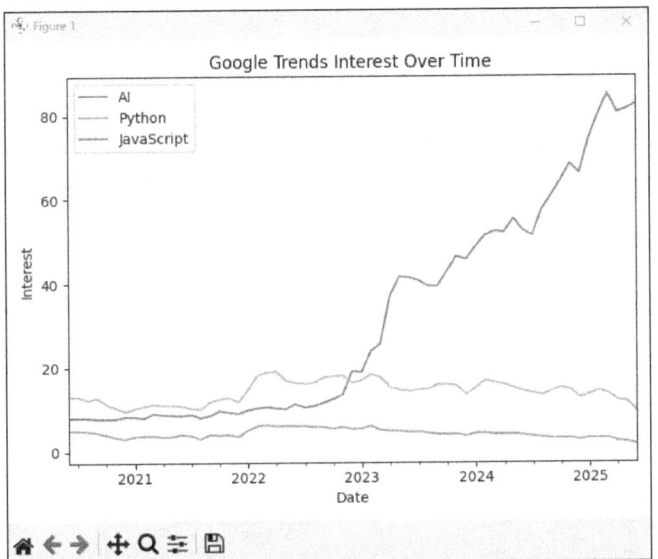

FIGURE 13-5:
Sample output from `analyze_trends.py`.

If you run the script while the chart is still open on the screen, nothing will seem to happen. Close the current chart shown onscreen before running the script to prevent that.

TIP

Setting your own keywords and timeframe

To adjust the script to your own keywords of interest and timeframe, set values for the `keyword_list` and `timeframe` variables in the `main()` function as follows:

```
keyword_list = ['AI', 'Python', 'JavaScript']
```

Make sure that you put each keyword you want to analyze in quotation marks, and separate them with commas, as shown in the example.

Defining your timeframe can be a little tricky, because you have to use syntax specified by the `pytrends` module. The current script provides examples using a week, a year, and the last five years, as follows:

```
# Set the timeframe here (change as desired).
# timeframe = 'now 7-d'   # One-week timeframe
# timeframe = 'today 12-m'   # For the last 12 months
timeframe = 'today 5-y'   # For the last 5 years
```

You can use any of those timeframes by un-commenting the one you want and commenting out the other two. For more details and options, see the pytrends README on GitHub at `https://github.com/GeneralMills/pytrends`.

4

Automating More Advanced Stuff

Chapter **14**

Scheduling Tasks

P ython is well-suited to scheduling tasks to run at specific dates and times, as well as at regular intervals. You can schedule system tasks like backups and logging. You can also schedule internet-related tasks like web scraping, email, and social media posting.

In this chapter, you learn about two libraries that are particularly well-suited to scheduling: `schedule` and `APScheduler`. First, I show you the features of each. Then I provide specific examples of how to use them to schedule Python automation tasks.

Using the Schedule Module

A popular module used for scheduling is aptly named `schedule`. The `schedule` module isn't part of the Python standard library. So, if you intend to use it in a script, make sure to create and activate your virtual environment and enter this command at the command prompt in the Terminal:

```
pip install schedule
```

You can use the `schedule` library to run tasks at specific times or at regular intervals. A simple way to get started is to write some simple scripts that just print some feedback in the Terminal, on schedule, so you know that your code works.

Here's a simple script that just displays some feedback in the Terminal every ten seconds, to show you the basic syntax and structure of such a script:

```python
# basic_schedule.py
# pip install schedule
import schedule
import time

# Function to be scheduled
def job():
    print("Task executed! Press Ctrl+C in Terminal to stop the script.")

# Schedule the job every ten seconds.
schedule.every(10).seconds.do(job)

# Main loop to run scheduled tasks with keyboard interrupt handling
try:
    while True:
        schedule.run_pending()
        time.sleep(1)  # Prevent high CPU usage.
except KeyboardInterrupt:
    print("\nScript terminated by user.")
```

The first function in the script, job(), displays some text on the screen when called. For testing and feedback purposes. When you run the script, you'll see that message appear every ten seconds. This is the line of code that sets up the scheduler to call the job() function every ten seconds:

```python
schedule.every(10).seconds.do(job)
```

Notice that when I'm using the schedule module, I refer to the function as job without the parentheses — in other words, job rather than job(). It may seem counterintuitive, because we usually call functions with those parentheses in the names. But in this syntax, I'm not calling on the function to return a value immediately — I'm simply telling the scheduler the name of the function to call when it starts running.

Below the line that defines the scheduled interval is a peculiar while True loop, inside an exception handler. You may be thinking that because True is always true, that loop will run forever. You're correct, and that's what we want in this case. Without the loop, the script would just end before the first ten seconds were up, and the script would do nothing. I explain why next.

Understanding how the schedule module works

The line `schedule.every(10).seconds.do(job)` never actually runs the job. Instead, every ten seconds, it updates the scheduled job list (or *queue* as it's sometime called) to say, "Please run the job when you get a chance." That prevents the scheduled task from trying to run when the central processing unit (CPU) is busy doing something else.

To actually run scheduled tasks that are ready to go, use the following line of code:

```
schedule.run_pending()
```

So, it really takes two lines of code to run scheduled tasks: one to set up the schedule, which simply lets the computer know that the task is to be run at its earliest convenience, and the second to actually run tasks that are waiting in the queue.

Now let's look at the entire loop for running scheduled tasks, along with the exception handler:

```
# Main loop to run scheduled tasks with keyboard interrupt handling
try:
    while True:
        schedule.run_pending()
        time.sleep(1)  # Prevent high CPU usage
except KeyboardInterrupt:
    print("\nScript terminated by user.")
```

Basically, the `while True` loop keeps the script running "forever." That loop repeats once per second, due to `time.sleep(1)`. That one second keeps the CPU freed up to do other tasks required by apps you may be using at the time. So, the scheduler runs "in the background," so to speak, occasionally taking a peek into the queue to see if any scheduled tasks need to run. But in the meantime, you can be doing other things with the computer because the scheduler isn't hogging all the CPU time.

Of course, in real life, you probably don't want to really run the script "forever." You may want to stop it to work with the code. That's where the `try...except` comes in. To stop the script, you can simply press Ctrl+C.

WARNING

Make sure you click inside the Terminal where the script in running inside VS Code before pressing Ctrl+C. The script won't detect keystrokes outside that Terminal window.

With that in mind, look at the code again. On the one hand, `schedule.every(10).seconds.do(job)` is adding the task to run the job every ten seconds to a queue. But it isn't actually running the task.

The `while True` loop is constantly running, but it repeats only once every second (not thousands of times a second). During that one second, the computer can be handling other demands from other apps. When the loop repeats and `schedule.run_pending()` is executed, then any scheduled tasks waiting in the queue can be executed (one at a time if there are several) without "crashing into" each other and overwhelming the CPU.

Thats how it all works, technically, behind the scenes. From your standpoint, as a user, when you run the script, nothing will happen for the first ten seconds. But after that, you'll see the following text repeated in the Terminal every ten seconds, indicating that the `job()` function is being executed on schedule:

```
Task executed! Press Ctrl+C in Terminal to stop the script.
```

As long as you see the message appear every ten seconds, you know the scheduler is working and your code is working. Of course, in real life, you'll probably want to do more than just display some text in the Terminal.

Scheduling tasks for intervals

In the first script, earlier, I had you schedule a task to run every ten seconds, just for easy testing purposes. Of course, you can use intervals other than seconds. Here's an example of scheduling a task to run every ten minutes:

```
# Schedule a task every ten minutes.
schedule.every(10).minutes.do(job)
```

Here's some code to run a task every two hours:

```
# Schedule a task every two hours
schedule.every(2).hours.do(job)
```

You can also use `.days` and `.weeks` to schedule tasks. Here's a line of code to run a task every other day:

```
# Schedule a task every two days.
schedule.every(2).days.do(job)
```

Here's an example of running a task every two weeks:

```
# Schedule a task every two weeks.
schedule.every(2).weeks.do(job)
```

You can also schedule for specific days of the week and month, and specific times of day. For example, here's code to run a task every day at 8:00 AM:

```
# Schedule a task daily at a specific time (for example, 8:00 AM).
schedule.every().day.at("08:00").do(job)
```

Here's an example of scheduling at 9:30 AM every weekday:

```
# Schedule a task every weekday at a specific time (for example, Monday through
    Friday at 9:30 AM).
schedule.every().monday.at("09:30").do(job)
schedule.every().tuesday.at("09:30").do(job)
schedule.every().wednesday.at("09:30").do(job)
schedule.every().thursday.at("09:30").do(job)
schedule.every().friday.at("09:30").do(job)
```

You have a lot of leeway in how often you want to run your scheduled task. However, the schedule module isn't the only game in town for scheduling tasks. In the next section, I introduce you to the APSchedule module, which can also schedule tasks and has a few extra tricks up its sleeve in terms of specifying schedules.

Using the APScheduler Module

The schedule module is a popular and relatively easy way to schedule tasks with Python. But out in the corporate world, many people use APScheduler (which stands for *Advanced Python Scheduler*). It works similarly to schedule but offers more flexibility for specifying dates and times for running tasks. APScheduler also lets you avoid the awkward while True loop in the previous script.

REMEMBER

APScheduler is not part of the Python standard library. So, if you intend to use it in a script, make sure to pip install APScheduler first.

Here's a script much like the first example — it calls a function named job() every ten seconds, but it uses APScheduler rather than the simple schedule module:

```python
# basic_apscheduler.py
# pip install apscheduler
from apscheduler.schedulers.blocking import BlockingScheduler


def job():
    print("Task executed! Press Ctrl+C in Terminal to stop the script.")


scheduler = BlockingScheduler()
scheduler.add_job(job, 'interval', seconds=10)


if __name__ == '__main__':
    try:
        scheduler.start()
    except (KeyboardInterrupt, SystemExit):
        print("Scheduler stopped")
        scheduler.shutdown()
```

TECHNICAL
STUFF

This script uses from apscheduler.schedulers.blocking import Blocking-Scheduler because APScheduler is actually a collection of modules offering many capabilities. For basic scheduling, you need only the BlockingScheduler, so importing just that one module is more efficient.

Let's look at the script in detail. The function named job() simply displays some text on the screen, so we can verify the script is working when we test it. Then come these two lines:

```python
scheduler = BlockingScheduler()
scheduler.add_job(job, 'interval', seconds=10)
```

The first line simply executes BlockingScheduler to create an object named scheduler. Throughout the rest of the code, the name scheduler refers to that instance of BlockingScheduler. After it's defined, you can schedule jobs to run using syntax like the following:

```python
scheduler.add_job(job, 'interval', seconds=10)
```

In that line of code, job refers to the job() function, and 'interval' specifies that we want to schedule the job to run at regular intervals. As you probably guessed, seconds=10 says to run the job every ten seconds. That line of code doesn't actually get the process going — it just defines what the schedule will be.

You can add as many scheduled tasks and intervals as you like using that `.add_job()` method.

With the `schedule` module, we had to add a `while True` loop to prevent the script from exiting immediately, but `BlockingScheduler` doesn't work that way. Instead you use the `.start()` method to get it going and keep the script from ending. But of course, you don't really want the script to run "forever." So, you still need some way to stop the scheduler when necessary. That's what the following lines are for:

```
try:
    scheduler.start()
except (KeyboardInterrupt, SystemExit):
    print("Scheduler stopped")
    scheduler.shutdown()
```

Those lines replace the `while True` loop, allowing you to stop the script by blocking inside the Terminal in VS Code and pressing Ctrl+C. The `scheduler.shutdown()` line stops the scheduler, cleans up any resources the scheduler was using, and allows the script to exit gracefully.

In the sample script, `except (KeyboardInterrupt, SystemExit)` ensures that the scheduler shuts down when you press Ctrl+C or if the script stops executing for any other reason (such as a bug in your Python code).

Using APScheduler with intervals

In the example script, I use `'interval'` as a keyword for indicating a schedule based on time intervals. In this section, I show you examples using different timeframes with the interval keyword.

Here's an example of running a job every five minutes:

```
scheduler.add_job(job, 'interval', minutes=5)
```

Here's an example of running a job every two hours:

```
scheduler.add_job(my_job, 'interval', hours=2)
```

Here's an example of running a job every three days:

```
scheduler.add_job(my_job, 'interval', days=3)
```

Here's one for running a job once a week:

```
scheduler.add_job(my_job, 'interval', weeks=1)
```

Here's one for running a job every two weeks:

```
scheduler.add_job(job_two_weeks, 'interval', weeks=2)
```

Using APScheduler with dates and times

One big advantage APScheduler has over schedule is the ability to specify dates and times for running tasks, rather than just intervals. To do this, use the cron keyword in place of interval. The syntax is as follows:

```
scheduler.add_job(job, 'cron', [year=], [month=], [day=], [week=], [day_of_
    week=], [hour=], [minute=], [second=], [start_date=], [end_date=],
    [timezone=], [jitter=], **kwargs)
```

You can omit any parameters in square brackets that you don't need. Examples are probably the easiest way to understand how to phrase things, so I'll show you a bunch of them next.

Here's a line of code to run a job every day at 8:00 AM:

```
scheduler.add_job(job, 'cron', hour=8, minute=0)
```

If you want to run a job several times an hour, you can use */ with minute= to specify an interval. For example, here's a line of code that will run a job every 15 minutes:

```
scheduler.add_job(job, 'cron', minute='*/15')
```

Here's one that runs a job once a week, every Wednesday at noon:

```
scheduler.add_job(my_job, 'cron', day_of_week='wed', hour=12)
```

TIP

When you're using the day_of_week parameter, you can use either numbers (0 through 6, where 0 is Sunday), or day name abbreviations in quotation marks ('sun', 'mon', 'tue', 'wed', 'thu', 'fri', 'sat') to specify days. Use commas to specify multiple values.

Here's a line of code to run a job every Monday, Wednesday, and Friday at noon:

```
scheduler.add_job(job, 'cron', day_of_week='mon,wed,fri', hour=12)
```

You can describe the days of the week as numbers, if you prefer, like this:

```
scheduler.add_job(job, 'cron', day_of_week='1,3,5', hour=12)
```

This next line of code runs a task once a month at midnight on the first day of each month:

```
scheduler.add_job(job, 'cron', day=1, hour=0, minute=0)
```

TIP

When using the day= parameter, specify the day of the month as a number, between 1 and 31.

APScheduler really gives you a lot of flexibility for scheduling. Here's an example where you run a task on the 1st and 15th of every month at midnight:

```
scheduler.add_job(job, 'cron', day='1,15', hour=0, minute=0)
```

With the day= parameter, you can use 'last' to specify the last day of each month. Here's an example to run a task at 11:59 PM on the last day of every month:

```
scheduler.add_job(job, 'cron', day='last', hour=23, minute=59)
```

To run a task on the first and last days of the month, use 1 for the first day and 'last' for the last day, like this:

```
scheduler.add_job(job, 'cron', day='1,last', hour=12)
```

If you want to run something hourly, set the hour parameter to '*'. For example, the following code runs a task at noon every Saturday and Sunday:

```
scheduler.add_job(job, 'cron', day_of_week='sat,sun', hour='*')
```

Here's a line of code that runs a task every 30 seconds on weekdays during business hours (8 AM to 5 PM).

```
scheduler.add_job(job, 'cron', day_of_week='mon-fri', hour='8-17',
    second='*/30')
```

There's almost no limit to how you can schedule things with APScheduler, which is a great thing for automation.

If you're having a hard time specifying your schedule, consider asking artificial intelligence (AI) for help. Phrase your prompt as "Using Python APScheduler, how can I specify . . ." and then express the schedule you want in plain language.

So far, I've shown you examples of calling a single simple function according to a schedule. That same strategy works for calling multiple functions on different schedules. Again, I'll use very simple functions to focus on the scheduling code. In the following code, you can see how three different scheduler.add_job() statements allow the script to execute code in the three different functions on three different schedules:

```python
# multi_functions.py
# pip install apschedule
from apscheduler.schedulers.blocking import BlockingScheduler

def job1():
    print("job1 - Press Ctrl+C in Terminal to stop")

def job2():
    print("job2")

def job3():
    print("job3")

if __name__ == "__main__":
    scheduler = BlockingScheduler()

    # Schedule job1 to run every ten seconds.
    scheduler.add_job(job1, 'interval', seconds=10)

    # Schedule job2 to run every 30 seconds.
    scheduler.add_job(job2, 'interval', seconds=30)

    # Schedule job3 to run every one minute.
    scheduler.add_job(job3, 'interval', minutes=1)

    try:
        # Keep the script running.
        scheduler.start()
    except (KeyboardInterrupt, SystemExit):
        scheduler.shutdown()
```

Automating Python Scripts

If you're running large Python scripts on a schedule, the thought of putting all the code from each script into a function may concern you. If you prefer to keep each task in its own script (its own .py file), you can still use the same techniques as I outline earlier to set up your schedule. Then just have each function run an external script.

To illustrate how it works, let's assume I have three scripts named script01.py, script02.py, and script03.py. Of course, you have as few, or as many, scripts as you like. Exactly what each script does isn't important. All that matters for this example is that each script does something that's useful for you when you run it.

There are two ways to run external scripts on a schedule. You can use the subprocess module, which I show you first, or you can import the scripts, which I show you later in this section.

Running scripts as subprocesses

The subprocess module, which is part of the Python standard library, is a great tool for running code outside of a Python script. In addition to external .py files, subprocess can run shell scripts (.bat, .cmd, and .sh files) and executables (.exe in Windows).

TECHNICAL STUFF

The subprocess module can run virtually any external code, though on a Mac you may need to grant permission. Refer to the subprocess documentation at https://docs.python.org/3/library/subprocess.html for details. Or ask any AI for help with the specific file type you intend to run with subprocess.

The easiest way to run multiple scripts is still to create a function for each job. But instead of having the function contain all the code to perform the task, the function just calls the script by its filename (and path, if the script isn't in the same folder as the scheduler script).

Here's an example where the scheduler runs three scripts named script01.py, script02.py, and script03.py, each on its own script, using code similar to the last example in the previous section.

```
# multi_scripts.py
# pip install apschedule
from apscheduler.schedulers.blocking import BlockingScheduler
import subprocess
```

```python
def job1():
    run_external_script('script01.py')


def job2():
    run_external_script('script02.py')


def job3():
    run_external_script('script03.py')


def run_external_script(script_path):
    try:
        # Run the external script.
        result = subprocess.run(
            ["python", script_path],  # Command as a list
            capture_output=True,      # Capture stdout and stderr.
            text=True,                # Return strings, not bytes.
            check=True                # Raise error on nonzero exit code.
        )
        # Show script output.
        print("Output:", result.stdout)
        # print("Error (if any):", result.stderr)
        # print("Return code:", result.returncode)
    except subprocess.CalledProcessError as e:
        print(f"Error running script: {e}")
        print("Error output:", e.stderr)
    except FileNotFoundError:
        print(f"Script or Python executable not found: {script_path}")


if __name__ == "__main__":
    scheduler = BlockingScheduler()

    # Schedule job1 to run every ten seconds.
    scheduler.add_job(job1, 'interval', seconds=10)

    # Schedule job2 to run every 30 seconds.
    scheduler.add_job(job2, 'interval', seconds=30)

    # Schedule job3 to run every one minute.
    scheduler.add_job(job3, 'interval', minutes=1)

    try:
        # Keep the script running.
        scheduler.start()
    except (KeyboardInterrupt, SystemExit):
        scheduler.shutdown()
```

Let's take a look at some specifics in the code. The `import subprocess` line near the top imports the `subprocess` module. That's part of the Python standard library, so you don't need to `pip install` it. The `subprocess` module allows you to run external code.

The script still contains three functions named `job1`, `job2`, and `job3`, but as you can see, each of them uses this syntax to run one of the external scripts — `script01.py`, `script02.py`, and `script03.py` — using syntax like this:

```
run_external_script('script01.py')
```

WARNING

The sample code assumes the external scripts are in the same folder as the scheduling script. If yours are in separate folders, make sure you include the path to the external folder in front of the filename.

That `run_external_script()` name refers to the function by the same name in the code:

```
def run_external_script(script_path):
    try:
        # Run the external script.
        result = subprocess.run(
            ["python", script_path], # Command as a list
            capture_output=True,     # Capture stdout and stderr.
            text=True,               # Return strings, not bytes.
            check=True               # Raise error on nonzero exit code.
        )
        # Show script output.
        print("Output:", result.stdout)
        # print("Error (if any):", result.stderr)
        # print("Return code:", result.returncode)
    except subprocess.CalledProcessError as e:
        print(f"Error running script: {e}")
        print("Error output:", e.stderr)
    except FileNotFoundError:
        print(f"Script or Python executable not found: {script_path}")
```

I've included exception handling in that script to gracefully handle any unforeseen errors. This next code is the part that actually runs the external script:

```
result = subprocess.run(
    ["python", script_path], # Command as a list
    capture_output=True,     # Capture stdout and stderr.
```

```
    text=True,              # Return strings, not bytes.
    check=True              # Raise error on nonzero exit code.
)
```

The line that reads ["python", script_path] basically says to use Python to run whatever script name was passed into the function (script_path). The line that reads capture_output=True captures any output that the script puts out through print() commands or error messages (but it doesn't display that output immediately). The text=True line ensures that any script output is stored as simple strings and not bytes. The check=True line prevents any errors in the script from stopping the scheduler script, so the error can be handled by the scheduler script.

Notice how the preceding function starts with result=. Any output from that function is stored in the result object. If you need to see any of that output, you can use standard print() statements with reference to the data you want.

Next, I'm only showing stdout (standard output, from print() statements). But you can uncomment the other print() statements below to see any error messages (stderr) and an exit code (returncode), where 0 is a normal exit:

```
print("Output:", result.stdout)
# print("Error (if any):", result.stderr)
# print("Return code:", result.returncode)
```

Most of the rest of the code is just the scheduling code and some extra exception handling for running external scripts.

Running scripts as imports

In the interest of being complete, I'll show you another way to run external scripts from Python, using the import statement. Personally, I recommend that you use subprocess from the previous example, where you can capture output from each script, and even run non-Python scripts and executables.

TECHNICAL STUFF

The subprocess module is safer than import, because it spawns a new operating system process for each external script, so there's no chance of collision between variables and such. It more closely resembles how things work when you manually start each script yourself.

To use the import statement, each script you want to run should have a main() function that kicks off the script execution. At the bottom, include an if __name__

== "__main__" block to prevent the script from running when you import it rather than run it. Here's an example:

```python
# script01.py
# Super-simple example to test scheduling

def main():
    print("Script01.py, press Ctrl+C in Terminal to stop")

if __name__ == "__main__":
    main()
```

Next I'll show you an APScheduler example similar to others you've seen in this chapter. But this one actually imports the Python scripts to run. Then it executes each one using *scriptname*.main() (where *scriptname* is the same as the filename without the .py extension):

```python
# multi_imports.py
# pip install apschedule
from apscheduler.schedulers.blocking import BlockingScheduler
# Import script01.py through script03.py.
import script01, script02, script03

def job1():
    script01.main()

def job2():
    script02.main()

def job3():
    script03.main()

if __name__ == "__main__":
    scheduler = BlockingScheduler()

    # Schedule job1 to run every ten seconds.
    scheduler.add_job(job1, 'interval', seconds=10)

    # Schedule job2 to run every 30 seconds.
    scheduler.add_job(job2, 'interval', seconds=30)

    # Schedule job3 to run every one minute.
    scheduler.add_job(job3, 'interval', minutes=1)
```

```
try:
    # Keep the script running.
    scheduler.start()
except (KeyboardInterrupt, SystemExit):
    scheduler.shutdown()
```

The scheduling code in this example is identical to the other examples. The code is simpler in that you don't need the run_external_script() function and other complications of the previous example. However, you may find using subprocess and run_external_script() to be easier, in the long run, if you're dealing with complex processes.

TIP

Yet another way to run Python on a schedule is to convert your .py script into a stand-alone executable file, and then use the operating system's scheduler (Task Scheduler in Windows or launchd or cron in macOS or Linux).

Chapter **15**

Integrating with Artificial Intelligence

A s you probably know, artificial intelligence (AI) is the latest big event in tech evolution, and it's evolving at a very fast rate. Most people interact with AI through simple chatbots, where you type a plain-English prompt into a text box and get a reply. However, you can interact with AI through Python, and that's what this chapter is all about.

Accessing Free AI through an API

Most popular AI chatbots provide an application programming interface (API) for integration with apps. Typically, you need a paid subscription to use it. But in this chapter, I stick to free AI APIs so you can practice without paying for access.

In this first section, you develop an AI chatbot using Python and Groq (https://groq.com).

WARNING

Groq is not the same as Grok, the AI associated with X and xAI. As of this writing, there is no free API access to Grok, which is why I'm using Groq.

In addition to being free, Groq is known for its ultrafast AI responses to your prompt, which is also great when you're first learning. Keep in mind that the general techniques you learn here will apply to all AI APIs to some extent. Any code in this chapter can easily be adapted to work with any paid service. Of course, you can also use just about any AI to write a Python script for you to access on any AI service.

Your first project will be a simple chatbot to get you warmed up. To start this project, create a folder and virtual environment as always. Activate your virtual environment and enter the following command to import the required dependencies:

```
pip install requests python-dotenv
```

You'll need a Groq API key. I discuss API keys in Chapter 9, so I won't repeat all the details here. To get a free API key for Groq, browse to `https://console.groq.com` and follow the onscreen instructions.

In keeping with security best practices, create a .env file for your Python project and store your own API key there. Figure 15-1 shows an example. Just make sure to replace the fake API key shown in Figure 15-1 with the actual API key that you get from Groq.

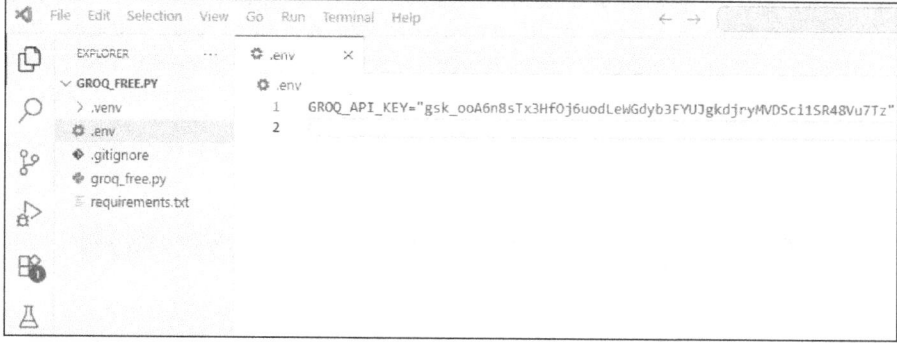

FIGURE 15-1:
Store your own key in a .env file for this code project.

Next, I'll show you all the code for interacting with the Groq chatbot for free through Python. Comments in the script help to explain some of the key components, which I discuss after the code listing.

```
# groq_free.py
# pip install requests python-dotenv
import requests
```

```python
import os
from dotenv import load_dotenv

# Load environment variables from .env file.
load_dotenv(dotenv_path=os.path.join(os.getcwd(), ".env"))
GROQ_API_KEY = os.getenv("GROQ_API_KEY")


# Groq Free AI Question Answering Tool
# Requires free API key from https://console.groq.com
class GroqFreeClient:
    def __init__(self, api_key: str):
        self.session = requests.Session()
        self.session.headers.update({
            'User-Agent': 'Mozilla/5.0 (Windows NT 10.0; Win64; x64)
AppleWebKit/537.36'
        })
        self.api_key = api_key


    def ask(self, question):
        try:
            url = "https://api.groq.com/openai/v1/chat/completions"
            headers = {
                "Authorization": f"Bearer {self.api_key}",
                "Content-Type": "application/json"
            }
            payload = {
                "model": "llama3-8b-8192",
                "messages": [
                    {"role": "user", "content": question}
                ],
                "max_tokens": 300,
                "temperature": 0.7
            }
            response = self.session.post(url, headers=headers, json=payload,
timeout=30)
            if response.status_code == 200:
                result = response.json()
                return result['choices'][0]['message']['content'].strip()
            else:
                print(f"Groq API error: {response.status_code} {response.text}")
        except Exception as e:
            print(f"Groq API error: {e}")
        return None
```

```python
def main():
    # Get API key from environment variable.
    api_key = GROQ_API_KEY
    if not api_key:
        print("Error: GROQ_API_KEY not provided. Exiting.")
        return
    client = GroqFreeClient(api_key)
    print("\nGroq Free AI Question Answering Tool")

    # Interactive mode
    question = ""
    while question.lower() not in ['quit', 'exit', 'q']:
        try:
            question = input("\nEnter your question (or 'quit' to exit): ").strip()
            if question.lower() in ['quit', 'exit', 'q']:
                break
            if not question:
                continue
            answer = client.ask(question)
            print(f"\nAnswer: {answer if answer else 'No answer received.'}")
            print("\n" + "="*50)
        except KeyboardInterrupt:
            print("\nGoodbye!")
            break
        except Exception as e:
            print(f"Error: {e}")

if __name__ == "__main__":
    # Start interactive mode.
    main()
```

Starting near the top of the script, you import the `requests` module for making HTTP requests to the internet. The `os` and `python-dotenv` modules allow you to retrieve the API key from the `.env` file using the following lines of code:

```python
# Load environment variables from .env file.
load_dotenv(dotenv_path=os.path.join(os.getcwd(), ".env"))
GROQ_API_KEY = os.getenv("GROQ_API_KEY")
```

The next line of code starts a class named `GroqFreeClient`. Subsequent code instantiates an object of that class, named `client`, by calling the class and passing in the API key that was obtained from the `.env` file:

```python
client = GroqFreeClient(api_key)
```

The GroqFreeClient class includes an `ask()` method, which accepts a question or prompt. That method sets up an HTTP request with the target URL, a headers block specifying the API key and content type, a payload indicating which AI model to use (for example, `"llama3-8b-8192"`), along with other required information for the API.

The following line then sends all that information to the specified URL and waits up to 30 seconds for a response:

```
response = self.session.post(url, headers=headers, json=payload, timeout=30)
```

TIP

Chapter 9 also discusses JavaScript Object Notation (JSON), which is commonly used when interacting with online APIs.

If the AI successfully responds to the question, it returns a response code of `200`, plus a JSON response. The start of the JSON response from `GrokFreeClient` looks something like the following example, where I'm using `...` as a placeholder for some information. Other AI APIs I've used return data in a similar format. I wanted to give you a sense of what to expect in your own responses.

```
{
  "id": "chatcmpl-...,
  "object": "chat.completion",
  "created": 1753730086,
  "model": "llama3-8b-8192",
  "choices": [
    {
      "index": 0,
      "message": {
        "role": "assistant",
        "content": "..."
      },
      "logprobs": null,
      "finish_reason": "stop"
    }
  ]...
}
```

TIP

To get the exact format of an API request for a different AI product, look at the developer documentation on the product's website.

In my sample script, the following `if` block checks to see whether the response code is `200` (successful). If so, it stores the entire JSON response in a variable named `result`. Then the function returns only the chatbot answer, identified by `'choices'][0]['message']['content']`, from that JSON response. The `.strip()` method at the end of that line simply removes any trailing spaces from the response:

```
if response.status_code == 200:
    result = response.json()
    return result['choices'][0]['message']['content'].strip()
```

In a nutshell, this is how you can send a prompt to an AI chatbot and get the results in a Python script. Of course, there's additional code for exception handling and the like. But that sending of the request, and isolating the answer in the response, is very typical of interacting with any online AI chatbot.

Warming Up to a Local Chatbot

You can run popular AI models like DeepSeek-R1, Gemma 3 from Google, Meta Llama 3, Qwen locally on your computer without internet access or paid subscriptions. These models can answer questions, generate text, analyze images, summarize data, help with coding, and more. Running these models is a great way to practice and learn AI coding.

Ollama, an open-source tool that lets you run powerful AI large language models (LLMs) directly on your own computer, is one of the best tools for this. To use Ollama effectively, your system should have a minimum of 8GB of RAM and at least 100GB of free disk space — LLM files can be huge. If your system includes an NVIDIA, AMD, or Apple Silicon graphics processing unit (GPU), or a neural processing unit — Ollama will use it automatically to accelerate performance. If you're using a CPU-only system, Ollama still functions, but processing may be significantly slower.

TIP

If you're using a CPU-only system, you'll get better performance from models with 1 to 7 billion parameters (1B–7B). TinyLlama 1.1B, Phi-2, and Mistral 7B are popular smaller models.

For Python, there's an Ollama module that makes it relatively easy to write Python code to interact with the local models you download via Ollama. But before you start writing any Python code, you'll need to download and install the Ollama app, which allows you to download models. Let's start there.

Installing and running Ollama

The first step to using Ollama is to download and install it on your computer. You can find versions for Linux, macOS, and Windows at `https://ollama.com/download`. You download and install it just like any other app.

After Ollama is installed, you can run it from the Windows Start menu, the macOS Launchpad, or however you normally launch apps on Linux. Ollama runs as a *background process,* which means you won't see any open windows or Taskbar/Dock icons while it's running. However, you may see a tiny llama icon in the Windows Notification Area (see Figure 15-2) or on the macOS menu bar (near the Wi-Fi, battery, and other icons on the right).

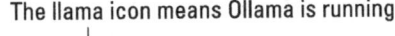
The llama icon means Ollama is running

FIGURE 15-2:
Ollama running in
the background.

Downloading AI models with Ollama

When Ollama is running in the background, you can interact with Ollama through a command-line interface (CLI). In other words, you can interact with it through the Terminal window in VS Code on any computer.

**TECHNICAL
STUFF**

Though not required, you can also access Ollama from a command line outside of VS Code. On Windows, you can use Command Prompt or PowerShell. On macOS or Linux, use the Terminal app.

To verify that Ollama is running and available, you can check its version number by entering the command `ollama –version` (see Figure 15-3). Optionally, use your web browser to browse to `127.0.0.1:11434` (a local address) and you'll see the message `Ollama is running`. If Ollama isn't running, entering `ollama serve` at the command line should start it.

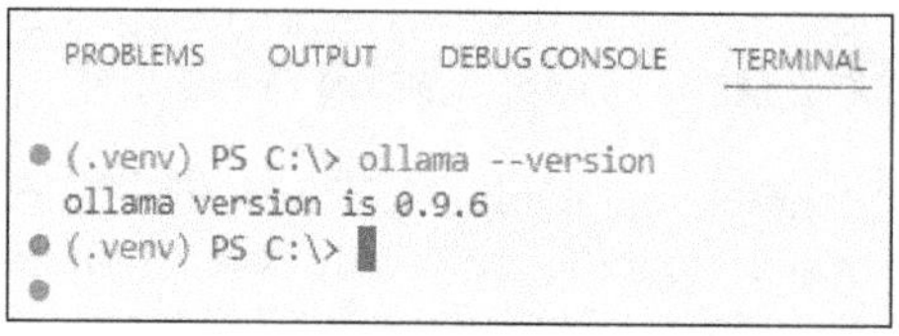

FIGURE 15-3:
Checking the
Ollama version
from the VS
Code Terminal.

```
PROBLEMS    OUTPUT    DEBUG CONSOLE    TERMINAL

● (.venv) PS C:\> ollama --version
  ollama version is 0.9.6
● (.venv) PS C:\> █
●
```

To use an AI model locally, first you have to download it. In the Terminal, enter the command `ollama pull` followed by a space and the name of the model you want to download. For example, entering the following command will download the popular `llama3.2` model:

```
ollama pull llama3.2
```

WARNING

Make sure you spell the model name correctly in your command. Browse to `ollama.com` and click the Models link to see the available models and their names. I mention it because many have weird names that are easy to misspell.

The models tend to be large; each one may take a minute or more to download. If at any time you want to check to see which models you've already downloaded, enter the command `ollama list`, as shown in Figure 15-4; you can see the sizes of the models I've downloaded.

```
PROBLEMS    OUTPUT    DEBUG CONSOLE    TERMINAL

● PS C:\> ollama list
● NAME                    ID              SIZE
  tinyllama:latest        2644915ede35    637 MB
  qwen2.5-coder:latest    dae161e27b0e    4.7 GB
  qwen3:latest            500a1f067a9f    5.2 GB
  deepseek-r1:latest      6995872bfe4c    5.2 GB
  llama3.2:latest         a80c4f17acd5    2.0 GB
  gemma3:latest           a2af6cc3eb7f    3.3 GB
○ PS C:\> []
```

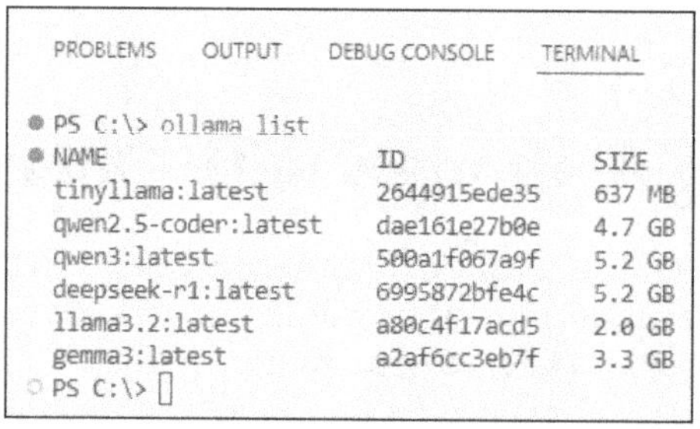

FIGURE 15-4:
The models I've
downloaded.

Building a simple local chatbot

A chatbot is a form of AI in which you submit a question or prompt, and AI returns an answer. ChatGPT, Claude, Google Gemini, Grok, Meta AI, and Microsoft Copilot are all examples of modern chatbots. You can create your own, albeit relatively simple, chatbot with a downloaded Ollama model and just a few lines of Python code.

Keep in mind that if your computer doesn't have a powerful GPU — such as an NVIDIA card or Apple Silicon chip such as the M1 Ultra, M2 Ultra, M3, or M4, or AMD MI-series chip — running AI models locally can be painfully slow. For this example, I recommend downloading a smaller model, `tinyllama`, which runs at a decent speed even without high-end hardware. That way, you can get some hands-on experience writing Python code to interact with AI no matter what hardware you're using.

To download `tinyllama`, make sure Ollama is running on your computer. Then at any command line, enter the following:

```
ollama pull tinyllama
```

You should be able to verify that `tinyllama` is installed by entering the command `ollama list`.

To set up your Python project, create your folder and virtual environment as usual. Activate your virtual environment and enter the following command in the Terminal to install the `ollama` Python module:

```
pip install ollama
```

Here's all the code for the simple chatbot:

```python
# simple_chatbot.py
# pip install ollama
import ollama

# Must be a model you have pulled with Ollama
model = "tinyllama"
print("\nSimple Ollama Chatbot (model: tinyllama)")
print("Type your prompt, or 'quit' to exit.\n")
while True:
    # Get prompt from user.
    prompt = input("You: ").strip()
    if prompt.lower() == "quit":
        print("Goodbye!")
        break
    try:
        # Get response from the Ollama model.
        response = ollama.chat(model=model, messages=[{"role": "user",
"content": prompt}], stream=False)
        print("Bot:", response["message"]["content"])
    except Exception as e:
        print(f"Error: {e}")
```

I'll step through key components of the code next.

The `import ollama` line is required to load the `ollama` module to simplify interacting with Ollama models from Python. The line `model = "tinyllama"` indicates which Ollama model you want to use. This must be a model you've already downloaded using `ollama pull`.

The line `prompt = input("You: ").strip()` puts the word `You` on the screen as a prompt (you can change that to any text you want). Then the script does nothing until the user types a prompt and presses Enter. When that happens, the user's text is stored in the variable named `prompt`, with any leading and trailing spaces removed by the `.strip()` method.

The next line sends that prompt to the chatbot, waits for a response, and stores the response in a variable named `response`:

```
response = ollama.chat(model=model, messages=[{"role": "user", "content": prompt}], stream=False)
```

Let's dissect that line:

Code	Description
`ollama.chat`	Uses the `chat` method of the `ollama` module to send a prompt to the AI mode and accept the resulting reply
`model=model`	Tells `ollama` to use the model previously stored in the variable named `model` (`tinyllama` in this example)
`messages=`	Defines a dictionary of information about the prompt
`"role": "user"`	Indicates that the prompt is coming from a human user rather than another model or system
`"content": prompt`	Defines the content of the prompt being sent as the text currently stored in the variable named `prompt`
`stream=False`	Ensures that the response is returned all at once, rather than in chunks, which makes it easier to store that information in the variable named `response`

This is a super simple chatbot that doesn't remember conversations, which may feel strange if you've been using conversation AI online for a while. But you can add some conversational ability to your own Python AI apps, as I explain in the next section.

Creating a Conversational Chatbot

Our super simple chatbot has one weakness: It doesn't remember anything about an ongoing conversation. For example, if my first prompt is "My name is Alan. Say hello," it will indeed say hello to me. If my second prompt is "What is my name?," it won't know.

Let's look at a local chatbot that can carry on a conversation for one session. For the sake of variety, I'll use the `llama3.2` model, which is more powerful than `tinyllama` but terribly slow if your computer lacks GPU or neural processing to speed things up. If it's too slow for you to even work with, you can use the `tinyllama` model instead. I'll start by showing you the script in its entirety:

```python
# converse_bot.py
# Install Ollama: Download and install Ollama from ollama.ai.
# pip install ollama.
import ollama
import sys

def initialize_model(model_name):
    # Initialize the Ollama model and check if it's available.
    try:
        # Strip any tag (for example, :latest) from the name for comparison.
        base_model_name = model_name.split(":")[0]

        # Get list of installed models.
        model_list = ollama.list()
        available_models = []

        if "models" in model_list:
            for model in model_list["models"]:
                name = model.get("model")
                if name:
                    # Strip any tag from installed model name for comparison.
                    installed_base_name = name.split(":")[0]
                    available_models.append(installed_base_name)

        if base_model_name not in available_models:
            print(f"Error: Model '{model_name}' not found. Available models:
{available_models}")
            sys.exit(1)

        return model_name
    except Exception as e:
```

```python
        print(f"Error connecting to Ollama: {e}")
        sys.exit(1)

def get_response(model_name, prompt, conversation_history):
    # Generate a response from the Ollama model with conversation context.
    try:
        # Prepare the messages with conversation history.
        messages = conversation_history + [{"role": "user", "content": prompt}]

        # Get the response from the model.
        response = ollama.chat(
            model=model_name,
            messages=messages,
            stream=False
        )

        # Extract and return the response content.
        return response["message"]["content"]
    except Exception as e:
        return f"Error generating response: {e}"

def main(model):
    # Main function to run the chatbot
    model_name = initialize_model(model)
    conversation_history = []

    print("Welcome to the Ollama Chatbot! Type 'exit' or 'quit' to stop.")
    print("Start chatting below:\n")

    # Initialize user prompt.
    user_prompt = ''
    while user_prompt.lower() not in ('quit', 'exit'):
        # Get user input.
        user_prompt = input("Type your prompt, or \"quit\": ").strip()

        # Check for exit commands.
        if user_prompt.lower() in ["exit", "quit"]:
            print("Goodbye!")
            break

        # Skip empty inputs.
        if not user_prompt:
            print("Please enter a message.")
            continue
```

```
        # Add user input to conversation history.
        conversation_history.append({"role": "user", "content": user_prompt})


        # Get response from the model.
        response = get_response(model_name, user_prompt, conversation_history)


        # Print the response.
        print(f"\n\nBot: {response}\n")


        # Add bot response to conversation history.
        conversation_history.append({"role": "assistant", "content": response})


if __name__ == "__main__":
    # Specify which Ollama model to use.
    model="llama3.2"
    main(model)
```

TIP

In this script, you can use any Ollama model you've already pulled by changing the model name in the line that reads `model="llama3.2"`. If the large model is too slow for your computer, try changing that to `model = "tinyllama"` as in the previous script example.

The real meat of the conversational AI script is virtually identical to the super-simple chatbot I show you in the previous section. You use this one line of code to send the prompts (messages) to the model and store its reply in a variable named `response`:

```
response = ollama.chat(
    model=model_name,
    messages=messages,
    stream=False
)
```

The main trick to this script is in the variable named `messages`, which no longer contains just what the user typed at the prompt. Instead, `messages` contains every prompt the user has entered since starting this session with the script. So, it's not really a matter of the model "remembering" the conversation; instead, the script "reminds" the model of every prompt entered prior to the current prompt.

In the `main()` function, the following line asks the user to type their prompt and stores what the user typed in the variable named `user_prompt`:

```
user_prompt = input("Type your prompt, or \"quit\": ").strip()
```

After the user types a prompt, the next line of code adds the key "role", the value "user", the key "content", and whatever prompt the user typed to a list named conversation_history:

```
conversation_history.append({"role": "user", "content": user_prompt})
```

Every time the chatbot responds, that response is also added to the conversation history. However, the chatbot's role is "assistant", not "user", so the chatbot can distinguish between user prompts and its own replies based on the role key. After a brief conversation, that list of dictionaries may look something like this:

```
{"role": "user", "content": "My name is Alan. Say hello."},
{"role": "assistant", "content": "Hi, Alan!"},
{"role": "user", "content": "I live in the USA. Where do you live?"},
{"role": "assistant", "content": "We both live in the USA!"},
{"role": "user", "content": "What is my name and where do I live?"},
{"role": "assistant", "content": "Your name is Alan. You live in the USA."}]
```

The user, of course, never sees that conversation history. From the user's perspective, the chatbot is remembering what the user said previously, on its own. But what's really going on, behind the scenes, is that the script is resubmitting every prompt and every response each time it queries the model, and the model uses that information to give the appearance of "remembering" the ongoing conversation.

This larger script example does significantly more exception handling than the super-simple script example did. Comments in the code should make it relatively easy to understand what's going on, but the main thing I want you to gain from this script is that the trick to making an LLM carry on a "conversation" (rather than just answer one prompt at a time) is to resubmit the entire conversation to the chatbot every time you post a prompt.

Of course, after you quit the script, the conversation history ceases to exist. The memory of that conversation won't carry over to the next time you run the script.

Developing an AI Image Generator

Creating images is another popular AI pastime, and a quick and easy way to get free — and copyright-free — images for a website or other project. In this section, I show you how to create your own Python script that can create images for free.

As I write this, Pollinations.AI (`https://pollinations.ai`) provides free access to online AI image generation without an API key or even requiring you to sign up. You can learn more about their products, and any current limitations, at their website. But to get started and try it out, you can just start here.

The first script allows you to type in a prompt describing the image you want to create, and then asks how many images you want. The script generates the requested number of images and saves them to a folder. Here's the entire script:

```python
# simple_images.py
# pip install requests
import requests
import os
import uuid
import time
from datetime import datetime


# Generate one image using pollinations.ai.
def generate_image(prompt, save_path, retries=3):
    # Adding a uuid ensures that the prompt and the generated image are unique.
    unique_prompt = f"{prompt}-{str(uuid.uuid4())}"
    url = f"https://image.pollinations.ai/prompt/{unique_prompt}"
    for attempt in range(retries):
        try:
            response = requests.get(url, stream=True)
            if response.status_code == 200:
                # Use current datetime for filename
                timestamp = datetime.now().strftime("%Y%m%d_%H%M%S_%f")
                image_path = os.path.join(save_path, f"{timestamp}.png")
                with open(image_path, "wb") as f:
                    for chunk in response.iter_content(chunk_size=8192):
                        f.write(chunk)
                return image_path
            else:
                print(f"Error: Status code {response.status_code}")
                time.sleep(5)
        except requests.RequestException as e:
            print(f"Request failed: {e}. Retrying {attempt + 1}/{retries}...")
            time.sleep(5)
    return None
```

```
def generate_all_images(prompt, save_path, num_images):
    print(f"\n\nGenerating {num_images} images...please wait.")
    # Create the save path if it doesn't exist.
    os.makedirs(save_path, exist_ok=True)
    # Generate each imaget.
    for i in range(num_images):
        image_path = generate_image(prompt, save_path)
        if image_path:
            print(f"Generated image {i+1} of {num_images} in {image_path}")
        else:
            print(f"Failed to generate image {i+1}")

if __name__ == "__main__":
    # Set the save path and prompt for generating images.
    save_path = "generated_images"

    # Prompt at runtime.
    prompt = input("Enter your image prompt: ").strip()
    while not prompt:
        prompt = input("Prompt cannot be empty: ").strip()
    while True:
        try:
            num_images = int(input("How many images? ").strip())
            if num_images > 0:
                break
            else:
                print("Please enter a positive integer.")
        except ValueError:
            print("Please enter a valid integer.")

    # Generate the images and show indicate when done.
    generate_all_images(prompt, save_path, num_images)
    print(f"{num_images} images added to {save_path}.")
```

The simple image generator uses the `request` moule to access the web, so make sure you `pip install requests` into your virtual environment before running this script.

When you run the script, you'll first see the following:

```
Enter your image prompt:
```

Describe the image you want to create. For example:

```
A rainbow-colored butterfly hovering near a giant red hibiscus flower. In the
    background a futuristic neon cyberpunk dystopian urban landscape.
```

Press Enter and you'll see the following prompt:

```
How many images?
```

As with any free AI, Pollinations.AI has some limitations. The limitations aren't specifically stated on their site as I write this, but I suggest limiting yourself to four images or so per prompt, so as not to overuse the system.

Press Enter after entering your number and wait a bit. You should see a message each time a new image is generated, and then a final message indicating when the image generation is done. The images will be stored in a subfolder named gener-ated_images in the same folder as your code. Each image will have a unique file-name based on the date and time it was created, as shown in Figure 15-5.

FIGURE 15-5:
AI-generated
images created
by simple_
images.py.

Let's look at the key components of the code related to connecting to the AI, generating the images, and saving them to a local folder. Down near the bottom of the code, this line specifies where to save the images (feel free to replace "generated_images" with a folder name or path of your own choosing):

```
save_path = "generated_images"
```

The generate_image() function does most of the work of generating one image and saving it. Near the top of that function are these two mysterious lines:

```
unique_prompt = f"{prompt}-{str(uuid.uuid4())}"
url = fhttps://image.pollinations.ai/prompt/{unique_prompt}
```

As it turns out, if you submit the exact same prompt to Pollinations.AI multiple times, you'll likely get four of the exact same image. The uuid4() method returns a unique string of random characters and appends them to the image prompt. This ensures a unique prompt for each submission, which helps to add some variety to the generated images.

The second line is the URL to which the code will send the prompt and then wait for it to return an image.

As with most scripts in this book, this one has plenty of exception handling to handle errors gracefully. Right off the bat, you may notice that the loop to generate one image starts with the following line:

```
for attempt in range(retries):
```

That retries value is defined in the function call as retries=3. For any one prompt, it will try three times to get one image. To get one image, the script uses the simple line:

```
response = requests.get(url, stream=True)
```

The url (shown earlier) is the URL for generating one image from a prompt. The stream=True allows a large image file to be downloaded in chunks, which helps to ensure the entire file is fully downloaded before the response variable gets its value.

The next lines execute only if the server sends the image and a response code of 200. That 200 number indicates that the transaction was successful. At the point the script generates a filename from the current datetime, with a.png extension, and saves the image file to that filename.

```
if response.status_code == 200:
    # Use current datetime for filename
    timestamp = datetime.now().strftime("%Y%m%d_%H%M%S_%f")
    image_path = os.path.join(save_path, f"{timestamp}.png")
    with open(image_path, "wb") as f:
        for chunk in response.iter_content(chunk_size=8192):
            f.write(chunk)
```

The `response.iter_content(chunk_size=8192)` reads the response body in chunks of 8KB, which is memory-efficient for large files. Each chunk is written to a file (`output_image.png`) in binary mode (`"wb"`).

When working with images, it's important to specify binary as the write mode (`wb`), because you're not dealing with textual data. The data is stored as raw bytes, which is essential to preserving the integrity of the image.

The script works fine as is. But you may be thinking that a purely textual interface for an app that deals in images is a bit strange. It would be nice to present a more graphical interface that would allow the user to see the image on the screen. In the next section, I show you how to display the image onscreen in a more graphical manner.

Showing the generated image onscreen

The purely text interface of Python at the command line is fine for automation. But now that we're dipping our toes into AI and images, a more graphical approach may be preferred.

For the next script, you'll use `gradio` to create a web page that presents a text box for typing a prompt, a button, and a place to show the generated image when it's done, as shown in Figure 15-6.

`gradio` is a Python library that allows you to write Python code to create interactive web interfaces, which are displayed as standard web pages in a browser. `gradio` also provides tools for interfacing with AI online, so it suits our needs perfectly here.

To use `gradio` in a script, you just set up your project folder and virtual environment as usual. Activate your virtual environment. Then use `pip install` to install `gradio`. You'll also use the `requests` module to access AI over the internet, and `Pillow` to help with downloaded images. So, before you get started, enter the following command in the Terminal:

```
pip install requests gradio Pillow
```

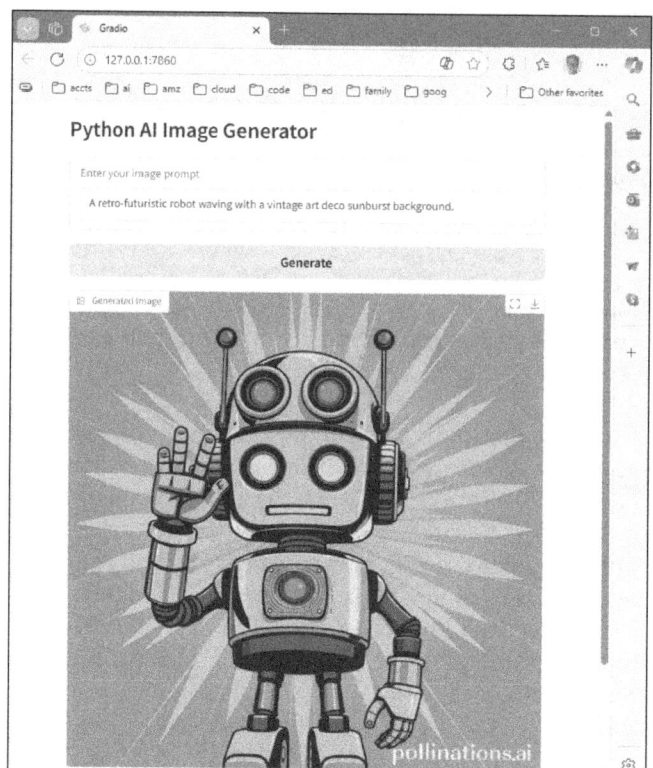

Next, I'll show you all the code for script. After the code, I explain the key components that make it work. You may be pleasantly surprised to see how little code it takes to pull off this feat.

```
# gradio_image.py
# pip install requests gradio Pillow
import requests
import gradio as gr
from PIL import Image
import time
import io


# Generate one image based on a prompt using Pollinations.AI.
def generate_image(prompt, status_box, retries=3):
    url = f"https://image.pollinations.ai/prompt/{prompt}"
    for attempt in range(retries):
        try:
            status_box = gr.update(value=f"Attempt {attempt+1}:
Requesting image...")
```

```
            yield None, status_box
            response = requests.get(url, stream=True)
            if response.status_code == 200:
                status_box = gr.update(value="Image generated.")
                yield Image.open(io.BytesIO(response.content)), status_box
                return
            else:
                status_box = gr.update(value=f"Error: Status code {response.
    status_code}")
                yield None, status_box
                time.sleep(2)
        except requests.RequestException as e:
            status_box = gr.update(value=f"Request failed: {e}. Retrying...")
            yield None, status_box
            time.sleep(2)
    status_box = gr.update(value=f"Failed to generate image after {retries}
    attempts.")
    yield None, status_box


# Call function to generate the image, then show results on page.
def gradio_generate(prompt):
    if not prompt.strip():
        yield None, gr.update(value="Prompt cannot be empty.")
        return
    yield None, gr.update(value="Starting generation...")
    for image, status in generate_image(prompt, status_box=None):
        yield image, status


# Create the interface with text boxes, buttons, and image output.
with gr.Blocks() as demo:
    gr.Markdown("# Python AI Image Generator")
    prompt = gr.Textbox(label="Enter your image prompt")
    generate_btn = gr.Button("Generate")
    output_image = gr.Image(label="Generated Image")
    status = gr.Textbox(label="Status / Error Messages", interactive=False)

    generate_btn.click(
        gradio_generate,
        inputs=prompt,
        outputs=[output_image, status]
    )


if __name__ == "__main__":
    demo.launch()
```

Running the script shows the following in the Terminal:

```
* Running on local URL:  http://127.0.0.1:7860
```

To see the web page, you need to browse to the URL shown in the first line. On Windows or Linux, you can just Ctrl+click the underlined link. On macOs, ⌘+click the link. Your default web browser should open, showing a page that looks like Figure 15-7.

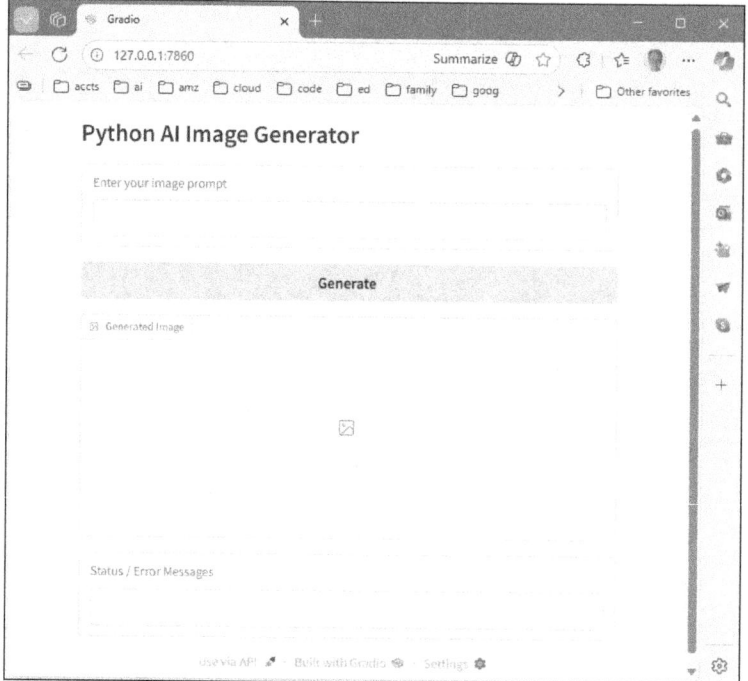

FIGURE 15-7: gradio web interface for generating an image.

When the web page opens, type your image prompt, click Generate, and wait a few seconds. When you see the image, you can download a copy by clicking the Download icon near the upper-right corner of the image control.

TIP

The official documentation for gradio can be found on the Gradio website at www.gradio.app/docs.

All the controls on the web page are created using this block of code. Note that in the imports section near the top of the script, I use the line import gradio as gr to import gradio, so gr is an abbreviated name I can use in the rest of the code to reference gradio.

```
# Create the interface with text boxes, buttons, and image output.
with gr.Blocks() as demo:
    gr.Markdown("# Python AI Image Generator")
    prompt = gr.Textbox(label="Enter your image prompt")
    generate_btn = gr.Button("Generate")
    output_image = gr.Image(label="Generated Image")
    status = gr.Textbox(label="Status / Error Messages", interactive=False)
```

The first line creates a gr.Blocks object, which is basically a collection of controls on a web page. In this case, that block is named demo. gr.Markdown() shows the page title. gr.Textbox() shows the text box and label "Enter your image prompt". gr.Button() creates the button. The gr.Image() creates the image control that will display the generated image (when available).

The last text box, named status, shows progress indicators and error messages. It's not interactive because it's not intended as a box where the user enters text, but rather as a way for the script to show information.

Then comes the following block of code:

```
generate_btn.click(
    gradio_generate,
    inputs=prompt,
    outputs=[output_image, status]
)
```

That block of code tells Python what to do when the user clicks the generate_btn button. When clicked, the button calls a function named gradio_generate() (which I show you in a moment). It passes into that function whatever prompt the user typed into the prompt text box. The last line, outputs=[output_image, status], indicates that the function will generate two outputs: one named output_image (which will be the generated image), and the other named status (a text message indicating status or an error message).

The very last line of code, demo.launch(), is what assembles the web page that the browser shows and then displays the instructions to access that page at the URL http://127.0.0.1:7860.

TECHNICAL
STUFF

In the web browser, you can right-click an empty spot on the generated web page and choose View Page Source (or the equivalent option in your browser) to see the Hypertext Markup Language (HTML), Cascading Style Sheets (CSS), and JavaScript that Python generated from your gradio code.

So, how does the rest work? Recall that clicking the Generate button calls a function named gradio_generate() and passes in the user's prompt as input. That function, in turn, does some quick exception handling to ensure that the prompt isn't empty.

```
# Call function to generate the image, then show results on page.
def gradio_generate(prompt):
    if not prompt.strip():
        yield None, gr.update(value="Prompt cannot be empty.")
        return
    yield None, gr.update(value="Starting generation...")
    for image, status in generate_image(prompt, status_box=None):
        yield image, status
```

Note the use of the keyword yield in that function. The word yield is a gradio keyword that creates a generator function that can return multiple values. In other words, it supports *streaming outputs* (where a function can return different values over time), which is exactly what you need if you want to show a progress indicator as a function is running.

In this example, the yield keyword returns two values each time it's called. The first value is placed in the image placeholder, where the generated image appears, after it's completed. The second value is displayed in the status box, which keeps the user informed of status or any error messages.

In the gradio_generate() function, this first yield line is as follows:

```
yield None, gr.update(value="Prompt cannot be empty.")
```

It shows nothing (None) in the image box, and an error message ("Prompt cannot be empty.") in the status text box if the user didn't provide a prompt. Otherwise, the following line executes:

```
yield None, gr.update(value="Starting generation...")
```

This line still leaves the image box empty. But the status text box displays the text to tell the user that image generation has started.

The next line sets up a for loop to call the function named in generate_image() repeatedly. The prompt parameter is the user's prompt for creating the image. The status_box parameter gets None as input, because there is no status to report at this moment in time.

```
for image, status in generate_image(prompt, status_box=None):
```

Within that loop, `yield image, status` simply updates that image box and status box as the `generate_image()` function is running.

The `generate_image()` function does the actual image generation. There's considerable exception handling in that function to manage unforeseen problems. In fact, for any one image the `retries=3` parameter will give the AI three chances to fully generate the image before giving up. The most important lines of code in the `generate_image()` function are the following:

```
if response.status_code == 200:
    status_box = gr.update(value="Image generated.")
    yield Image.open(io.BytesIO(response.content)), status_box
    return
```

The response code of `200` indicates that no errors have occurred and an image was returned. When that happens, the `status_box` text is set to `"Image generated."`, and the generated image is displayed in the image box via `Image.open(io.BytesIO(response.content))` where `response.content` is the content of what the AI image generator returned to the calling code.

TIP

As a user, after the image appears in the browser, you can hover the mouse pointer over the image and click Download to save a copy.

Be aware that closing the browser window doesn't end the Python script. To get back to a normal command line, click inside VS Code's Terminal window and press Ctrl+C or ⌘+C on macOS, to interrupt the current session and end the script.

Hitting up Hugging Face

Hugging Face (`https://huggingface.co`) is a popular website for sharing AI models and applications that you're free to use. They offer an inference API that you can access via Python to generate AI text and images using a variety of models.

Unfortunately, you can't use Hugging Face to generate images entirely for free. They do offer a free tier where you can generate a few images using a script like the one shown in this chapter, so at least you can learn some things and try out your code for free. But if you want to continue using Hugging Face AI, you'll need to set up a paid account. See the Hugging Face website for more information on switching to a paid account if you run out of free credits and want to pursue this type of coding further.

To use Hugging Face, even for free, you'll need to first set up a free account. Then you'll need an API token, which is basically the same thing as an API key. You can get one at `https://huggingface.co/settings/tokens` after you set up your account.

TIP

Chapter 9 discusses APIs and API keys in detail.

I'll show you a complete script for generating images from Hugging Face in a moment. But to get started with this script, set up a folder and virtual environment as you normally would. Activate your virtual environment, and enter the following command to install all the required dependencies:

```
pip install gradio requests Pillow python-dotenv
```

In keeping with security best practices (and good habits), I suggest you also create a .env file and store your API key there. Figure 15-8 shows an example.

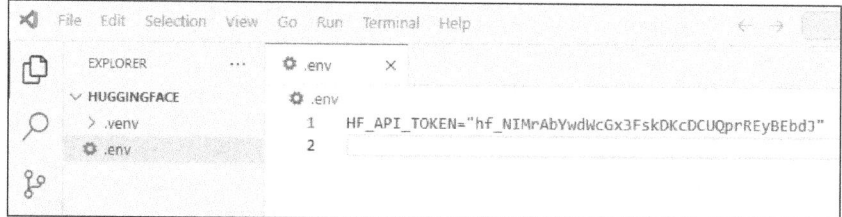

FIGURE 15-8:
A .env file with
an API token for
Hugging Face.

REMEMBER

The API key in Figure 15-8 is fake and used only as an example. Make sure to put your own API key in your own .env file.

Here's all the code for the script to generate images using a Hugging Face model. As in the previous code example, I use `gradio` to provide a nice graphical interface that can show the generated image.

```
# hugging_face.py
# pip install gradio requests Pillow python-dotenv
import gradio as gr
import requests
from PIL import Image
import io
import os
from dotenv import load_dotenv

# Get API token from https://huggingface.co/settings/tokens.
```

```python
# Load environment variables from .env file
load_dotenv()
HF_API_TOKEN = os.getenv("HF_API_TOKEN")

# Using Stable Diffusion XL, a reliable free model on Hugging Face
MODEL_URL = "https://api-inference.huggingface.co/models/stabilityai/stable-
    diffusion-xl-base-1.0"
def generate_image(prompt):
    # Generate an image from a text prompt using Hugging Face API.
    if not HF_API_TOKEN:
        return None, "Error: Please set your HF_API_TOKEN environment variable"

    if not prompt or prompt.strip() == "":
        return None, "Error: Please enter a prompt"

    headers = {
        "Authorization": f"Bearer {HF_API_TOKEN}"
    }

    # For the inference API, we send the prompt as simple JSON.
    payload = {
        "inputs": prompt
    }

    try:
        # Make request to Hugging Face API.
        response = requests.post(MODEL_URL, headers=headers, json=payload,
timeout=120)

        if response.status_code == 200:
            # Convert response to PIL image.
            image = Image.open(io.BytesIO(response.content))
            return image, f"Image generated successfully for: '{prompt}'"
        elif response.status_code == 503:
            return None, "Model unavailable, please try again later"
        elif response.status_code == 401:
            return None, "Authentication error, check your API token"
        elif response.status_code == 400:
            return None, f"Bad request: {response.json() if response.content
    else 'Invalid prompt'}"
        else:
            error_msg = response.json() if response.content else response.text
            return None, f"Error {response.status_code}: {error_msg}"
```

```python
        except requests.exceptions.Timeout:
            return None, "Request timed out. Please try again."
        except Exception as e:
            return None, f"Error: {str(e)}"


def create_interface():
    # Create and configure the Gradio interface
    with gr.Blocks(title="AI Image Generator", theme=gr.themes.Soft()) as
    interface:
        gr.Markdown("# AI Image Generator")
        gr.Markdown("Generate images from text prompts using Hugging Face")

        with gr.Row():
            with gr.Column(scale=2):
                prompt_input = gr.Textbox(
                    label="Image Prompt",
                    placeholder="Enter your image description (e.g., 'a sunset
    over mountains')",
                    lines=3,
                    max_lines=5
                )

                generate_btn = gr.Button(
                    "Generate Image",
                    variant="primary",
                    size="lg"
                )

                status_output = gr.Textbox(
                    label="Status",
                    interactive=False,
                    show_label=True
                )

            with gr.Column(scale=2):
                image_output = gr.Image(
                    label="Generated Image",
                    type="pil",
                    interactive=False
                )

        # Set up the button event handler.
        generate_btn.click(
            fn=generate_image,
```

```
            inputs=[prompt_input],
            outputs=[image_output, status_output],
            show_progress=True
        )


        # Allow Enter key in lieu of clicking button.
        prompt_input.submit(
            fn=generate_image,
            inputs=[prompt_input],
            outputs=[image_output, status_output],
            show_progress=True
        )

    return interface

if __name__ == "__main__":
    # Create and launch the interface.
    interface = create_interface()

    # Launch with public sharing disabled by default.
    # Set share=True if you want a public link.
    interface.launch(
        server_name="127.0.0.1",
        server_port=7860,
        share=False,
        show_error=True,
        quiet=False
    )
```

The gradio code for generating the user interface is in the bottom half of the script, starting with the create_interface() function. That function contains the code necessary to create the web interface shown in Figure 15-9, which includes a text box for typing an image prompt, a button to submit the prompt, a Status text box for showing a progress indicator or error messages, and an image control for showing the generated image.

The code indented under if __name__ == "__main__" is the code that launches the script and initially shows the following prompt in the Terminal.

```
* Running on local URL:  http://127.0.0.1:7860
```

When you see that prompt, just Ctrl+click the link in Windows or Linux or ⌘+click the link on macOS. The interface will open in your default web browser. Type in your prompt, click Generate Image, and wait for the image to appear.

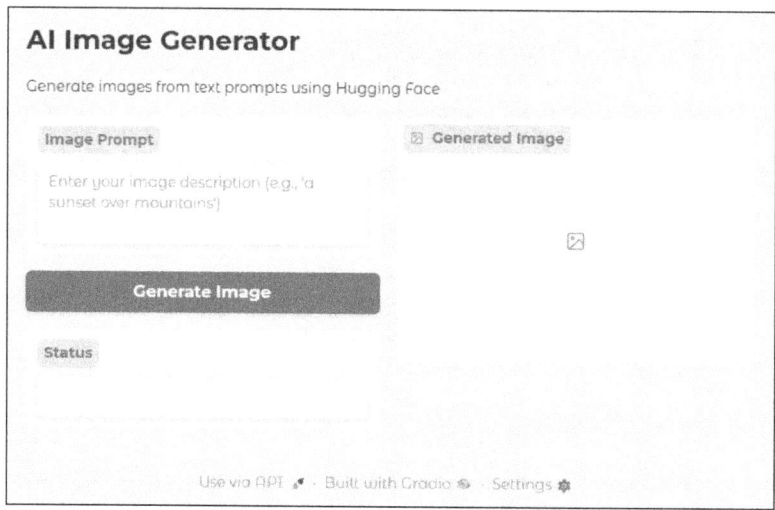

FIGURE 15-9:
gradio user
interface for
generating
AI images.

The actual image generation takes place higher up in the script. These first lines get the API token from the .env file and set up the URL for accessing a Hugging Face image generator. I used an older Stable Diffusion model because it's reliable and likely to give you successful results on your first try. But you can change the URL to use any image generation model that Hugging Face offers.

```
# Load environment variables from .env file.
load_dotenv()
HF_API_TOKEN = os.getenv("HF_API_TOKEN")

# Using Stable Diffusion XL, a reliable free model on Hugging Face
MODEL_URL = https://api-inference.huggingface.co/models/stabilityai/
    stable-diffusion-xl-base-1.0
```

The function that starts with def generate_image(prompt) generates the image from the user's prompt. There's quite a bit of exception handling in there to handle all the things that could go wrong (but hopefully won't). The next lines set up the headers and payload that need to be sent to Hugging Face. The headers provide your authorization (API token), and the payload is the image prompt:

```
headers = {
    "Authorization": f"Bearer {HF_API_TOKEN}"
}

# For the inference API, we send the prompt as simple JSON.
payload = {
    "inputs": prompt
}
```

This next line sends the request to Hugging Face and stores the response in a variable named response:

```
response = requests.post(MODEL_URL, headers=headers, json=payload, timeout=120)
```

The response includes a response.status_code, which will be 200 if all went well. Otherwise, that response.status_code will be some other number, and you can see lots of exception handling for those other numbers as well. Assuming all went well, this line put the generated image into a variable named image:

```
image = Image.open(io.BytesIO(response.content))
```

TECHNICAL STUFF

The io.BytesIO(response.content) wraps the raw image bytes in the response content into an object that's more like what you'd get when opening an image file. This allows the bytes to be treated as if they were read from a file, which is necessary because Image.open expects a file-like object or a file path to put into that image variable.

Assuming all went will with image generate and you have a viable image in the image variable, the following line in the function returns the image and some status text to the calling code:

```
return image, f"Image generated successfully for: '{prompt}'"
```

That function was called by gradio down in that section of code, which tells Python what to do with the two returned values.

Not to confuse things, but you actually call generate_image() from two different gradio blocks, and each block contains code telling Python what to do with the returned image and status text:

```
# Set up the button event handler
generate_btn.click(
    fn=generate_image,
    inputs=[prompt_input],
    outputs=[image_output, status_output],
    show_progress=True
)

# Allow Enter key in lieu of clicking button
prompt_input.submit(
    fn=generate_image,
```

```
    inputs=[prompt_input],
    outputs=[image_output, status_output],
    show_progress=True
)
```

I use two blocks of `gradio` code where the first block responds to a click on the Generate Image button, and the second responds to the user pressing Enter in the Image Prompt text box (because I don't know which of those two things the user is likely to do after typing a prompt). The outputs=[image_output, status_output] in each of those blocks direct the returned image to the image control named image_output and direct the returned text to the status_output text box.

As I mention in the previous example, closing the browser doesn't end the Python script. Click inside the Terminal window in VS Code and press Ctrl+C or ⌘+C on macOS to end the script and current session before modifying and rerunning the script.

5

The Part of Tens

Appreciate the top ten Zen of Python aphorisms.

Know what to do with the top ten error messages.

Chapter **16**

Top Ten Zen of Python Guidelines

The Zen of Python is a philosophy of writing code that emphasizes clarity, simplicity, and practicality — code that's easy for you, and perhaps other developers, to understand, modify, and maintain. Being Pythonic means writing code that adheres to the Zen of Python principles.

The Zen of Python consists of 19 aphorisms or principles. Entering the command `import this` at a Python command prompt lists these 19 aphorisms, but you won't get any details or examples that way. In this chapter, I go through the top ten Zen of Python principles, with some explanations and examples to give you a better understanding.

Beautiful Is Better than Ugly

This principle emphasizes that code should be aesthetically pleasing, readable, and elegant, prioritizing clarity and simplicity over convoluted or messy solutions. In the context of Python, "beautiful" code is intuitive, maintainable, and aligns with the language's idiomatic style, whereas "ugly" code is overly complex, hard to read, or unnecessarily obscure.

So, what are some things that can make code beautiful? Think in terms of being able to read and instantly understand its intent. Think in terms of:

>> **Readability:** Beautiful code is easy to understand at a glance, even for someone unfamiliar with the project.

>> **Simplicity:** Beautiful code avoids unnecessary complexity, favoring straight-forward solutions.

>> **Expressiveness:** Beautiful code leverages Python's features to convey intent clearly and concisely.

>> **Maintainability:** Beautiful code is easier to debug, extend, and col-laborate on.

In contrast, ugly code sacrifices these qualities for quick fixes, clever tricks, or overengineered solutions that obscure intent.

Sometimes being beautiful is simply a matter of using fewer words. For example, the following code below uses an `if` statement to determine whether the length of a list is greater than zero:

```
my_list=[1,2,3,4,5]
if len(my_list)>0:
    print("list is not empty")
```

Technically, there's nothing wrong with the code, and it will run as expected. However, Python automatically makes any empty list return `False` when you refer to the list by name in an `if` statement. The name of a non-empty list always returns `True`. So, you could make that code more beautiful by taking advantage of that fact, like this:

```
my_list=[1,2,3,4,5]
if my_list:
    print("list is not empty")
```

That tiny change on the second line may seem insignificant. But when you're working at a professional level and dealing with thousands of lines of code, small changes like that add up.

Here's another example:

```
# Clunky and repetitive
my_dict = {"a": 1, "b": 2}
if "c" in my_dict:
```

```
        value = my_dict["c"]
    else:
        value = 0
    print(value)
```

Again, that code works as written. It creates a dictionary named `my_dic` and populates it with two keys named `"a"` and `"b"`, giving each key a value. Then an `if` statement checks to see whether the dictionary contains a key named `"c"` and assigns `c` a value of `0` if that key doesn't exist.

TIP

If you're wondering whether there's a more beautiful way to write some code you already have, consider copying and pasting the code into artificial intelligence (AI), and asking whether there is a more beautiful or Pythonic way to write that code.

A more elegant way to handle this example would be to use Python's `.get()` method, which allows you to assign a default value to any missing key, on the fly. For example, the following example does exactly what the previous code does, but with fewer lines, making it more beautiful:

```
# Clean and succinct using get()
my_dict = {"a": 1, "b": 2}
value = my_dict.get("c", 0)
print(value)
```

This version is beautiful because it's simpler, cleaner, and easier to read.

Let's look at an example where I create a function named `check_number` that returns `True` if a positive number is passed in; otherwise, it returns `False`:

```
def check_number(n):
    if n > 0:
        return True
    else:
        if n <= 0:
            return False
```

The code, as written, works properly and contains no errors. But here's a more beautiful version of the function that also returns `True` if a positive number is passed in or `False` for any other number:

```
def is_positive(number):
    return number > 0
```

The latter function is more beautiful because its name, `is_positive`, is more descriptive than `check_number` in terms of what the function does and returns. The parameter name, `number`, is more descriptive than just using `n` as a variable name. Performing the test and returning a value is handled by the single line `return number > 0`, as an alternative to the complex `if...else` statement.

Here's one more example where we use some code to create a list of numbers. The additional code creates a second list, containing only even numbers from the original list:

```
my_list = [1, 2, 3, 4, 5]
new_list = []
for i in range(len(my_list)):
    if my_list[i] % 2 == 0:
        new_list.append(my_list[i])
print(new_list)
```

The code works fine as is, but it's bulky and difficult to read. It isn't very pretty to look at either. The following code accomplishes the same thing with far fewer lines and no indentations:

```
numbers = [1, 2, 3, 4, 5]
even_numbers = [num for num in numbers if num % 2 == 0]
print(even_numbers)
```

Not only is the latter code more succinct and easier to read, but using names like `numbers` and `even_numbers` helps to make the code more readable and easier to understand — and, thus, more beautiful!

Explicit Is Better than Implicit

This principle is a way of saying that code should clearly express its intent, avoiding hidden or assumed behavior. Implicit code relies on defaults, side effects, or unclear assumptions, which can obscure meaning and lead to errors. Explicit code, by contrast, makes actions, types, and intentions obvious, improving readability and maintainability.

To clarify the difference between explicit and implicit consider the following:

>> **Explicit code** clearly states what the code does, using precise names, types, or operations.

>> **Implicit code** relies on defaults, magic behavior, or context that isn't immediately obvious to all developers.

Being explicit encourages writing code that is self-documenting and predictable, reducing the need for developers to guess or dig into documentation to understand it.

Let's work through an example of making code more explicit. We'll start with this "ugly" code (referring to the preceding section):

```
def tot(x,y):
    st =x * y
    return x + st
```

The code works — it returns the original value of x with st added, where st is that x value multiplied by y. But what exactly does that get us? Here's a rewrite of the code that's more explicit in terms of what the code does:

```
def total_with_tax(total_sale,sales_tax_rate):
    return round((1 + sales_tax_rate) * total_sale.2)
```

It's easier to tell what's going on in this version. The function name, total_with_tax, gives you a hint as to what the function returns. The names total_sale and sales_tax_rate are much more explicit than x and y, and they give you some clue as to what to pass into the function.

WARNING

Intentionally using abbreviations and single-letter variable names to keep your code compact works against explicitness. Follow PEP 8 guidelines (https://peps.python.org/pep-0008) and use all lowercase variable names that are meaningful, with underscores in place of spaces, to keep your code's meaning explicit.

To add the sales tax amount to the total sale, the function adds the sales tax rate (say, 0.07) to 1, and then multiples that value by the total sale, a simple and accurate way to add sales tax to total_sale. The code is more descriptive just by using better names for things. But we can do more to make the code even more explicit.

Using type hints

Python doesn't require you to declare a type for every value you create. Instead, it uses *dynamic typing,* where you simply enter a value (for example, 10, 123.45, or "Hello") and Python figures out its data type automatically. Although this feature is convenient, it can make code harder to read because the type isn't explicitly shown.

Python *type hints* allow you to specify data types for values passed into and returned from functions. That way, anybody working with your code knows exactly what kind of value to pass into and expect from a function. To use type hints in a function's parameter list, follow the parameter name with a colon and the data type, using one of the abbreviations (int, float, bool, str, list, dict, object, None, and so on).

REMEMBER

If you need a reminder of data types, turn to Chapter 3.

Here is the total_with_tax() function with type hints added to the top line:

```
def total_with_tax(total_sale: float, sales_tax_rate: float) -> float:
    return (1 + sales_tax_rate) * total_sale
```

The type hints show that both total_sale and sales_tax_rate should be the float type, and that the function returns a float as well.

Using comments

Python code comments are ideal for making code more explicit. Referring to the previous example, it may not be clear how to pass in a sales tax rate. A comment for the return type may be useful. You can put the comments above the code, if you like, or you put the comments right inside the function as shown here:

```
def total_with_tax(total_sale: float, sales_tax_rate: float) -> float:
    # total_sale (float): The taxable sale amount (positive number)
    # sales_tax_rate (float): Tax rate as decimal (for example, 0.07 for 7%)
    # Returns float rounded to pennies (two decimal places)
    return round((1 + sales_tax_rate) * total_sale,2)
```

The comments provide info about the values you'd pass into the function and what to expect in return.

Handling errors

Building exception handling into your code helps make code more explicit, by leaving no doubt as to what data isn't acceptable. The sample automation scripts in this book all use exception handling to handle errors gracefully. For this simple example with sales tax calculations, we can add some exception handing to reject negative sales amounts or invalid percentages, like this:

```
def total_with_tax(total_sale: float, sales_tax_rate: float) -> float:
    # total_sale (float): The taxable sale amount (positive number)
    # sales_tax_rate (float): Tax rate as decimal (for example, 0.07 for 7%)
    # Returns float rounded to pennies (two decimal places)
    # Exception handling
    if total_sale < 0:
        raise ValueError("Total sale cannot be negative")
    if not 0 <= sales_tax_rate <= 1:
        raise ValueError("Sales tax rate must be between 0 and 1")
    return round((1 + sales_tax_rate) * total_sale, 2)
```

You could add even more comments to the code, to explain the exception handling, though the error messages in the code ("Total sale cannot be negative" and "Sales tax rate must be between 0 and 1") are self-explanatory.

TIP

Turn to Chapter 3 for more information on exception handling. Chapter 17 also provides information on common exceptions and how to handle them.

With the function written the way it is now, any Python programmer can call the function and handle any errors using a try...except block, like this:

```
if __name__ == "__main__":
    total_sale = 10.00
    sales_tax_rate = 0.07
    try:
        result = total_with_tax(total_sale, sales_tax_rate)
        print(f"Total with tax: ${result}")
    except ValueError as e:
        print(f"Error: {e}")
```

Being specific (and explicit) in your coding makes it easier for others (and perhaps your future self) to really understand the intent of the code and how best to use it.

Simple Is Better than Complex

This principle emphasizes that clear, straightforward solutions are preferable to overly complicated ones. For a beginning programmer, this means writing code that's easy to read, understand, and maintain. Simple code reduces bugs, makes collaboration easier, and helps you focus on solving the problem rather than wrestling with the code itself. To summarize:

- » **Choose clear logic.** Avoid convoluted approaches when a direct one works.

- » **Use readable code.** Write code that others (or your future self) can understand quickly.

- » **Avoid over-engineering.** Don't add unnecessary features or layers of abstraction.

For example, here's a function that accepts a number and returns that number squared:

```
def calculate_square(number):
    result = number ** 2
    return result
```

This function works, but it's unnecessarily verbose. It uses a temporary variable (`result`) and a function when a simpler approach would suffice, like this:

```
def square(number):
    return number * number
```

This version is concise, has a clear name, and directly returns the result. It's easier to read and does the same thing.

TIP

Large functions that perform many operations before returning a value can add to code complexity. Consider decomposing complex functions into smaller, simpler ones. Each function should ideally do one thing well, making testing, debugging, and maintenance easier.

Here's another example where the function returns `True` if passed an even number; otherwise, it returns `False`:

```
def is_number_even(num):
    if num % 2 == 0:
        return True
    else:
        return False
```

This code is overly verbose because it uses an `if...else` structure to return `True` or `False` when the condition itself is already a Boolean. In other words, the expression `num % 2 == 0` returns `True` if `num` is evenly divisible by 2 (that is, if the remainder is zero); otherwise, the expression returns `False`. Here's a much simpler, cleaner way to write this function:

```
def is_even(num):
    return num % 2 == 0
```

This version is shorter and clearer. The expression num % 2 == 0 already evaluates to `True` or `False`, so the function just returns that result.

TIP

If you're looking at your own code, wondering if there's a simpler way to achieve a result, consider copying and pasting that code into AI and asking "Is there a simpler, more Pythonic way to do what this code does?"

Here's an example where the function totals all the numbers in any list that's passed to the function:

```
. def sum_list(numbers) :
     total = 0
     for i in range(len(numbers)):
         total += numbers[i]
     return total
```

The function works. When you're first learning Python, you may see code like this as an example of using a loop. However, lists have a built-in sum() function, which accomplishes the same thing, but with a single line of code:

```
def sum_list(numbers):
    return sum(numbers)
```

To clarify exactly what should be passed into the function, you can add a type hint, like this:

```
def sum_list(numbers: list):
    return sum(numbers)
```

The beauty of this version is that the both the input (a list of numbers) and the output (the sum of numbers) is clearly stated in the minimal code. Python's built-in sum() function is both simpler and more efficient.

REMEMBER

Beginning programmers are often tempted to write complex code to feel "clever" or because they're mimicking something they saw somewhere else. But complex code often leads to more bugs, difficult debugging, and other people misusing your code because they don't understand what the code is about. If you keep things simple, you make your code more reliable and easier to work with.

Complex Is Better than Complicated

For a newbie Python developer, this principle means that it's okay for your code to handle complex tasks or ideas, but it should avoid being unnecessarily complicated. Here's the difference:

>> **Complex code** deals with intricate problems but is structured, readable, and logical. It embraces the necessary complexity of the task while keeping things as straightforward as possible.

>> **Complicated code** is overly tangled, hard to follow, or unnecessarily obscure, making it difficult to understand or maintain.

As a beginner, think of this as choosing a clear path to solve a problem, even if the problem requires multiple steps, rather than creating a messy, hard-to-follow solution. As an example, let's look at a sum of squares function, that calculates the sum of squares for numbers from 1 to n (for example, for $n = 3$, compute $1^2 + 2^2 + 3^2 = 1 + 4 + 9 = 14$). Here's the code:

```
def sum_squares(n):
    result = 0
    for i in range(1,n+1):
        if i != 0:
            result = result + (i * i)
    return result
```

The function works fine as written, but it's a little overcomplicated because:

>> The code includes an unnecessary check (if i != 0) because range(1, n+1) would exclude 0 anyway.

>> The loop iterates one extra time (n+1) and compensates with logic, making it harder to follow.

>> The variable update (result = result + (i * i)) is verbose.

Here's an alternative function that accomplishes exactly the same thing as the original function, but in a cleaner, simpler way:

```
def sum_squares(n):
    return sum(i ** 2 for i in range(1, n + 1))
```

The latter code uses the sum() function, which is a more Pythonic way to handle summation than a loop. For a beginner, the second version may look advanced, but it's actually simpler when you learn basic Python constructs like range and sum. It avoids extra logic and is easier to maintain.

Shortcut methods like sum() are sometimes referred to as *idioms* in Python. Writing code that way is sometimes referred to as *idiomatic programming.* If you're interested in exploring other idioms, consider asking an AI for examples of Python idiomatic programming.

Flat Is Better than Nested

As you probably know by now, code indentations are critical in Python. Unlike other languages that use { and } or other characters to delimit blocks of code, Python relies entirely on indentation level. At times, the indentations can become so deep that it's difficult to read and follow the code.

This principle means avoiding deeply nested layers of logic, such as multiple levels of loops, conditionals, or function calls, because *flat* (less nested) code is easier to read, understand, and maintain. Complex conditionals (nested if statements) and nested loops often contribute to deep indentations, so we'll look at alternatives in the next sections.

Flattening nested conditionals

As an example of nested conditionals, consider this next function, named check_ discount(). It accepts some values and returns one of several possible messages ("You get a 20% discount", "You get a 10% discount", and so on) based on age:

```python
def check_discount(age, member, items):
    if age >= 18:
        if member:
            if items > 5:
                return "You get a 20% discount!"
            else:
                return "You get a 10% discount!"
        else:
            return "No discount for nonmembers."
    else:
        return "No discount for under 18."
```

The code works fine as is — there are no errors in the code — but the deep nesting in all the if...else logic makes the code look complicated. A quick and easy way to flatten (and simplify) that code is to simply not wait until the very end to return a value. Use return statements inside the code to exit the function and return a value when there is no need to check other possibilities. For example, applying that principle to the preceding code yields the less complicated-looking function here:

```
def check_discount(age, member, items):
    if age < 18:
        return "No discount for under 18."
    if not member:
        return "No discount for nonmember."
    if items > 5:
        return "You get a 20% discount!"
    return "You get a 10% discount!"
```

In this flat version, I use *early returns* (return statements inside the if block) to exit the function as soon as a condition is met. Nonmembers are handled and dismissed on discovery. Then it's just a matter of calculating the discount. The code is flattened (and simplified) by checking each condition at the same level of indentation. The logic is easier to follow because you don't need to drill down through nested if statements.

REMEMBER

If your code is too deeply nested, it's difficult to read. Consider copying and pasting that code into any AI and ask AI for tips on how best to flatten that code.

Using list comprehension

In Python, nested loops can create complex, deeply nested code. When dealing with lists, Python's list comprehension can greatly simplify things. *List comprehension* is a concise way to create a new list by applying expression to each item in an existing list (or another iterable, like tuple or range) and (optionally) filtering items based on a condition. It's a flat and readable alternative to using loops for list creation. Here's the syntax for list comprehension:

```
new_list = [expression for item in iterable if condition]
```

Here's what each italicized name represents:

Code	Description
new_list	The resulting list created by the comprehension
expression	The operation or value to include in the new list
item	The variable representing each element in the iterable
iterable	The source of data (for example, a list, tuple, range, or string).
condition	Optional; a filter that includes only items where the condition evaluates to True (for example, item > 0).

Let's look at an example of flattening a couple of nested loops. The following code contains a list of lists. The code uses an outer loop to loop through each item in the list as a whole. The inner loop deals with numbers in one sublist.

```
numbers = [[1, 2, 3], [4, 5, 6], [7, 8, 9]]
evens = []
for sublist in numbers:
    for num in sublist:
        if num % 2 == 0:
            evens.append(num)
print(evens)
```

The code works fine, as written. However, if you wanted to flatten things out to avoid all the deep indentations, this code would do the trick:

```
# Get all even numbers using a list comprehension.
numbers = [[1, 2, 3], [4, 5, 6], [7, 8, 9]]
evens = [num for sublist in numbers for num in sublist if num % 2 == 0]
print(evens)  # Output: [2, 4, 6, 8]
```

The list comprehension flattens the nested loop structure into a single, concise line. It is more Pythonic and easier to read when you're familiar with the syntax. The code creates a new list named evens, consisting of the even numbers from all sublists:

```
evens = [num for sublist in numbers for num in sublist if num % 2 == 0]
```

That expression basically says, "For each num in each sublist in the list numbers, add it to evens if the number is even (that is, if the remainder after division by 2 is zero)." So, you get the new list without the indented nested loops.

Sparse Is Better than Dense

This principle emphasizes that code should avoid unnecessary complexity or clutter. For a beginning programmer, this means writing code that is straightforward and focused, with only the essential elements needed to solve the problem. It prioritizes clarity over cramming too much into a single line or function.

Think of it like writing a short, clear sentence instead of a long, wordy paragraph to explain a simple idea. In programming, this may mean using a simple loop instead of a nested mess of conditions or choosing a clear variable name over a cryptic one. Let's look at a simple task: calculating the square of numbers in a list.

```
numbers = [1, 2, 3, 4, 5]
squared = []
for i in range(len(numbers)):
    squared.append(numbers[i] * numbers[i])
print("The squares are: " + str(squared))
```

This code creates a list of numbers and an empty list named squared, and then it uses a loop to append each number squared to the squared list before printing the result.

The following code accomplishes the same thing but with less code.

```
numbers = [1, 2, 3, 4, 5]
squared = [num * num for num in numbers]
print(f"The squares are: {squared}")
```

In this second example, I'm using list comprehension rather than a loop to create the list named squared, and an f string instead of clunky string concatenation to display the result.

TIP

For sparseness, think in terms of making your code readable at a glance. If there's too much packed into a single line of code, consider breaking it into multiple lines.

This principle encourages you to write code that is as simple and clear as possible while still getting the job done. As a beginner, focus on

» Using clear variable names (for example, num instead of i)

» Leveraging Python's built-in features (like list comprehension) to avoid verbose loops or conditions

» Avoiding unnecessary steps or overcomplicated logic

By keeping your code sparse, you make it easier for yourself (and others) to understand and maintain it later.

Readability Counts

This principle emphasizes that code should be written in a way that is easy for humans to read and understand, prioritizing clarity over cleverness or complexity. Think in terms of people reading your code (teammates in a programming team, or your future self). If you work in a team, consider junior developers who are new to the project and not already familiar with how your team does things. Focus on

>> **Clarity over obscurity:** Use meaningful variable names, clear structure, and straightforward logic.

>> **Human-first design:** Code is read more often than it's written, so optimize for the reader's comprehension.

>> **Pythonic style:** Follow all the guidelines in this chapter to develop a consistent style like you've seen throughout this book.

For readability by humans, descriptive names for variables probably contribute more to readability than any other factor. For example, take a look at the following code. It's not so clear or obvious what the code is doing:

```python
def x(y):
    z=0
    for i in y:
        z+=i
    return z/len(y)
```

The purpose of the code becomes much more apparent when you replace short one-letter variable names with more descriptive names:

```python
def calculate_average(numbers):
    total = 0
    for number in numbers:
        total += number
    return total / len(numbers)
```

Although that code is clear in terms of names of things, it's quite a bit longer than it needs to be. This next function performs the exact same task as the previous one, using a single line of code within the function:

```
def calculate_average(numbers):
    return sum(numbers) / len(numbers)
```

The beauty of the last example is that it simply returns the sum of the numbers passed in by the length of the numbers list, and the code makes that clear without even using any comments.

You can think of code as basically an electrical circuit expressed in words. For readability, think in terms of making those words easy for a human to read rather than easy for a computer to read.

Special Cases Aren't Special Enough to Break the Rule

This principle emphasizes consistency in coding practices, even when you're tempted to make exceptions for unique situations. It urges beginning programmers to stick to established rules, conventions, or patterns in their code, even when a specific situation feels like it deserves a unique solution. In programming, consistency makes code easier to read, maintain, and debug.

In its simplest form, this includes following basic naming conventions, like *snake case* for all variable names (all lowercase letters, underscores in place of spaces). For example, you could easily make up some variables names on the fly, as follows, and your code would run perfectly fine:

```
Dog-Name = "Buddy"
CAT_AGE = 3
snakeLength = 5.2
```

In the long run, your code will be easier to read and understand if you always stick to the snake case convention, like this:

```
dog_name = "Buddy"
cat_age = 3
snake_length = 5.2
```

There's a general rule in Python that a function should always return a consistent data type, such as always returning an integer or always returning a string. Often when writing functions, people are tempted to take the lazy route for handling errors, and just return an error message (string) if the data passed into a function is no good. For example, the following square() function will return a number, squared, as long as you pass in a positive number. But if you pass in a negative number, the function returns a string containing the error message:

```
def square(num):
    if num < 0:
        return "Negative numbers not allowed"  # Special case
    return num * num
```

The preferred way to handle this sort of thing is to always use exception handling, where the function raises an error instead of returning a string.

```
def square(num):
    if num < 0:
        raise ValueError("Negative numbers not allowed")
    return num * num
```

Now the code is consistent with Python's built-in functions: It either returns a valid, consistent data type, or it raises an error when it can't. You can use a try . . . except block to call the function and handle any errors, as follows:

```
if __name__ == "__main__":
    number = -9
    try:
        print(f"{number} squared is {square(number)}")
    except Exception as e:
        print(f"Error: {e}")
```

This approach matches the kind of error handling you see throughout this book. The function consistently returns a number (when it can); otherwise, it returns an error with an explanation of what caused the error. Then the script ends gracefully with no additional error messages.

TIP

The PEP 8 guidelines basically define the rules you don't want to break. When you need a quick summary, ask any AI to summarize the PEP 8 guidelines.

Practicality Beats Purity

This principle emphasizes that real-world usability and effectiveness should take precedence over rigid adherence to idealized rules, standards, or theoretical perfection. In other words, when you're faced with a choice between a "pure" or theoretically correct solution and a practical one that gets the job done efficiently, the practical approach is preferred. Here's a summary:

>> **Purity** refers to following strict rules, conventions, or theoretical ideals, such as adhering to a specific design pattern, enforcing type safety everywhere, or writing code that is academically "perfect."

>> **Practicality** focuses on what works best given constraints like time, resources, readability, or project requirements, even if it means bending rules or using less "elegant" approaches.

A common mistake in this realm is trying to use a class, in honor of object-oriented programming (OOP), to make the code look more modern, even when a simple procedural approach (a function) is simpler and more straightforward for the task at hand. For example, here's a class named DataProcessor that returns a list of numbers with each number squared:

```
# Purist approach: Define a class
class DataProcessor:
    def __init__(self, data):
        self.data = data

    def process(self):
        return [x * 2 for x in self.data]
```

There's nothing wrong with OOP. The code works fines, as shown, and an OOP purist would likely see that as the "correct" way to write the code. To use the class, a programmer would first need to create a DataProcessor object and then calculate a result:

```
processor = DataProcessor([1, 2, 3])
result = processor.process()
```

Python supports OOP programming, but it doesn't demand you use it. Here, a function would likely be a cleaner, simpler approach involving less code and complexity:

```
def process_data(data):
    return [x * 2 for x in data]
```

Using a simple function removes the added step of instantiating an object first. You can get a result with a single line of code:

```
result = process_data([1, 2, 3])
```

The latter approach is more practical and avoids the "purity" of trying to strictly follow a paradigm like OOP.

TECHNICAL STUFF

Using classes makes sense when creating application programming interfaces (APIs) and larger modules that involve a lot of data input and output. There would be nothing impractical about using a class that way. This principle is more about using classes for small, general procedures that are easily handled with simple functions.

Errors Should Never Pass Silently

Most of the scripts you see in this book use considerable exception handling to prevent unforeseen problems from causing a program to crash unexpectedly. This principle emphasizes writing robust, reliable programs that always handle errors properly and gracefully. In other words, a script should always alert the user to any error condition in a way that allows the user (or a programmer, if you're still writing the code) to remedy the situation.

Perhaps the best way to explain this is with a super simple example where a script just asks for two numbers and then returns the result of the first number divided by the second number:

```
# Bad example: Ignoring errors
number1 = float(input("Enter the first number: "))
number2 = float(input("Enter the second number: "))
result = number1 / number2  # This crashes if number2 is 0.
print(f"Result: {result}")
```

The script works fine, as long as the user enters two valid numbers and the second number isn't zero — but that's not the Pythonic way. There are two possible error conditions here: The user doesn't enter two valid numbers, or the user enters a zero for the divisor number. Here's the same code with exception handling added to gracefully handle both kinds of errors:

```
try:
    number1 = float(input("Enter the first number: "))
    number2 = float(input("Enter the second number: "))
```

```
    result = number1 / number2
    print(f"Result: {result}")
except ZeroDivisionError:
    print("Error: You cannot divide by zero!")
except ValueError:
    print("Error: Please enter valid numbers!")
```

Catching and explaining each potential error prevents the script from crashing with an obscure error message.

Chapter 17 covers many common Python errors and includes examples of using exception handling to manage those errors.

Let's look at another example. Here's some code to open a file named sample_data.csv (in the same folder as the script). It does not handle potential errors.

```
# Bad example: Ignoring errors
file_name = "sample_data.csv"
with open(file_name, 'r') as file:
    content = file.read()
print(content)
```

This script, like any script that accesses external files, is prone to problems where the file doesn't exist at the specified location, or the script needs to write something to a file but doesn't have sufficient permissions from the operating system. Adding some basic exception handling to the script solves both problems, informing the user exactly what will happen if the script is unable to perform its task:

```
try:
    file_name = "sample_data.csv"
    with open(file_name, 'r') as file:
        content = file.read()
    print(content)
except FileNotFoundError:
    print(f"Error: The file '{file_name}' was not found!")
except PermissionError:
    print("Error: You don't have permission to read this file!")
```

If you're a beginning programmer, take some time to learn about exception handling, and especially the more common exceptions. Chapter 3 describes the basics of exception handling. Chapter 17 lists the ten most common error messages and includes examples of using exception handling to prevent such errors from crashing your code.

Chapter **17**

Top Ten Python Error Messages

When it comes to tech creativity, error messages are just a fact of life, especially when you're first learning Python and programming. Error messages appear onscreen to alert you when something is wrong. They're usually good at pinpointing the problem, but not so good at telling you what to do about it.

This chapter presents the ten most common Python error messages and what to do to fix the problem and get back on track. Of course, you can also get help from artificial intelligence (AI). When asking AI about a problem with your code, include the code that's giving you problems in your prompt. Often AI can spot and fix the error quite quickly.

Command Not Found

When you're first learning Python, you may often see the following error message in VS Code's Terminal:

```
command not found: python
```

This message is unnerving when you're intending to write Python code. But keep in mind that VS Code is a generic code editor, not tied to any one programming language and not tied to any specific version of Python.

When you first open VS Code, in Windows, you can use py as a stand-in for the python command; use python3 on macOS. For example, in the VS Code Terminal, entering the command py –V on Windows or python3 –V on macOS will reveal the current Python version.

To select a Python version choose View ⇨ Command Palette. If you don't see the option to select an interpreter, type **sel** and then click Python: Select Interpreter. Then click whichever Python version displays as Recommended (unless you regularly work with multiple Python versions and have good reason to choose some older version of Python).

Using the python command directly at the command line in VS Code won't work until you activate a virtual environment. If you've already created one, its folder name will be visible in VS Code's Explorer pane (see Figure 17-1). You don't need to create another virtual environment if the current project already has one.

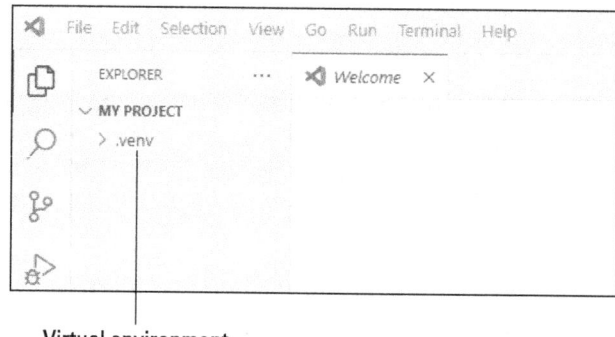

FIGURE 17-1:
A virtual environment is represented by a folder in the Explorer pane.

Virtual environment

If you haven't yet created a virtual environment, create one. In Windows you can enter the following command:

```
py –m venv .venv
```

In Linux or macOS, use the following:

```
python3 –m venv .venv
```

After the virtual environment is created, make sure to activate it. In Windows, enter the following command in the Terminal:

```
.venv\scripts\activate
```

In Linux or macOS, enter this command:

```
source .venv/bin/activate
```

WARNING

Both of these activation examples assume the virtual environment folder is named .venv. If you've named yours differently, use your name in place of .venv in your own command. If it still doesn't work in Windows, try using activate.ps1 rather than activate at the end of the command.

After it's activated, the name of the virtual environment (.venv in this example) will show as part of the command line in VS Code. VS Code will now recognize python as a recognized command, and it will use whatever Python version is associated with that virtual environment. So, on either macOS or Windows, you can enter the following command in the Terminal to determine your working Python version (make sure to use an uppercase letter V):

```
python -V
```

TECHNICAL STUFF

You can also get the current Python version using the following command (all lowercase):

```
python --version
```

No Module Named . . .

If you run a Python and script and see this error message, it usually means you're trying to import a module that isn't part of the Python standard library and isn't available in your virtual environment.

If you already have a virtual environment for your project, activate it (.venv/scripts/activate on Windows, source .venv/bin/activate on macOS). Then try running the script again. If it still fails, most likely you never used pip install to install the module to your virtual environment. You can pip install it into your active virtual environment, if you want, and that should resolve the problem.

If you've never created a virtual environment for your project, you should do so first. Then activate that environment, and `pip install` any dependencies you'll need that aren't part of the Python standard library.

If you're not sure about a module, you can always ask AI about it, including whether you need to `pip install` it and how to write the `import` statement in your code.

A related error, `ModuleNotFoundError`, is covered later in this chapter. You may want to look at that section for clues as well.

SyntaxError

In Python, a `SyntaxError` is typically a typographical error in your code. A `SyntaxError` isn't an exception that you want to catch. Instead, you need to fix each `SyntaxError` as it occurs. Often, VS Code will show a wavy red underline or other marker to show that the error is located in the code. The error message itself may provide additional information.

Here's a simple function that, at first glance, may seem perfectly legitimate:

```
def calculate_sum(a, b)
    result = a + b
    return result
```

When you run the code that contains that function, you'll get an error message that reads `"SyntaxError: expected ':'"`. Python syntax requires that you end a line that starts with `def` with a colon (`:`), and the sample function is missing that. The correction here is to simply add the colon where it's required, as shown here:

```
def calculate_sum(a, b):
    result = a + b
    return result
```

Here's another example where the error may not be apparent at first glance:

```
def greet(name):
    message = "Hello, " + name +
    return message
```

Running that code produces the error "SyntaxError: invalid syntax". VS Code also tells me that the error is in line 2, and it shows a wavy red line at the end of that line. The problem here is that the last + isn't appending anything to the string, so that last + should be removed. The corrected code is simply as follows:

```
def greet(name):
    message = "Hello, " + name
    return message
```

TIP

VS Code usually shows a red wavy line near bad code that may contain a SyntaxError. Touching the mouse pointer to that wavy line provides some information about the error. You can then click Quick Fix (if available) near the error text to get help fixing the problem.

NameError

In Python, a NameError occurs when you call something (a function, a variable, or whatever) by name, but that name doesn't exist. Take a look at the following code:

```
def sum_nums(numlist):
    return sum(numlist)


if __name__ == "__main__":
    numlist = [34, 7, -5, 22.4]
    result = sumnums(numlist)
    print(result)
```

Running that code displays an error message that reads:

```
NameError: name 'sumnums' is not defined. Did you mean: 'sum_nums'?
```

The error is that the first line defines the function name as sum_nums (with an underscore). The subsequent code result = sumnums(numlist) attempts to call sumnums (no underscore), so that name isn't recognized. The solution is to simply call the function by its defined name, result = sum_nums(numlist).

WARNING

Names are case-sensitive in Python. When calling a function, make sure to use the same uppercase/lowercase letters you used in the def statement when creating the function.

TypeError

In Python, a `TypeError` occurs when you try to perform an operation on a data type that isn't supported for that operation. Think of it as Python saying, "I don't know how to do this with these types of values!" It's one of the most common errors you'll encounter when first learning Python.

Confusing strings and numbers are one of the most common `TypeError` mistakes. Here's a simple example:

```
# Code that causes TypeError
x = "5"
y = 10
result = x + y
```

Running that code produces the following error:

```
TypeError: can only concatenate str (not "int") to str
```

The problem here is that the x variable is defined as a string (because it's enclosed in quotation marks). Python doesn't allow you to join a string to a number. You would either have to make both x and y numbers (by removing the quotation marks around 5) or make them both strings, as in "5" and "10".

Here's another example of a `TypeError`:

```
extended_price= 98.99
print (len(extended_price))
```

The error message for this code is `TypeError: object of type 'float' has no len()`. The variable `extended_price` is the `float` data type, because its value is a number with a decimal point, not enclosed in quotation marks. The `len()` function returns the length of a string and causes an error if you try to get the length of a number.

If you're going to allow users to put in their own data while running your code, you can use both `TypeError` and `ValueError` in a `try...except` block to catch either type of error. (A `ValueError` is the correct data type, but a bad value, such as a negative number when a positive number is expected.) The following code shows an example where the user can input a total sale price and tax rate. The code then calls a function named `total_with_tax` to add sales tax to the total, but notice the `try...except` block near the end, to catch both `ValueError` and `TypeError` exceptions if they arise:

```
# Function expects floats and returns a float
def total_with_tax(price: float, tax_rate:float) -> float:
    # Require positive numbers for price and tax_rate
    if price < 0 or tax_rate < 0:
        raise ValueError("Price and tax rate must be non-negative numbers.")
    # Calculate total price with tax if no error.
    total_price = price * (1 + tax_rate)
    return total_price

if __name__ == "__main__":
    try:
        total_sale = float(input("Enter the total sale amount: "))
        tax_rate = float(input("Enter the tax rate (0.065 for 6.5%): "))
        # Get total with sale tax added
        total = total_with_tax(total_sale, tax_rate)
        print(f"The total price with tax is: {total:.2f}")
    except ValueError:
        print("Invalid input. Please enter numeric values for price and
    tax rate.")
    except TypeError as e:
        print(e)
```

IndexError

In Python, an IndexError occurs when you try to access an element in a sequence (like a list, tuple, or string) using an index that's out of range. In simpler terms, you're trying to reach a position that doesn't exist in the sequence. For example, let's say you have a list of five items, and your code asks for the sixth item. Python will throw an IndexError exception because there is no sixth item.

In Python (and most programming languages), the first item in a list is always item 0 (zero), not 1 (one). We humans don't usually think that way. For example, you may think the following code is perfectly legitimate:

```
fruits = ['Apple', 'Banana', 'Cherry']
print(fruits[3])
```

Running that code produces the following error message:

```
IndexError: list index out of range
```

You would expect fruits[3] to be Cherry, the third item in the list. But that's not how Python sees it. Python sees it like this:

```
fruits[0] = 'Apple'
fruits[1] = 'Banana'
fruits[2] = 'Cherry'
```

There is no fruits[3] as far as Python is concerned. That's why the code generates an error.

One way to get around that problem is to try to avoid using loops with range() or some other kind of counter when working with a list. The simplest way to loop through a list using this syntax, which will never encounter an IndexError (because it repeats once for each item in the list and knows to start at 0) is as follows:

```
fruits = ['Apple', 'Banana', 'Cherry']
for fruit in fruits:
    print(fruit)
```

You can do that more compactly using list comprehension like this:

```
fruits = ['Apple', 'Banana', 'Cherry']
[print(fruit) for fruit in fruits]
```

If you need to keep a counter going as you're moving through a list, you can use Python enumeration, which allows you to automatically assign a number to each item in a list. For example, look at this code:

```
my_list = ['apple', 'banana', 'cherry']
for index, value in enumerate(my_list, start=1):
    print(f"Index: {index}. {value}")
```

The syntax here uses a for loop with the name index (which is a counter), and value (an item from the list). The word enumerate lets Python know you want index to be a counter. The name my_list is a reference to the original list. The start=1 lets Python know you want to start counting at 1. The output from that is:

```
1. apple
2. banana
3. cherry
```

Python (and most other programming languages) start lists at 0 rather than 1, because it's more efficient for computers to handle lists that way. If you use enumeration without start=1, items will be numbered starting at 0.

KeyError

In Python, a `KeyError` happens when you try to access a key in a dictionary that doesn't exist. Think of a dictionary like a real-world dictionary: You look up a word (the *key*) to find its definition (the *value*). If the word isn't in the dictionary, you get nothing. In Python, trying to access a nonexistent key raises a `KeyError`.

Here's a simple example where a dictionary named `my_dict` contains two keys — one named `"name"` and the other named `"age"`. Each of those keys has a value assigned to it — `"Annabelle"` for `"name"`, and `65` for `"age"`. That code is then followed by three `print` statements attempting to display data from the dictionary:

```
# A simple dictionary
my_dict = {"name": "Annabelle", "age": 65}

print(my_dict["name"])
print(my_dict["age"])
print(my_dict["gender"])
```

Running that code produces the following output:

```
Annabelle
65
...
KeyError: 'gender'
```

The `KeyError` happens because there is no key named `"gender"`, just keys named `"name"` and `"age"`.

If you're working with keys that are generated by other code, you don't always have great control over the dictionaries. You can use the `.get()` method to request a key value and specify a default if the key doesn't exist. That way, you always get some value for a key and don't risk crashing the entire script. Here's a modified version of the code, where the `"gender"` value becomes `"not specified"` if the `"gender"` key is missing.

```
# A simple dictionary
my_dict = {'name': 'Annabelle', 'age': 65}

print(my_dict['name'])
print(my_dict['age'])
print(my_dict.get('gender', 'not specified'))
```

Now take a look at the following code:

```
# A simple dictionary
my_dict = {'name': 'Annabelle', 'age': 65}

print(my_dict[name])
print(my_dict[age])
```

At first glance, that code may look perfectly fine. But running it produces a NameError. Why? Because the print statements treat name and age as variable names (no quotation marks), not key names. You can easily fix that error by adding quotation marks:

```
print(my_dict['name'])
print(my_dict['age'])
```

If you're working with a lot of imported JavaScript Object Notation (JSON) data that isn't always as reliable as you'd like, and you want to catch KeyError with a try...except block, you can use the standard syntax for try...except, instead of defaulting to some other value:

```
# A simple dictionary
my_dict = {'name': 'Annabelle', 'age': 65}

print(my_dict['name'])
print(my_dict['age'])
try:
    print(my_dict['gender'])
except KeyError:
    print('No gender specified')
```

This is useful when you expect a key may be missing and you want to handle the error without crashing your program and without presuming a default value for the missing key.

AttributeError

In Python, an AttributeError occurs when you try to access or use an attribute (method or property) that doesn't exist on an object. In Python, objects have attributes (data) and methods (functions) associated with their class. Common causes of errors include the following:

- ⟩⟩ Misspelling an attribute or method name

- ⟩⟩ Accessing an attribute that doesn't exist for the object's type

- ⟩⟩ Using a method or attribute on the wrong type of object

- ⟩⟩ Forgetting to initialize an attribute in a class

Here's a super-simple example of creating a list and then trying to add another item to the list:

```
my_list = [1, 2, 3]
my_list.add(4)
```

Running that code generates the following error message:

```
AttributeError: 'list' object has no attribute 'add'
```

In other words, you can't use the word add. The attribute for adding a new item to a list is append( ). So, correcting the error in this case is a simple matter of changing add to append, as follows:

```
my_list = [1, 2, 3]
my_list.append(4)
```

In Python, you can create your own classes, with attributes of your own choosing. Here's an example of a custom class I've created named Car. Each instance of a Car object can have make, model, and year attributes:

```
class Car:
    def __init__(self, make, model, year):
        self.make = make
        self.model = model
        self.year = year
```

With that code, you can create objects using a syntax like my_car = Car("Toyota", "Camry", 2020). Let's say you then try to execute this command:

```
print(f"My car is a {my_car.year} {my_car.make} {my_car.modal}.")
```

That code would fail with the following error message:

```
AttributeError: 'Car' object has no attribute 'modal'. Did you mean: 'model'?
```

The problem here is that in the class, `self.model` defines the attribute name as `model` (with an e). The faulty code attempts to access `my_car.modal` (a misspelling of `model`).

TIP

If you need a quick reminder of attributes for an object, you can always ask AI. Just make sure to use the terms *Python* and *attribute* in your prompt, such as "What are attributes of Python lists?" or "What are attributes of Python dictionaries?"

ModuleNotFoundError

The `ModuleNotFoundError` happens when you try to import a module that doesn't exist, either because you misspelled the filename or because the module isn't part of the Python standard library and you haven't yet installed the module to the active virtual environment. This error can also happen when a filename in the VS Code Explorer pane is the same as a module name, but with a `.py` extension. For example, maybe you're trying to use `matplotlib` as a module, but you have a file named `matplotlib.py` in the current folders.

The simplest example could be a misspelling or case error. For example:

```
import OS
```

That one line of code can fail because you need to spell the name with all lower-case letters, as in:

```
import os
```

Here's another example where the code looks perfectly fine, but it generates a `ModuleNotFoundError`:

```
import requests
```

Here the problem is likely that `requests` isn't part of the Python standard library. The `requests` module needs to be installed before you use it in your code. If you haven't already done so, you should create a virtual environment. Activate your virtual environment, and then enter the command `pip install requests` to bring that module into the virtual environment.

If you've created a virtual environment in the past, activate the virtual environment, and then enter the command `pip list` in the Terminal. If you don't see requests listed in the results, `pip install requests` into the active virtual environment.

A `ModuleNotFoundError` can happen when a filename in the current folder matches a module name. That name may be followed by description, something along the lines of:

```
No module named 'matplotlib'; 'matplotlib' is not a package
```

Check the filenames in the VS Code Explorer pane to see if any of them matches the module name in the error message. For example, Figure 17-2 shows a file named matplotlib.py. That filename conflicts with the `matplotlib` import, which is why the error says it's not a package. To fix this, rename matplotlib.py so it doesn't match the module name — but make sure to keep the .py filename extension.

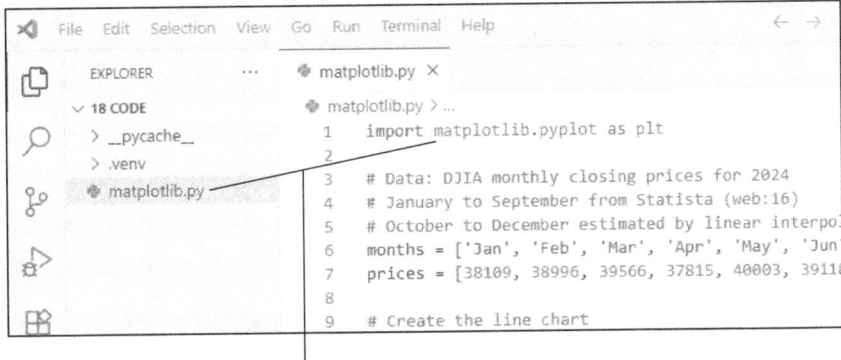

FIGURE 17-2: Make sure filenames don't match module names.

Filename must not match module name

FileNotFoundError

If your Python code needs to access a file, but that file can't be found in the specified location, Python throws a `FileNotFoundError`. Here are the most common causes of this error:

>> You misspelled the filename in your code.

>> The file doesn't exist in the specified directory.

Here's a line of code that tries to open a file named data.json from the current working directory (the same directory that contains the script that contains the code):

```
with open('data.json', 'r') as file:
```

Keep in mind that file and folder names are case-sensitive on macOS and Linux, so watch your uppercase/lowercase letters, too!

The current working directory is assumed because no other directory is specified in the path. If the file is in another location, you can specify the path using the proper syntax for your operating system. For example, if the file is in a folder named assets on a disk or USB drive in drive D: on Windows, you could write the code like this:

```
file_path = r"D:\assets\data.json"
with open(file_path, 'r') as file:
```

On macOS, that would look like this (assuming the name of the USB drive is MyUSB):

```
file_path = "/Volumes/MyUSB/assets/data.json"
with open(file_path, 'r') as file:
```

On Linux, the path may look more like this (but replace Alan with your username and MyUSB with the name of your USB drive):

```
file_path = "/media/Alan/MyUSB/assets/data.json"
with open(file_path, 'r') as file:
```

Working with external files can also produce PermissionError, which happens when you try to write to a file that's open in read-only mode or a file that's already open in some other app. To fix the error, you need to set permissions on the file, or its directory, so your script has whatever rights it needs. Typically, you can set permissions on a file by right-clicking the file's icon and choosing Properties ⇨ Security on Windows, choosing Get Info ⇨ Sharing & Permissions on macOS, or using the chmod command on Linux.

In Python code that works with files, you'll often see exception handlers in place to handle both FileNotFoundError and PermissionError problems, as well as a generic handler like this:

```
import json

def read_json_file(filepath):
    try:
        with open(filepath, 'r') as file:
            data = json.load(file)
            print("File loaded successfully.")
            return data
```

```
    except FileNotFoundError:
        print(f"Error: The file '{filepath}' was not found.")
    except PermissionError:
        print(f"Error: Permission denied when trying to read '{filepath}'.")
    except Exception as e:
        print(f"Unexpected error: {e}")


# Example usage
file_path = "data.json"
content = read_json_file(file_path)
```

It's a good idea to get in the habit of always including exception handling for errors related to files outside your own code, because in many environments you may not have control over what's happening in those other directories.

IndentationError

Many programming languages use different kinds of braces and brackets to delimit blocks of code within a larger script. For example, in the following JavaScript code, the code inside the greet() function is surrounded by curly braces:

```
function greet(name) {
    alert("Hello " + name);
}


// Call the function with the name "wilma"
greet("wilma");
```

Python doesn't use braces or brackets to define blocks of code. Instead, it relies solely on indentations to determine what's inside a block of code. For example, the following greet() function contains the one line of print code, as indicated by the indentation. The remaining code is outside the function, because it's not indented:

```
def greet(name):
    print("Hello " + name)


# Call the function with the name "wilma"
greet("wilma")
```

When you see `IndentationError` in a script, it means Python can't quite figure out what to do with your code. In some cases, the problem may be easy to identify:

```
def greet(name):
print("Hello", name)
```

When you understand that the `def` command defines a function, and only indented code below that line is part of the function, you can see the problem here. There is no indented code under `def`, so nothing is in the function. The exact error message for that error reads like this, so you know the problem starts below a function definition line (which always starts with `def`):

```
IndentationError: expected an indented block after function definition
```

Loops and `if` statements also require indentation below the first line. For example, here's an example of proper indentation for a loop (starting with `for`) and an `if` inside the loop (starting with `if`):

```
# Create a list of numbers
numbers = [1, 2, 3, 4, 5, 6, 7, 8, 9, 10]

# Loop through each item in the list
for number in numbers:
    # Check if the number is odd
    if number % 2 != 0:
        print(f"{number} is odd")
```

The code works fine as written. But the following code would generate an `IndentationError` because it lacks indentations under the `for` and `if` statements:

```
# Create a list of numbers
numbers = [1, 2, 3, 4, 5, 6, 7, 8, 9, 10]

# Loop through each item in the list
for number in numbers:
# Check if the number is odd
if number % 2 != 0:
print(f"{number} is odd")
```

TIP

Inconsistent indentation using the Tab key sometimes and spaces at other times, can also lead to `IndentationError` problems. The PEP 8 guidelines generally recommend using four spaces for indentation level. In VS Code, pressing Tab also indents by four spaces. Try to be consistent when indenting (for example, always use Tab in VS Code) to minimize the likelihood of messing up your indentations.

Index

Numerics

A

B

directories (folders) and files. *See* files and folders, automating

divide_numbers() function, 66

dotenv module, 230, 237, 246

drives, 71–72

.dump method, 188

dunder (double underline) names, 66

duplicate files, 103–109
  calculating file hash, 106
  deleting, 108
  finding, 107–108
  tweaking the find duplicates script, 108–109

dynamic typing, 315

E

ehlo (Extended Hello), 233

elif statement, 56

else statement, 53, 54, 63, 66

email, sending automatically, 229–236
  collecting account information, 230
  creating .env file, 230–231
  creating script, 231–234
  putting email recipient addresses in file, 235
  sending HTML mail, 234–235
  throttling problems, dealing with, 236

.env file, 182, 183, 230–231, 237, 245, 252, 278, 302

environment variables, 184

EOFError, 63

error messages, Python, 331–346
  AttributeError, 340–342
  Command Not Found, 331–333
  FileNotFoundError, 343–345
  IndentationError, 345–346
  IndexError, 337–338
  KeyError, 339–340
  ModuleNotFoundError, 342–343
  NameError, 335
  No Module Named . . ., 333–334
  SyntaxError, 334–335
  TypeError, 336–337

errors, handling, 316–317

Escape key, 150–151, 152

Excel. *See* Microsoft Excel

except: and try: statements, 53, 63, 64–66, 263, 340

Exception as e, 64

exception handling, 63–66, 87, 316–317, 329–330

exit_script function, 154–155

extract_frames() function, 133–135

F

file management
  automating, 93–117
  backing up files, 98–103
  compressing files, 109–113
  decompressing files, 114–117
  deleting old and temporary files, 93–98
  finding and removing duplicate files, 103–109

FileNotFoundError, 63, 343–345

file.path.match(pattern) syntax, 97

files and folders
  automating, 69–91
  drives, 71–72
  File Explorer directories, 70
  moving files with shutil, 86–87
  navigating, 74–81
  organizing, by type, 81–87
  Practice folder, used to work on file scripts safely, 74
  renaming files, 87–91
  script customization, 87
  subfolders, 81
  using mkdir for subfolders, 86
  See also file management; image and video files

finally (optional), 63, 66

find_duplicates() function, 107–108

.find_element() method, 207

Finder, 70

flip() method, 125

flipping images, 126–127

floating point, 37

About the Author

Alan Simpson is the award-winning author of more than 100 tech books covering Python, web design, and database design. His books have been published in dozens of languages throughout the world and have sold millions of copies. Alan also has more than 20 years' experience as an online instructor and consistently gets rave reviews from his students for helping to make complex topics understandable.

Dedication

To Susan, Ashley, and Alec.

Author's Acknowledgments

Many thanks to Margot Maley, my literary agent at Waterside Productions. To Steve Hayes at Wiley for bringing me this opportunity and to Elizabeth Kuball and Doug Holland for supporting me through the process.

Publisher's Acknowledgments

Managing Editor: Murari Mukundan
Executive Editor: Steve Hayes
Editor: Elizabeth Kuball
Technical Editor: Doug Holland

Production Editor: Tamilmani Varadharaj
Cover Image: © Roman Samborskyi/Shutterstock
Special Help: Carmen Krikorian, Kristie Pyles